# A Century of Sovereign Ratings

Norbert Gaillard

# A Century of Sovereign Ratings

Norbert Gaillard
Economic Policy and Debt Department
The World Bank
1818 H Street, NW
Washington, DC 20433, USA
gaillard@alumni.princeton.edu

ISBN 978-1-4614-0522-1      e-ISBN 978-1-4614-0523-8
DOI 10.1007/978-1-4614-0523-8
Springer New York Dordrecht Heidelberg London

Library of Congress Control Number: 2011937968

© Springer Science+Business Media, LLC 2012
All rights reserved. This work may not be translated or copied in whole or in part without the written permission of the publisher (Springer Science+Business Media, LLC, 233 Spring Street, New York, NY 10013, USA), except for brief excerpts in connection with reviews or scholarly analysis. Use in connection with any form of information storage and retrieval, electronic adaptation, computer software, or by similar or dissimilar methodology now known or hereafter developed is forbidden.
The use in this publication of trade names, trademarks, service marks, and similar terms, even if they are not identified as such, is not to be taken as an expression of opinion as to whether or not they are subject to proprietary rights.

Printed on acid-free paper

Springer is part of Springer Science+Business Media (www.springer.com)

# Acknowledgments

I would like to thank Sara Bertin, Marc Flandreau, Harold James, Frank Packer, and Frederic Zumer for their strong support and encouragement.

I am grateful to David Levey, Richard Sylla, Richard Cantor, and several rating analysts for their helpful comments and conversations.

Washington, DC                                                                 Norbert Gaillard

# Contents

| | | |
|---|---|---|
| **1** | **Introduction** | 1 |
| **2** | **The Booms and Busts of the Sovereign Rating Activity** | 3 |
| | 2.1 Expansion of the Sovereign Rating Activity During the Interwar Years | 4 |
| | 2.2 The Decline of Sovereign Rating | 6 |
| | 2.3 The Recovery from the Mid-1970s | 8 |
| | References | 10 |
| **3** | **Definition, Typology, and Refinement of Sovereign Ratings** | 13 |
| | 3.1 Definition of Ratings | 13 |
| | 3.2 Significance of Rating Scales | 14 |
| |     3.2.1 The Meaning and the Widening of Rating Scales | 14 |
| |     3.2.2 The Dividing Line Between Investment Grade and Speculative Grade | 17 |
| | 3.3 Main Credit Rating Policies and Procedures | 20 |
| |     3.3.1 Short-Term Ratings | 20 |
| |     3.3.2 Reviews for Possible Rating Change | 22 |
| |     3.3.3 Rating Outlooks | 23 |
| | 3.4 Local and Foreign Currency Ratings | 23 |
| | 3.5 The Country Ceiling | 24 |
| | 3.6 Rating Sovereigns That Default | 25 |
| | 3.7 Sovereign Recovery Ratings | 27 |
| | References | 29 |
| **4** | **How Are Sovereign Ratings Assigned?** | 31 |
| | 4.1 Introduction | 31 |
| | 4.2 The Sovereign Rating Teams | 31 |
| |     4.2.1 The Interwar Years | 31 |
| |     4.2.2 The Modern Era | 33 |

|     |       |                                                                                 |     |
| --- | ----- | ------------------------------------------------------------------------------- | --- |
|     | 4.3   | The Sovereign Rating Process                                                    | 34  |
|     |       | 4.3.1 Shifting from Unsolicited to Solicited Ratings                            | 35  |
|     |       | 4.3.2 Importance of the Rating Committee                                        | 36  |
|     | References                                                                              | 38  |

## 5 Moody's Sovereign Ratings: 1918–1939 and 1986–2006 Compared ... 39
- 5.1 Review of the Literature ... 39
- 5.2 Moody's Rating Policy ... 40
- 5.3 Moody's Official Methodologies ... 44
- 5.4 Empirical Analysis of the Determinants of Moody's Sovereign Ratings ... 50
- 5.5 Concluding Remarks ... 60
- References ... 60

## 6 Sovereign Rating Methodologies: From Theory to Practice ... 63
- 6.1 Evolution and Comparison of Official Rating Criteria ... 63
  - 6.1.1 Common and Unchanged Methods for Assessing Sovereign Risk ... 64
  - 6.1.2 More Crises Lead to Expanded Criteria ... 64
  - 6.1.3 Modeling Sovereign Risk ... 67
- 6.2 Determinants of Sovereign Ratings ... 72
  - 6.2.1 Conventional Determinants ... 72
  - 6.2.2 Determinants Specific to Low- and Middle-Income Countries ... 72
- 6.3 Rating Gaps Across Agencies ... 76
  - 6.3.1 Split Ratings Among Fitch, Moody's, and S&P ... 76
  - 6.3.2 Split Ratings Between Leading Agencies and Smaller Non-U.S. Firms ... 85
- References ... 90

## 7 Consistency and Performance of Sovereign Ratings During the Interwar Years ... 95
- 7.1 Review of the Literature ... 95
- 7.2 Analysis of Rating Changes ... 96
- 7.3 Analysis of Average Cumulative Default Rates ... 101
- 7.4 Concluding Remarks ... 106
- References ... 107

## 8 Consistency and Performance of Sovereign Ratings Since the 1980s ... 109
- 8.1 Review of the Literature ... 109
- 8.2 Sovereign Rating Reviews and Outlooks ... 110
  - 8.2.1 Sovereign Rating Reviews ... 111
  - 8.2.2 Sovereign Rating Outlooks ... 115
  - 8.2.3 Outlook/Watchlist Status Prior to Rating Change Announcements ... 122

|     |       |                                                                                   |     |
| --- | ----- | --------------------------------------------------------------------------------- | --- |
|     | 8.3   | Stability of Sovereign Ratings                                                    | 125 |
|     |       | 8.3.1 Frequency and Magnitude of Rating Changes                                   | 125 |
|     |       | 8.3.2 Rating Migration Matrices                                                   | 127 |
|     |       | 8.3.3 Rating Reversals                                                            | 133 |
|     | 8.4   | Accuracy of Sovereign Ratings                                                     | 136 |
|     |       | 8.4.1 Ratings Prior to Default                                                    | 136 |
|     |       | 8.4.2 Average Cumulative Default Rates                                            | 138 |
|     |       | 8.4.3 Cumulative Accuracy Profiles and Accuracy Ratios                            | 141 |
|     | 8.5   | Conclusions                                                                       | 146 |
|     | References                                                                               | 147 |
| 9   | **Fitch, Moody's, and S&P Sovereign Ratings and EMBI Global Spreads: Lessons from 1993–2007** | 149 |
|     | 9.1   | Review of the Literature                                                          | 150 |
|     | 9.2   | Correlations Between EMBIG Spreads and Fitch, Moody's, and S&P Ratings            | 150 |
|     |       | 9.2.1 Data Description                                                            | 150 |
|     |       | 9.2.2 A Univariate Model of Spreads                                               | 152 |
|     | 9.3   | Adjustments of Ratings to Market Spreads                                          | 153 |
|     |       | 9.3.1 Adjustments of Ratings to Excessively High/Low Spreads                      | 153 |
|     |       | 9.3.2 Adjustments of Ratings to Strong Increase/Decrease in Spreads               | 158 |
|     | 9.4   | Reaction of Market Spreads to Rating Changes                                      | 160 |
|     | 9.5   | Conclusions                                                                       | 169 |
|     | References                                                                               | 169 |
| 10  | **The Limits of Sovereign Ratings in Light of the Greek Debt Crisis of 2009–2010**        | 171 |
|     | 10.1  | Review of the Literature                                                          | 171 |
|     | 10.2  | Perception of Sovereign Risk During the Greek Debt Crisis: Ratings vs. CDS-IRs    | 173 |
|     |       | 10.2.1 Chronicle of a Debt Crisis Foretold                                        | 173 |
|     |       | 10.2.2 Data Description and Methods                                               | 174 |
|     |       | 10.2.3 "Sticky" Ratings vs. Volatile CDS-IRs                                      | 175 |
|     | 10.3  | How CRAs Were Cornered                                                            | 183 |
|     |       | 10.3.1 The Daedalean Labyrinth                                                    | 183 |
|     |       | 10.3.2 The Icarus Syndrome                                                        | 184 |
|     | 10.4  | Concluding Remarks                                                                | 185 |
|     | References                                                                               | 186 |

| 11 | Conclusion | 189 |
|---|---|---|
| **Appendix 1** | **Sovereign Bonds in USD or in GBP Listed on the NYSE That Defaulted in 1931–1938** | 191 |
| **Appendix 2** | **Sources Used in Chap. 5** | 193 |
| **Appendix 3** | **List of the 135 Bonds Included in the Sample Used in Chap. 7** | 195 |

# Chapter 1
# Introduction

The credit rating agencies (CRAs) have been under criticism since the Asian crisis. At that time, they were held responsible for aggravating the liquidity crises of several Asian countries by downgrading these issuers' ratings by as many as ten notches within 2 months. This controversy shed light on what was then a little-known activity: the rating of sovereign credit. Since 1997, many questions have arisen about sovereign ratings. How can countries be rated like any private entity? What are the criteria used by the CRAs' analysts to assess sovereign risk? Are sovereign ratings accurate? Do the CRAs' views simply echo those reflected in market yield spreads?

This book is the first research work to answer these questions by providing a unique analysis of the sovereign credit opinions issued by the CRAs. Two periods are examined: the interwar years and the period 1986–2010 (hereafter, the "modern era") because the sovereign rating was moribund from the 1940s through the mid-1980s. For the interwar period, the analysis focuses on the ratings assigned by the four principal CRAs at that time [Fitch, Moody's Investors Service (Moody's), Poor's Publishing Company (Poor's), and Standard Statistics] to the sovereign bonds denominated in US dollars (USD) and GB pounds (GBP) that were listed on the New York Stock Exchange (NYSE). For the modern era, this study's scope is the foreign currency long-term credit ratings assigned by the three leading CRAs: Fitch Ratings (Fitch), Moody's, and Standard & Poor's (S&P).

The core of this book consists of nine chapters. Chapters 2–4 provide the key notions to understand sovereign ratings. Chapter 2 presents an overview of sovereign rating activity since the first such ratings were assigned in 1918. Chapter 3 analyzes the meaning of sovereign ratings and the significance of rating scales; it also describes the refinement of credit rating policies and tools. Chapter 4 focuses on the sovereign rating process.

Chapters 5 and 6 open the black box of sovereign ratings. Chapter 5 compares sovereign rating methodologies in the interwar years with those in the modern era. After examining how rating agencies have amended their methodologies since the 1990s, Chap. 6 scrutinizes rating disagreements between CRAs.

Chapters 7 and 8 measure the performances of sovereign ratings by computing default rates and accuracy ratios: Chap. 7 looks at the interwar years and Chap. 8 at the modern era. The two chapters assess which CRA assigns the most accurate ratings during the respective periods.

Chapters 9 and 10 compare the perception of sovereign risk by the rating agencies and market participants. Chapter 9 focuses on the relation between JP Morgan Emerging Markets Bond Index Global spreads and emerging countries' sovereign ratings for the period 1993–2007. Chapter 10 compares the eurozone members' sovereign ratings with Credit Default Swap-Implied Ratings (CDS-IRs) during the Greek debt crisis of November 2009–May 2010.

Finally, Chap. 11 summarizes prominent results and draws general conclusions.

# Chapter 2
# The Booms and Busts of the Sovereign Rating Activity

In previous centuries, sovereigns often went bankrupt. For example, Spain defaulted three times during the Golden Century; it defaulted seven more times in the seventeenth, eighteenth, and nineteenth centuries. France defaulted eight times between 1500 and 1800. In the nineteenth century, Austria-Hungary and Prussia defaulted five times. These defaults, which involved both colonial and continental powers, show how difficult it has been to assess sovereign creditworthiness (see Reinhart and Rogoff 2009; Suter and Stamm 1992; Winkler 1933; Wynne 1951 for an exhaustive view of sovereign defaults occurred before the twentieth century).

Unlike conditions in the corporate area, until the late nineteenth century there were no external firms that provided economic and financial information concerning sovereign borrowers. Consequently, the few data and criteria used to assess sovereign creditworthiness came from bankers themselves. For instance, in the 1810s, the King of Prussia was informed after applying for a loan from Nathan Rothschild that his premium would be higher because his kingdom was not a rule-of-law regime (Ferguson 1998). Several decades later, in 1898, the Service des Etudes Financières of the Crédit Lyonnais classified foreign states into three categories according to their sovereign risk index, which was essentially based on the ratio of debt service to revenues (Flandreau 2003). However, this rudimentary rating system was for internal use only and was not subsequently updated.

The first sovereign risk report released by a nonbanking entity is Moody's first manual, in 1900. This publication, entitled *Manual of Industrial and Miscellaneous Securities*, established a list of sovereign bonds and provided public finance data, but did not include any ratings.[1] This 1,100-page book mainly compiled information about corporations, public utilities, railroad companies, and foreign governments. Actually, this manual was the first step towards the rating of sovereigns.

---

[1] The list of sovereign securities consisted of Argentinean, Austrian, Belgian, Brazilian, British, Canadian, Danish, Dutch, German, and Mexican bonds (Moody 1900, pp. 275–293).

## 2.1 Expansion of the Sovereign Rating Activity During the Interwar Years

Ratings first appeared in 1909 in *Moody's Analyses of Railroad Investments*, but these ratings concerned corporate bonds (for an overview of the rating history, see Sylla 2002). Moody's started rating foreign government bonds in March 1918, becoming the first firm in the world to measure the creditworthiness of sovereign issuers. The *Moody's Analyses of Investments – Government and Municipal Securities of 1918* contained statistics on approximately 30,000 different bonds, 85% of which had been issued by the United States and its political subdivisions. The remaining 15% were obligations issued by foreign governments, states, counties, and cities: 189 foreign government bonds were rated,[2] of which 24 were denominated in USD or in GBP and listed on the New York Stock Exchange (NYSE). Ten foreign issuer countries were covered: Argentina, Canada, Cuba, the Dominican Republic, France, Japan, Norway, Panama, Switzerland, and the United Kingdom (Table 2.1).

These first sovereign ratings were assigned at a particularly opportune moment when the United States experienced a turning point with regard to its economic and financial position: it had just become the first lending nation in the world (Madden et al. 1937). Meanwhile, New York was about to become the most capitalized stock exchange, contributing to the boom in lending to European and Latin American nations (Rippy 1950). Moody's also benefited from the laissez-faire of the 1920s: in a statement issued on 3 March 1922, the U.S. Department of State clearly affirmed that American bankers were not obliged to consult with any particular legal power in regard to their foreign lending policy (Dulles 1926). Moreover, although the quality of foreign bonds could have been monitored by an American bondholders association such as the U.K. Corporation of Foreign Bondholders or the French Association Nationale des Porteurs Français de Valeurs Etrangères, no such organization was set up in the United States until December 1933, when the Foreign Bondholders Protective Council was established to implement debt restructuring programs with defaulting countries (Adamson 2002). As a result, ratings issued by Moody's and then by Poor's, Standard Statistics, and Fitch (starting 1922, and 1924, respectively) were the only indicators that enabled investors to discriminate among the increasing number of foreign government issues on the NYSE in the 1920s (Fig. 2.1).

By 1929, more than 120 sovereign bonds were rated by the four CRAs. From that year, the drying up of the foreign government bond market, the wave of sovereign defaults in 1931, and the Johnson Act of 1934 – which made it unlawful for U.S. bankers to lend to countries in default – contributed to the slowdown of the sovereign rating business in the 1930s. Between 1935 and 1938, 73% of issues came from

---
[2] Author's computations.

## 2.1 Expansion of the Sovereign Rating Activity During the Interwar Years

**Table 2.1** First sovereign ratings ever issued: USD and GBP foreign government bonds listed on the NYSE and rated by Moody's in 1918

| Bonds | Date of issue | Date due | Rating |
|---|---|---|---|
| Argentine Government 6% Gold Treasury Bonds | 1915 | 1920 | A |
| Canada Public Service Loan 5s | 1916 | 1921, 1926, 1931 | Aaa |
| Republic of Cuba 6% Notes 1915 | 1915 | 1918 | Aa |
| Republic of Cuba External Gold 5s | 1904 | 1944 | Aa |
| Republic of Cuba External Gold 4½s | 1909 | 1949 | Aa |
| Republic of Cuba External Gold 5s | 1914 | 1949 | Aa |
| Dominican Republic 5% Customs Admin. Gold Bonds | 1908 | 1958 | A |
| Dominican Republic 6s SF Treasury Gold Notes | 1913 | 1918 | A |
| France – Anglo-French 5s | 1915 | 1920 | Aaa |
| France – American Foreign Securities 5s | 1916 | 1919 | Aaa |
| France – Convertible Gold Notes 5½s | 1917 | 1919 | Aaa |
| Japanese Sterling 4s | 1905 | 1931 | A |
| Japanese Sterling 4½s first issue | 1905 | 1925 | Aa |
| Japanese Sterling 4½s second issue | 1905 | 1925 | A |
| Norwegian External 6% Loan | 1916 | 1923 | A |
| Panama – 5% Sinking Fund 30-Year Gold | 1914 | 1944 | Aa |
| Panama – 5% Secured Serial Gold Bonds | 1915 | 1922–1925 | Aa |
| Switzerland – 5% Gold Notes | 1915 | 1920 | A |
| United Kingdom – Anglo-French 5s | 1915 | 1920 | Aa |
| United Kingdom Collateral 5s | 1916 | 1918 | Aaa |
| United Kingdom Collateral 5½s | 1916 | 1919 | Aaa |
| United Kingdom Collateral 5½s | 1916 | 1921 | Aaa |
| United Kingdom Conversion Collateral 5½s | 1917 | 1919 | Aaa |
| United Kingdom 90-day Treasury Bills | 1917–1920 | 1917–1920 | Aaa |

*Sources*: Author's classification from *Moody's Manual* (1918)

Argentina, Canada, and Norway. In view of strained international relationships, beginning in 1936, Fitch withdrew the ratings of Germany, Austria, China, Czechoslovakia, Italy, and Japan.[3] The other three agencies followed suit in 1939 and 1940. In fact, World War II was the deathblow to sovereign rating activity. By 1940, the four agencies withdrew all ratings assigned to USD bonds issued by Australia or by European and Asian countries, deciding to rate North American and Latin American bonds only (i.e., 17 countries and 64 bonds).[4]

---

[3] *Fitch Bond Books* (1936, 1938, 1939).

[4] *Moody's Manual of Investments – American and Foreign Government Securities* (1940), *Poor's Volume* (1940), *Standard Bond Descriptions* (1940), *Fitch Bond Book* (1940).

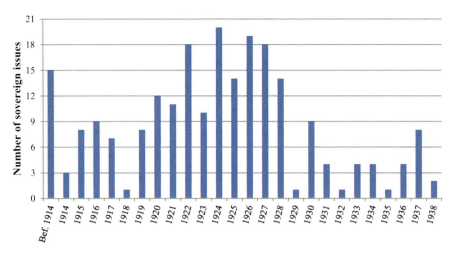

**Fig. 2.1** USD and GBP securities listed on the NYSE and rated between 1918 and 1938 according to their issuance year (total of 225 sovereign bonds). *Sources*: Author's calculations from *Moody's Manuals* (1918 through 1939)

## 2.2 The Decline of Sovereign Rating

The sovereign rating business was in the doldrums for more than 3 decades. This fact is closely related to the low number of foreign government bonds issued in the United States between the 1940s and the 1970s. This low level of activity stems from various root causes.

The first cause is linked to the world economic and financial situation in the postwar years. In 1946, more than 20 countries had not yet resumed payment of their debt.[5] The gradual return to growth and creditworthiness was made possible by two major series of initiatives. The new international financial architecture launched at Bretton Woods led to the creation of the World Bank and the International Monetary Fund (IMF), institutions that together replaced the financial markets providing capital to the developing countries. Next, the Marshall Plan was the primary instrument for rebuilding and creating a stronger foundation for the Allied countries of Europe. This plan, which operated for 4 years beginning in July 1947, helped the recovery of Western European countries and was complementary to the bilateral loans granted by the Export–Import Bank to Latin American and European countries. The second cause of reduced sovereign rating activity in this period was the implementation of the Interest Equalization Tax (IET) in 1963. This U.S. domestic tax, which was designed to reduce the outflow of U.S. capital,

---

[5] Foreign Bondholders Protective Council (1950), *Report 1946 through 1949*, p. 362.

## 2.2 The Decline of Sovereign Rating

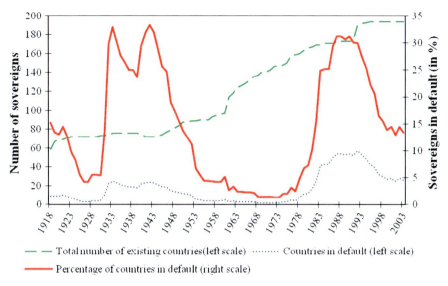

**Fig. 2.2** Percentage of sovereigns in default. *Sources*: Author's computations from http://www.cia.gov, Suter and Stamm (1992), and S&P (1999, 2004)

restricted considerably the foreign debt issued in the U.S. bond market. Finally, that so few countries defaulted in the 1960s and 1970s (see Fig. 2.2) led investors to suppose that the risk of sovereign default had subsided.[6] This belief partly explains the overlending cycle to the developing countries during 1973–1982, the effect of which was to reduce the motivation of countries to tap financial markets (Folkerts-Landau 1985).

These three causes account for the continuing decrease in the number of sovereigns rated: 7, 13, and 14 in 1955 for S&P, Moody's, and Fitch, respectively.[7] Between 1968 and 1974, S&P suspended its sovereign activity, and rated only Canada and the United States. In 1975, Moody's rated only five countries (Australia, Canada, United States, New Zealand, and Panama) vs. seven for S&P (Australia, Austria, Canada, United States, France, Japan, and Norway). In the meantime, Fitch had already given up rating sovereigns.

During these 3 decades of low activity in the sovereign rating business, Moody's was the only CRA that continued to release reports on the macroeconomic situation of both rated and unrated countries[8] and on the 1967–1973 international monetary

---

[6] See Strange (1967) for an unconventional yet correct argument that sovereign defaults were likely to increase.

[7] *Standard & Poor's Corporation Records* (1955), *Moody's Municipal and Government Manual* (1955), *Fitch Bond Book* (1955).

[8] For instance: *Moody's Bond Survey*, "Brazilian Government, State & Municipal Dollar Bonds," 19 June 1944, and *Moody's Bond Survey*, "Peru's Final Debt Settlement Offer," 26 January 1953.

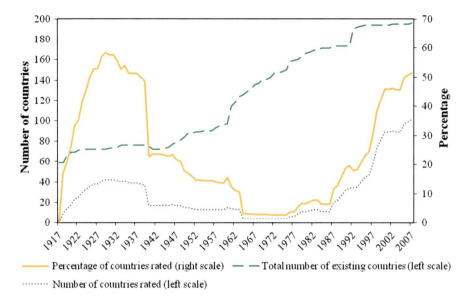

**Fig. 2.3** Percentage of countries rated by Moody's. *Notes*: Ratings of USD and GBP bonds listed on the NYSE for 1917–1985 and FC (foreign currency) ratings for 1986–2007. All data are as of 31 March. *Sources*: Author's calculations from *Moody's Manuals* (1918–1987), http://www.moodys.com, and http://www.cia.gov

crisis.[9] Figure 2.3 illustrates the near extinction of the sovereign rating activity during the 1940s–1970s.

## 2.3 The Recovery from the Mid-1970s

The recovery of sovereign rating activity was gradual and can be presented as a four-step process.

The abrogation of the IET in 1974 was the first step; this contributed to the resumption of sovereign bond issuances on the NYSE as early as 1975, when the securities issued by three countries (Australia, Austria, and Norway) were assigned a rating by Moody's.[10] In 1977, three other countries tapped the U.S. market and were rated both by Moody's and S&P: Finland, Venezuela, and Sweden each issued two series of bonds for amounts of USD 100, 150, and 200 million, respectively.[11]

---

[9] For instance: *Moody's Bond Survey*, "International & Foreigns – Currencies Again in Crisis," 25 November 1968; and *Moody's Bond Survey*, "International Monetary Conditions and the U.S. Economy," 31 May 1971.

[10] *Moody's Bond Survey*, "International Bonds Rated During 1975," 5 January 1976.

[11] *Moody's Bond Survey*, 3, 10, and 31 October 1977.

However, the number of sovereigns rated did not increase during subsequent years because new sovereign issuances came from countries that were already rated. Also, the wave of sovereign defaults beginning in 1982 (see Fig. 2.2) increased risk aversion, constrained access to the market, and precluded CRAs from assigning new sovereign ratings.

Yet, sovereign rating activity rebounded in 1986 after the decision by Moody's to rate countries issuing securities in other than USD (e.g., Germany, Hong Kong, the Netherlands, and Switzerland).[12] This shift in rating practices, which was followed by S&P, contributed to the increasing number of countries rated.[13] It is hardly surprising that sovereign ratings were assigned to highly creditworthy countries,[14] but they were also assigned as a prerequisite to a subnational rating. For example, Malta was rated for the first time by S&P so that Freeport Terminal (Malta) Ltd., a state-guaranteed firm that had issued a bond on the U.S. market, could receive its own rating.[15]

The Brady Plan was the third step in the recovery of sovereign rating activity in the early 1990s. Implemented in 1989 under the auspices of Secretary of Treasury Nicholas Brady, the first deal aimed to restructure the Mexican debt by issuing sovereign bonds. Other Brady deals had the effect of increasing the size of sovereign bond markets,[16] which spurred developing and emerging countries to request ratings.[17]

The last step of the expansion of sovereign rating occurred in the early 2000s, though it concerned only S&P and Fitch. In 2002, Fitch and the U.S. Department of State signed an agreement for the purpose of assigning ratings to 15 Sub-Saharan African countries (the first sovereign rated was Lesotho in September 2002; then Gambia in 2002; Malawi, Mozambique, Cape Verde, Cameroon, and Ghana in 2003; Mali and Benin in 2004; Uganda and Namibia in 2005; Nigeria and Rwanda in 2006; and Kenya and Gabon in 2007).[18] In 2003, a new initiative was launched by the United Nations Development Programme (UNDP) with S&P to help Sub-Saharan African countries obtain ratings. The first of these ratings was assigned to Ghana, Cameroon, and Benin in 2003; then Burkina Faso, Mali, and Mozambique in 2004; Nigeria and Kenya in 2006; Gabon in 2007; and Uganda in 2008.[19] These two initiatives involving Fitch and S&P have enabled many African countries to receive their first rating.

---

[12] Interview with David Levey (Managing Director, Sovereign Risk Unit, Moody's Investors Service until July 2004), 16 December 2003, New York.

[13] This evolution accelerated as new countries issued bonds in USD (Italy in 1986 and Hungary in 1989): *Moody's Bond Surveys*, 20 October 1986 and 24 July 1989.

[14] *Moody's Bond Survey*, "Sovereign Outlook 1988," 18 January 1988.

[15] *Standard & Poor's CreditWeek*, 28 March 1994.

[16] In 1994, Brady bonds represented 61% of the negotiable debt of emerging countries (http://www.emta.org).

[17] Most Brady bonds were assigned a rating shortly after their issuance.

[18] http://www.worldbank.org, Fitch (2002) and http://www.fitchratings.com.

[19] S&P (2003) and http://www.standardandpoors.com.

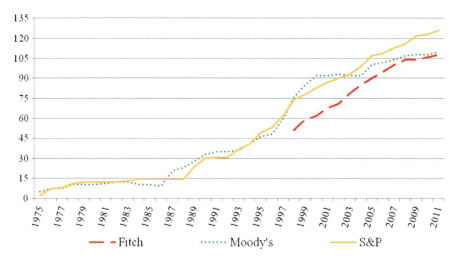

**Fig. 2.4** Number of sovereigns rated by the big three CRAs. *Notes*: Number of sovereigns rated as of 1 January. Fitch curve starts in 1998, after its merger with IBCA. *Sources*: http://www.fitchratings.com, http://www.moodys.com, and http://www.standardandpoors.com

Other factors – such as the dismantling of capital controls during the 1980s–1990s, the advent of capitalism in Eastern Europe and Russia, and the implementation of market-oriented macroeconomic policies – increased the size of sovereign bond markets and boosted sovereign rating activity.

In conclusion, it is worth noting that the recovery of sovereign rating was profitable to the big three CRAs: Fitch, Moody's, and S&P. Two firms, IBCA and Duff & Phelps, managed to rate nearly 40 countries in the mid-to-late 1990s before they were purchased by Fitch in 1997 and 2000, respectively (Huhne 1996). In January 2011, Japan Credit Rating Agency (JCR) and Rating & Investment (R&I) rated 35 and 46 sovereigns, respectively, but they remain small players. As shown in Fig. 2.4, Fitch made up for lost time within a decade and is now rating almost as many sovereigns as Moody's.

## References

Adamson M. R. (2002), "The Failure of the Foreign Bondholders Protective Council Experiment, 1934–1940", *Business History Review*, Vol.76.
Dulles J. F. (1926), "Our Foreign Loan Policy", *Foreign Affairs*, Vol.5.
Ferguson N. (1998), *The House of Rothschild: Money's Prophets, 1798–1848*, Viking, New York.
Fitch (various issues), *Fitch Bond Book*.
Fitch Ratings (2002), "Sovereign Ratings and the HIPC Initiative", 27 August.
Flandreau M. (2003), "Caveat Emptor – Coping with Sovereign Risk under the International Gold Standard, 1871–1913", in *International Financial History in the Twentieth Century: System*

# References

*and Anarchy*, edited by Flandreau M., Holtfrerich C.-L. and James H., Cambridge University Press, Cambridge.

Folkerts-Landau D. (1985), "The Changing Role of International Bank Lending in Development Finance", *IMF Staff Papers*, Vol.32, No.2.

Foreign Bondholders Protective Council (1950), *Report 1946 through 1949*, New York.

Huhne C. (1996), "Rating Sovereign Risk", *Bank of England, Financial Stability Review*, Autumn.

Madden J., Nadler M. and Sauvain H. (1937), *America's Experience as a Creditor Nation*, Prentice-Hall Inc, New York.

Moody J. (1900), *Manual of Industrial and Miscellaneous Securities*, New York.

Moody's Investors Service (various years), *Moody's Manual of Investments – American and Foreign Government Securities*, New York.

Moody's Investors Service (various years), "Moody's Bond Surveys".

Moody's Investors Service (various years), "Moody's Investment Letters".

Poor's (various years), *Poor's Volume*.

Reinhart C. and Rogoff K. (2009), *This Time is Different – Eight Centuries of Financial Folly*, Princeton University Press, Princeton.

Rippy J. F. (1950), "A Bond-Selling Extravaganza of the 1920's", *Journal of Business of the University of Chicago*, Vol.23, No.4.

Standard & Poor's (various years), *Standard & Poor's Corporation Records*.

Standard & Poor's (various years), "Standard & Poor's CreditWeek".

Standard & Poor's (1999), "Sovereign Defaults: Hiatus in 2000?", *Standard & Poor's CreditWeek*, 22 December.

Standard & Poor's (2003), "First Sovereign Credit Ratings Assigned under New UNDP Initiative for Africa", 4 September.

Standard & Poor's (2004), "Sovereign Defaults Set to Fall Again in 2005", 28 September.

Standard Statistics (various years), *Standard Bond Descriptions*.

Strange S. (1967), "Debts, Defaulters and Development", *International Affairs*, Vol.43, No.3.

Suter C. and Stamm H. (1992), "Coping with Global Debt Crises: Debt Settlements, 1820 to 1986", *Comparative Studies in Society and History*, Vol.34, No.4.

Sylla R. (2002), "An Historical Primer on the Business of Credit Rating", in *Ratings, Rating Agencies and the Global Financial System*, edited by Levich R., Majnoni G. and Reinhart C., Kluwer Academic Publishers, Boston.

Winkler M. (1933), *Foreign Bonds – An Autopsy*, Roland Swain Company, Philadelphia.

Wynne W. (1951), *State Insolvency and Foreign Bondholders – Volume II*, Yale University Press, New Haven.

# Chapter 3
# Definition, Typology, and Refinement of Sovereign Ratings

## 3.1 Definition of Ratings

In its first *1918 Manual* and *Investment Letters*, Moody's defined its sovereign ratings as the relative creditworthiness of government. This measure has two components: the *ability* and the *willingness* (or the "good faith") to repay the debt.[1] In 1919, Moody's claimed that its measure of creditworthiness was valid generally and it established a credit scale of main sovereigns. The United States led this classification with 100% ("probability" that the country will take care of its debt in every respect), ahead of Canada (95%), the United Kingdom (90%), Belgium (85%), France (75%), Italy (70%), Germany (65%), Austria (60%), and Russia (55%). The agency indicated that its ratings conveyed the probability of country respecting its financial obligations. The manuals published by Poor's, Fitch and Standard Statistics, gave a similar definition of their ratings.[2]

Although none of the four CRAs defined "default" precisely, this notion can be understood as the absence of (or the delay in) payments of principal or interest, or a modification of contract terms that leads the borrower to reduce the value of the bonds issued, to extend their maturity, or to reduce the interest rate. This definition, which may be inferred from the rating practices and rating scales of the time, is much the same as today. However, a careful analysis of ratings assigned by the four agencies to defaulting bonds reveals that ratings measured not only a default probability but also a recovery rate. This critical characteristic of the rating policy during the interwar period is explored more fully in Sect. 3.6.

Focus now on more recent times, the 1990s–2000s. Moody's officially affirms that its ratings measure both a default probability and an estimate of financial losses

---

[1] "The Credit of Foreign Governments," *Moody's Investment Letter*, 3 April 1919. The other three agencies did not mention these notions of ability and willingness to pay, which are now commonly accepted.

[2] *Poor's Rating Services* (1922, 1925); *Fitch Bond Book* (1924, 1930); *Standard Bond Book* (1924).

in the event of a default (Moody's 2010b). Yet, given the difficulty of quantifying losses ex ante, the Moody's ratings primarily reflect the default probability.[3] The S&P definition is close to that of Moody's: its ratings measure a default probability and may also take into account the relative seniority of bonds when measuring the severity of loss in the event of default. These factors are not actually part of the S&P rating scale, which officially classifies issuers solely in terms of their default probability (S&P 1979, pp. 327–328; 2010b). Until 2005, Fitch ratings reflected a default probability and took financial losses into account only for defaulting issuers (Fitch IBCA 1998). Thereafter, Fitch suppressed the three categories (DDD, DD, and D) used to evaluate this recovery rate, replacing them with a two-part scale (similar to that used by S&P that indicated whether the default involved all or only part of the debt). In the meantime, the agency created a new type of rating applicable to low-grade sovereign bonds that measured the recovery rate; of course, this specific rating is likely to influence issuer's overall rating (Fitch 2005a). This feature of Fitch ratings is examined in Sect. 3.7.

## 3.2 Significance of Rating Scales

### 3.2.1 *The Meaning and the Widening of Rating Scales*

During the interwar years, Moody's foreign government bond rating scale included nine categories (Aaa, Aa, A, Baa, Ba, B, Caa, Ca, C).[4] The significance of this hierarchy was explained at the beginning of every *Manual* in a section entitled "Key to the Ratings." Explanations given to illustrate the degree of risk inherent in each rating category changed little throughout this time.

Aaa: "intrinsic strength and security," "assurance of the prompt payment of principal and interest."
Aa: "strong investments and generally fundamentally secure," "subject to some qualification in security or stability."
A: bonds in this category are "well established but have not yet acquired the full development necessary for higher ratings."
Baa: "bonds of this rating require close discrimination." "They cannot as a group be uniformly recommended but they often represent opportunities for persons who are willing to concede some investment quality for the sake of attractive yields." Nevertheless, such bonds "are liable to become largely speculative."

---

[3] E-mail exchange with Richard Cantor (then Team Managing Director, Moody's Investors Service), 17 November 2004.
[4] Between 1918 and 1929, this rating scale differed from the Moody's corporate bond rating system, which contained fourteen and later twelve categories (Aaa, Aa, A, Baa, Ba, B, Caa, Ca, C, Daa, Da, D, E, F; the E and F categories were retired in 1923).

Ba: "a security of this type is purchased for its speculative possibilities rather than its investment quality."
B: "imminent danger of defaulting."
Caa: "obligations of dangerous[ly] weakened communities."
Ca: "little or no hope of any substantial improvement short of partial repudiation."
C: "practically worthless."

Fitch classified securities into twelve categories: AAA, AA, A, BBB, BB, B, CCC, CC, C, DDD, DD, and D. Unlike the Moody's ratings, the Fitch rating category definitions referred to features characteristic of corporate, not sovereign, bonds.[5] This is because Fitch gathered all rated securities in a single volume that consisted mostly of corporate bonds. For instance, the *Fitch Bond Book 1924* reported on seven types of securities: the US government and municipal bonds, foreign government and municipal bonds, railroad bonds, public utilities bonds, industrial bonds, investment trust bonds, and real estate bonds. Fitch's explanations of its ratings were short and self-evident: bonds rated AAA are of higher quality than bonds rated AA, which are safer than A bonds. Fitch classified securities of grades AAA–A securities as "sound" investments. Bonds rated in the BBB–B range are "semi-investment" securities: Fitch regards BBB bonds as being fairly safe, although unfavorable economic changes may lead to threatened or actual default of BB and B bonds. Securities in the CCC–C categories are clearly hazardous and in actual or immediately anticipated default. Finally, bonds rated DDD, DD, or D are in default; there are high expectations for recovery with DDD securities and little hope for bonds rated D.

As with Fitch, the Standard Statistics rating scale is based on its corporate risk assessments. The scale is composed of fourteen ratings: A1+, A1, A, B1+, B1, B, C1+, C1, C, D1+, D1, D, E, and F.[6] The A whole category (ratings A1+, A1, and A) applies to high grade bonds. The B whole category comprises the "businessman's bonds" (i.e., the lowest-grade investment bonds). This category is characterized by heterogeneity: a bond in the B1+ class is considered a "good" bond but is likely to be affected by adverse economic conditions; bonds in the B1 class are considered to be fairly safe investments, and the B class includes the better grade of speculative issues. Securities in the C whole category (C1+, C1, and C) are all speculative. The D whole category consists of defaulted issues. The best of these issues (those rated D1+) have the highest possibility of recovery; the worst of them (those rated D) have a low recovery expectancy. Securities rated E and F have little or virtually no value.

Poor's rating scale requires further attention because it changed in the late 1930s. From 1922 to 1937, the scale ran as follows.[7] The rating A***** (assigned only to securities of the US government) is the best rating. The subsequent hierarchy is

---

[5] *Fitch Bond Book* (1924).
[6] *Standard Bond Book* (1924).
[7] *Poor's Volume* (1922, 1924); *Poor's Bank, Government and Municipal Volume* (1933); *Poor's Fiscal Volume* (1937). Note that the corporate scale included the ratings D**, D*, and D.

A\*\*\*\*, A\*\*\*, A\*\*, A\*, A, B\*\*, B\*, B, C\*\*, C\*, and C. The A\*\*\*\* category is the highest class for foreign bonds. Bonds rated between A\*\*\* and A are viewed as extremely safe obligations. The B\*\* class consists of businessman's bonds; bonds rated B\* are at the top of the speculative grade class, and securities rated B are clearly speculative. The C\*\* and C\* categories apply to highly speculative bonds and bonds regarded as being in temporary default; the C class indicates a risk of serious and persistent default. In 1938 and 1939, the ratings A\*\*\*\*\*, A\*\*\*\*, and A\*\*\* were dropped; thus, just before World War II, the Poor's rating scale (like that of Moody's) consisted of nine categories.[8]

None of these four CRAs provided information to explain or justify the thresholds. It is worth noting that Poor's once added a "salability" (marketability) indicator for every bond rated. The numeral 1 was assigned to bonds whose difference between bids and offers was less than 1 point. Likewise, the numeral 2 was appended to ratings of securities for which the bid–offer gap did not exceed 3 points, and the numeral 3 applied to bonds that were listed but whose bid–offer gap was more than 3 points. The numeral 4 was assigned to unlisted securities.

Two remarks follow from this overview of the interwar rating scales and definitions. First, the granularity of rating scales differs from one agency to another, so that ratings are not strictly comparable. For instance, Moody's Baa does not correspond exactly to Fitch's BBB, to Standard Statistics B1+, or to Poor's B\*\*. Second, this lack of strict correspondence implies that upgrades and downgrades are not equivalent from one agency to another.

Following the merger of Standard Statistics and Poor's in 1941, S&P adopted the Fitch rating scale. The only exception was for the rating of defaulting bonds, where the three ratings DDD, DD, and D were replaced by D for general defaults and SD for selective (i.e., partial) defaults.

Starting in 1973, Fitch and S&P began to refine their rating scale by dividing their AA–CCC rating categories into three subratings: a plus (minus) sign modified the most (least) creditworthy subrating; no modifier applied to the middle subrating (Kliger and Sarig 2000). This new rating scale did not affect any Fitch sovereign ratings until the 1990s, when Fitch reentered the sovereign rating business. The new scale was first applied to the S&P sovereign ratings in April 1983, when New Zealand was downgraded to AA+ from AAA. Moody's refined its corporate and sovereign ratings in April 1982 and August 1986, respectively, announcing the attachment of numerical modifiers to its ratings. Moody's rating modifiers were 1 for the best subrating, 2 for the middle subrating, and 3 for the worst subrating.

So the situation now is much different than in the interwar years. Today, the rating systems of Fitch, Moody's, and S&P enable global comparisons of rated securities, regardless of the type of rated entity, its geographical origin, or the obligation's denomination currency.

---

[8] During the two-step reduction of the rating range, bonds with highest ratings were artificially downgraded and assigned the new current highest rating (these rating actions concerned the US, British, and Canadian government bonds in 1938 and 1939).

## 3.2.2 The Dividing Line Between Investment Grade and Speculative Grade

The emergence of a cutoff between investment grade and speculative grade securities was a major event in the history of rating agencies.[9] As emphasized previously, Standard Statistics and Poor's were the only two CRAs that, as early as the 1920s, established a dividing line between investment and speculative grade bonds: B1/B for Standard Statistics and B**/B* for Poor's. In contrast, there was no such clear cutoff point in the ratings from Moody's and Fitch.

In fact, the first two regulatory rules using credit ratings, enacted in September 1931 and February 1936, contributed to the appearance of such a cutoff point. These two rules established a dividing line between "high" and "good" bonds (first four rating categories) on the one hand and, on the other hand, speculative grade bonds (securities rated below the fourth rating category). However, given that the agencies had different rating scales, there was still some uncertainty as to whether some bonds were of investment or speculative grade.

After the first regulatory rule was enacted, Moody's promptly established a clear dividing line (Baa/Ba). The other agencies did not clear matters up until 1937, when Fitch, Poor's, and Standard Statistics set up an explicit cutoff for investment vs. speculative grade in their methodologies (BBB/BB, B**/B*, and B1+/B1, respectively). In 1939, after Poor's introduced its new rating scale, the first four rating categories of each agency corresponded to investment grade securities, and those with lower ratings were viewed as speculative grade. This cutoff has remained unchanged to date.

The homogenization of scales is evident when one examines the current definitions of the Fitch, Moody's, and S&P ratings; see Tables 3.1–3.3.

**Table 3.1** Current meanings of Fitch ratings

| Category | Rating | Significance |
| --- | --- | --- |
| Investment grade | AAA | Denotes the lowest expectation of credit risk. Assigned only in case of an exceptionally strong capacity for timely payment of financial commitment that is highly unlikely to be adversely affected by foreseeable events |
| | AA | Denotes a very low expectation of credit risk. Indicates a very strong capacity for timely payment of financial commitment that is not significantly vulnerable to foreseeable events |
| | A | Denotes a low expectation of credit risk. The capacity for timely payment of financial commitments is considered to be strong yet more vulnerable to changes in circumstances or in economic conditions than is the case for higher ratings |
| | BBB | Indicates that there is currently a low expectation of credit risk. The capacity for timely payment of financial commitments is considered adequate, although adverse changes in circumstances and economic conditions are more likely to impair that capacity. This is the lowest investment grade category |

(continued)

---

[9] See Harold (1938) and Moody's (2004) for discussion of the problems that investors had distinguishing between investment grade and speculative grade bonds.

**Table 3.1** (continued)

| Category | Rating | Significance |
|---|---|---|
| Speculative grade | BB | Indicates that there is a possibility of credit risk developing, particularly as the result of adverse economic change over time; however, business or financial alternatives may be available to allow financial commitments to be met. Securities rated in this category are not of investment grade |
| | B | Indicates that significant credit risk is present though a limited margin of safety remains. Financial commitments are currently being met; however, capacity for continued payment is contingent upon a sustained, favorable business and economic environment |
| | CCC, CC, and C | Default is a real possibility. Capacity for meeting financial commitments is entirely reliant upon sustained, favorable business, or economic developments. A rating of CC indicates that default of some kind appears probable; a C rating signals imminent default |
| Default | RD | Securities are not meeting current obligations; RD designates default on part of the debt |
| | D | Securities are not meeting current obligations; D designates default on all of the debt |

*Source*: http://www.fitchratings.com

**Table 3.2** Current meanings of Moody's ratings

| Category | Rating | Significance |
|---|---|---|
| Investment grade | Aaa | Denotes obligations that are judged to be of the highest quality, with minimal credit risk |
| | Aa | Denotes obligations that are judged to be of high quality and are subject to very low credit risk |
| | A | Denotes obligations that are judged to be of upper-medium grade and are subject to low credit risk |
| | Baa | Denotes obligations that are subject to moderate credit risk; they are considered medium grade and as such may possess certain speculative characteristics |
| Speculative grade | Ba | Denotes obligations that are judged to have speculative elements and be subject to substantial credit risk |
| | B | Denotes obligations that are considered to be speculative and subject to high credit risk |
| | Caa | Denotes obligations that are judged to be of poor standing and are subject to very high credit risk |
| | Ca | Denotes obligations that are highly speculative and that are likely in (or near) default, with some prospect of recovering the principal and interest. |
| | C | Denotes obligations that are the lowest-rated class of bonds; they are typically in default, with little prospect of recovering the principal or interest |

*Source*: http://www.moodys.com

## 3.2 Significance of Rating Scales

**Table 3.3** Current meanings of S&P ratings

| Category | Rating | Significance |
|---|---|---|
| Investment grade | AAA | The highest rating assigned by S&P. The obligor's capacity to meet its financial commitment on the obligation is extremely strong |
| | AA | Differs from the highest-rated obligations only in small degree. The obligor's capacity to meet its financial commitment on the obligation is very strong |
| | A | Somewhat more susceptible to the adverse effects of changes in circumstances and economic conditions than obligations in higher categories. However, the obligor's capacity to meet its financial commitment on the obligation remains strong |
| | BBB | Obligations that exhibit adequate protection parameters; although adverse economic conditions or changing circumstances are more likely to lead to a weakened capacity of the obligor to meet its financial commitment on the obligation |
| Speculative grade | BB | An obligation that is less vulnerable to nonpayment than other speculative issues. However, it faces major ongoing uncertainties or exposure to adverse business, financial, or economic conditions that could lead to inadequate capacity of the obligor to meet its financial commitment on the obligation |
| | B | An obligation that is more vulnerable to nonpayment than are obligations rated BB although the obligor currently has the capacity to meet its financial commitment on the obligation. However, adverse business, financial, or economic conditions will likely impair the obligor's capacity or willingness to meet that commitment |
| | CCC and CC | An obligation rated CCC is currently vulnerable to nonpayment and is dependent upon favorable business, financial, and economic conditions for the obligor to meet its financial commitment on the obligation. In the event of adverse conditions, the obligor will likely not have the capacity to meet that commitment. An obligation rated CC is currently highly vulnerable to nonpayment |
| Default | SD and D | An obligor rated SD (selective default) or D has failed to pay one or more of its financial obligations. A D rating is assigned when S&P believes that the default will be a general default and that the obligor will fail to pay all or substantially all of its obligations as they come due. An SD rating is assigned when S&P believes that the obligor has selectively defaulted on a specific issue or class of obligations but it will continue to meet its payment obligations on other issues or classes of obligations in a timely manner |

*Source*: http://www.standardandpoors.com

## 3.3 Main Credit Rating Policies and Procedures

Since the first sovereign bond ratings were assigned in 1918, the rating systems of Fitch, Moody's, and S&P have evolved in response to the increasing depth and breadth of capital markets. Although most credit rating services launched so far have concerned financial institutions and the corporate and structured finance areas, sovereign ratings are now much more sophisticated than in the 1920s.

For instance, rating agencies in the interwar years assigned ratings to bonds exclusively. At that time, the bond issuers themselves were not rated; creditworthiness was assessed through the quality of the securities they issued. CRAs started rating sovereign bond issuers in the 1980s. These issuer credit ratings are opinions about the obligor's overall financial capacity to pay its financial obligations and do not apply to any specific financial obligation. Although CRAs continue to rate sovereign bonds, issuer credit ratings are the most commonly used credit opinions.[10]

Since the 1970s, CRAs have made efforts to inform investors also regarding the likely short-term evolution of ratings.

### 3.3.1 Short-Term Ratings

Moody's and S&P issued first short-term ratings to sovereigns as early as 1971 and 1975, respectively. Fitch did the same in 1995.

Short-term ratings, which are assigned to sovereign issuers and short-term securities, are opinions about the ability of issuers to honor short-term financial obligations (i.e., bonds that generally have an original maturity not exceeding 12 months). Fitch and Moody's short-term ratings are derived from their long-term ratings (see Table 3.4).

The F1+, F1, F2, and F3 ratings by Fitch indicate respectively "exceptionally strong," "strongest," "good," and "fair" short-term credit quality. The B and C short-term ratings indicate a speculative short-term credit quality and a high short-term default risk, respectively. The RD and D short-term ratings indicate, respectively, a partial and a broad-based default. Moody's Prime-1 rating signifies a superior ability to repay short-term debt, while Prime-2 and Prime-3 ratings indicate, respectively, "a strong ability" and "an acceptable ability" to repay short-term debt obligations. Issuers rated "Not Prime" do not fall within any of the "Prime" rating categories. S&P short-term rating scale is displayed in Table 3.5. It is worth noting that short-term rating changes are connected to long-term rating changes.

---

[10] Unless otherwise stated, the remaining of this book addresses the long-term credit ratings of sovereign issuers when discussing the sovereign ratings assigned by the agencies since the 1980s.

## 3.3 Main Credit Rating Policies and Procedures

**Table 3.4** Fitch and Moody's rating correspondence tables

| Fitch | | Moody's | |
|---|---|---|---|
| Long-term ratings | Short-term ratings | Long-term ratings | Short-term ratings |
| AAA | F1+ | Aaa | Prime-1 |
| AA+ | F1+ | Aa1 | Prime-1 |
| AA | F1+ | Aa2 | Prime-1 |
| AA− | F1+ | Aa3 | Prime-1 |
| A+ | F1+ or F1 | A1 | Prime-1 |
| A | F1 | A2 | Prime-1 or Prime-2 |
| A− | F1 or F2 | A3 | Prime-1 or Prime-2 |
| BBB+ | F2 | Baa1 | Prime-2 |
| BBB | F2 or F3 | Baa2 | Prime-2 or Prime-3 |
| BBB− | F2 or F3 | Baa3 | Prime-3 |
| BB+ | B | Ba1 | Not Prime |
| BB | B | Ba2 | Not Prime |
| BB− | B | Ba3 | Not Prime |
| B+ | B | B1 | Not Prime |
| B | B | B2 | Not Prime |
| B− | B | B3 | Not Prime |
| CCC | C | Caa | Not Prime |
| CC | C | Ca | Not Prime |
| C | C | C | Not Prime |
| RD | RD | | |
| D | D | | |

*Source*: http://www.fitchratings.com and http://www.moodys.com
*Note*: The RD short-term rating applies only to issuers

**Table 3.5** Current meanings of S&P short-term ratings

| Category | Short-term rating | Significance |
|---|---|---|
| Investment grade | A-1+ | The obligor's capacity to meet its financial commitments is extremely strong |
| | A-1 | The obligor has strong capacity to meet its financial commitments |
| | A-2 | The obligor has satisfactory capacity to meet its financial commitments; however, it is somewhat more susceptible to the adverse effects of changes in circumstances and economic conditions than obligors in the highest rating category |
| | A-3 | The obligor has adequate capacity to meet its financial obligations; however, adverse economic conditions or changing circumstances are more likely to lead to a weakened capacity of the obligor to meet its financial commitments |

(continued)

**Table 3.5** (continued)

| Category | Short-term rating | Significance |
|---|---|---|
| Speculative grade | B-1 | The obligor has a relatively stronger capacity to meet its financial commitments over the short-term compared with other speculative grade obligors |
| | B-2 | The obligor has an average capacity to meet its financial commitments over the short-term compared with other speculative grade obligors |
| | B-3 | The obligor has a relatively weaker capacity to meet its financial commitments over the short-term compared with other speculative grade obligors |
| | C | The obligor is currently vulnerable to nonpayment and is dependent upon favorable business, financial, and economic conditions to meet its financial commitments |
| Default | SD D | An SD rating is assigned when S&P believes that the obligor has selectively defaulted on a specific issue or class of obligations but that it will continue to meet its payment obligations on other issues or classes of obligations in a timely manner. A D rating is assigned when S&P believes that the default will be a general default and that the obligor will fail to pay all or substantially all of its obligations as they come due |

*Source*: http://www.standardandpoors.com

## 3.3.2 Reviews for Possible Rating Change

S&P, Moody's, and Fitch began placing sovereign credit ratings on review for possible rating change in 1991, 1992, and 1995, respectively. Although the terminology differs from one agency to the next ("creditwatch" for S&P, "watchlist" for Moody's, and "ratingwatch" for Fitch), this procedure indicates that a rating is under review for possible change in the short term.[11]

A rating can be placed on review for possible upgrade, for possible downgrade, or (more rarely) with direction uncertain,[12] which means the rating may be raised, lowered, or confirmed. A credit rating is removed from the watchlist once it has been upgraded, downgraded, or confirmed. A watchlist is often driven by events and is usually resolved over a relatively short period. Note that ratings can be raised or lowered without first being placed on creditwatch. Chapter 8 provides an exhaustive analysis of the creditwatch placements of Fitch, Moody's, and S&P sovereign ratings.

---

[11] The three terms are equivalent and are used interchangeably thereafter.

[12] This is Moody's term; S&P and Fitch use the terms "developing" and "evolving," respectively.

## 3.3.3 Rating Outlooks

S&P, Moody's, and Fitch started issuing rating outlooks for sovereign entities in 1989, 1997, and 2000, respectively. Rating outlooks indicate the likely direction of an issuer's rating over the medium term.[13]

There are four categories of rating outlooks. A "positive" outlook means that a rating may be raised, and a "negative" outlook means that a rating may be lowered. A "stable" outlook means that a rating is not likely to change. A "developing" outlook (termed "evolving" by Fitch) means a rating is contingent upon an event and thus may be raised or lowered. A positive (negative) outlook does not imply that an upgrade (a downgrade) is inevitable. Similarly, ratings with stable outlooks can be raised or lowered without a prior revision of the outlook. Chapter 8 also analyzes the sovereign rating outlooks assigned by Fitch, Moody's, and S&P.

## 3.4 Local and Foreign Currency Ratings

Traditionally, sovereigns can issue debt in local (i.e., domestic) currency (LC) or in foreign currency (FC).[14] During the interwar years, Fitch, Poor's, and Standard Statistics assigned ratings only to bonds denominated in US dollars (USD) or British pounds (GBP) that were listed on the New York Stock Exchange (NYSE). In contrast, Moody's rated both LC and FC securities, but it did not use this terminology, referring instead to the currency denomination of the securities.

Moody's explained the rationale behind its LC and FC policy in 1921 as follows: "the fact must be borne in mind that the ratings of all foreign government obligations are based on the point of view of the American investor (the investor who thinks and acts in 'dollars' and not in sterling, francs, mark or lira). From the standpoint of the Frenchman a franc investment (other things, such as yield and security being equal) is more desirable than a dollar bond; but from the American standpoint, the dollar bond is the best investment. If an American purchases a franc bond [...], he does it as a speculator in franc exchange, and not as an investor."[15] For this reason, Moody's rated the USD bonds issued by a sovereign higher than those denominated in LC or in any other currency. The rating gap between USD and non-USD sovereign bonds was typically one or two notches.[16]

---

[13] Moody's rating outlooks indicate the likely direction of the rating over "the medium term" (Moody 2010b). The time horizons of Fitch and S&P rating outlooks are "one- to two-year" and "six-month to two-year" periods, respectively (Fitch 2009; S&P 2010b).

[14] See Eichengreen et al. (2005) for a focus on the "original sin" hypothesis (i.e., the inability of a country to use its domestic currency to borrow abroad or to borrow long-term even domestically); see Hausmann and Panizza (2010) for an updated analysis.

[15] *Moody's Analyses of Investments and Security Rating Books – Government and Municipal Securities* (1921).

[16] Foreign governments whose USD bond rating was Aaa, Aa, or A had non-USD bonds rated one notch lower. For the sovereigns with a USD bond rating lower than A, there could be a two-notch gap.

**Table 3.6** LC–FC sovereign issuer rating differentials (in notches)

| CRA | As of 1 January 2001 | As of 1 January 2011 |
|---|---|---|
| Fitch | +1.26 | +0.43 |
| Moody's | +0.72 | +0.05 |
| S&P | +1.21 | +0.41 |

*Sources*: Author's computations from http://www.fitchratings.com, http://www.moodys.com, and http://www.standardandpoors.com
*Notes*: Ratings are transformed numerically. The differential calculation is: LC rating minus FC rating

The rebound of the sovereign rating activity in the 1980s was accompanied by a radical shift in policies regarding LC vs. FC. The wave of sovereign bankruptcies that occurred in Latin American countries in 1982–1983 demonstrated how FC debt was likely to default. Rating agencies drew lessons from this episode and revised their methodology. Moody's and S&P first assigned FC ratings to the most creditworthy sovereign issuers. Afterwards, they covered speculative grade issuers and published LC ratings in the 1990s.[17]

Since then, the LC rating of most sovereign issuers has been higher than the FC rating. This policy is underpinned by: (a) the greater capacity of governments to tax and appropriate LC vs. FC income and assets to pay their debt (Moody's 1999); and (b) the lower frequency of sovereign defaults on LC than on FC debt (S&P 2003). In 2001, the LC rating of sovereign issuers was, on average, one notch higher than the FC rating (see Table 3.6).

However, the LC–FC rating gap diminished in the 2000s for various reasons (see Fitch 2008; Moody's 2008; S&P 2005). First, financial liberalization increased the risk of spillover from FC debt crisis to LC debt. Second, emerging countries managed to accumulate massive FC reserves, which boosted their FC rating. Third, several governments became members of a monetary union (e.g., the European Economic and Monetary Union) or adopted another currency domestically (e.g., dollarization). For these countries, there is no longer a gap between FC and LC ratings.

Fitch, Moody's, and S&P today all tend to consider that governments are almost equally likely to default on either type of debt.

## 3.5 The Country Ceiling

Until the early 2000s, the FC rating of sovereigns served as a ceiling for the ratings of FC debt obligations of domestic issuers. In 2001, Moody's began to relax this "sovereign ceiling" policy in light of its belief that, "in an external payments/

---

[17] LC (resp., FC) ratings reflect the ability and willingness of a government to raise resources in its own currency (resp., in a foreign currency) to repay its debt.

currency crisis, a government would choose to default on its own external bonds without imposing a blanket debt moratorium on FC borrowers within its jurisdiction" (Moody's 2001).

As a result, in 2001 Moody's began to assign a ceiling for FC bonds and notes to every country in which there were rated entities; Fitch did the same in 2004. The "country ceiling" establishes the highest rating attainable for an issuer of long-term, FC-denominated bonds. These ceilings, which are expressed on the long-term issuer scale, reflect the "risk of capital and exchange controls being imposed by the sovereign authorities that would prevent or materially impede the private sector's ability to convert LC into FC and transfer to non-resident creditors (transfer and convertibility (T&C) risk)" (Fitch 2009; Moody's 2010b).[18]

S&P issues T&C assessments that reflect the "likelihood of a sovereign restricting nonsovereign access to foreign exchange needed to satisfy the nonsovereign's debt service obligations" (S&P 2010a). These T&C assessments, which are also expressed using the symbols of the long-term issuer scale, first appeared in 2005.

The FC country ceiling (or T&C assessment) is above the FC sovereign rating when the likelihood of the sovereign restricting access to foreign exchange needed for nonsovereign debt service is perceived as being significantly lower than the likelihood of the sovereign defaulting on its FC debt. Examples of such sovereigns include the Baltic states, Hungary, and Panama. In contrast, the two ratings are equal when a sovereign (e.g., China or Serbia) is likely to restrict access to FC and thereby constrain the FC rating of domestic issuers.

## 3.6 Rating Sovereigns That Default

The analysis of ratings assigned to defaulting sovereign bonds and defaulting sovereigns is useful for two reasons. First, it supports the view that ratings reflect not only a default probability but also a recovery rate.[19] Second, it discloses contradictions between official methodologies and actual rating practices.

During the interwar years, a few countries had several Moody's ratings that depended on whether or not their bonds had (a) sinking funds or (b) were pledged. This indicates that Moody's took the appropriate characteristics of bonds into account and was likely to issue higher ratings for bonds with guarantees. Also in

---

[18] Nonetheless, some ratings may pierce the country ceiling if the securities benefit from special characteristics that reduce the T&C risk.

[19] This finding was confirmed by David Levey (former Managing Director, Sovereign Risk Unit, Moody's Investors Service) in an interview with the author on 16 December 2003. In practice, Moody's ratings have traditionally reflected a probability of default for investment grade; whereas the recovery rate has been taken into account only for speculative-grade issuers (e-mail from Richard Cantor to the author, 17 November 2004).

this period, two defaulting securities or countries might have different ratings. The most significant example was the four-notch gap between Mexican and Russian bond ratings in 1924 and 1925; even though both countries were in default (their respective Moody's ratings were Ba and C). This gap, all the more impressive given that Moody's ratings were based on a nine-notch scale, was explained by Moody's forecasting that the Russian default would impose larger losses on investors than would the Mexican default.[20] Similar rating gaps among defaulting bonds were also observed in ratings issued by Fitch, Poor's, and Standard Statistics.

Note also that the ratings of defaulting securities may occasionally be no less than those of nondefaulting issues. In 1923 and 1924, for example, ratings of several defaulting Mexican bonds (issues of 1899, 1910, and 1913) were higher than those of nondefaulting Polish bonds. More recently, in 2003, the defaulting Dominican Republic was rated higher (B3) than Ecuador and Moldova (both rated Caa1), which actually met their debt obligations.[21]

It is worth remarking that, during the interwar years, the three CRAs other than Moody's assigned a speculative grade rating to defaulting bonds. For instance, Dominican securities were rated B by Fitch, Poor's, and Standard Statistics in the late 1930s despite the default status of those securities.

There are several similar illustrations for the 1990s–2000s. Indonesia was rated B– by Fitch between March 1998 and August 2002 despite several payment disruptions during that period. Fitch's rating rationale was that the risk of restructuring was low given the small FC bond debt (Fitch 2002). In contrast, Fitch did not explain why defaulting Russia was rated CCC for the period August 1998 to May 2000.

Moody's rating scale is interesting to analyze because it does not stipulate a separate category for defaults. In particular, of the fourteen sovereign defaults listed by Moody's during 1998–2009, only three (Argentina in 2001–2003, Moldova in 2002–2003, and Ecuador in 2008–2009) resulted in a downgrade to Ca.[22] For other defaulting issuers, the ratings assigned ranged between B3 and Caa3. No defaulting sovereign was downgraded to C (i.e., the lowest rating assigned by Moody's).

Moody's ratings policy contrasts with that at S&P and Fitch, where all sovereign borrowers defaulting since the mid-1990s were automatically downgraded to the default rating category.[23] From this perspective, the rating policy of Fitch evolved over time in that there were several examples of defaulting sovereigns rated higher

---

[20] *Moody's Investment Letter* (1922), "Defaulted Foreign Government Bonds," 28 December. *Moody's Investment Letter* (1923), "Mexican Debt Agreement," 8 February.

[21] This practice contradicts the rating definitions for Moody's, described previously, where the lowest two rating categories are based on the prospects of recovery (Ca rating for defaulting bonds with high recovery prospects; C rating for defaulting bonds with low recovery prospects).

[22] Author's computations based on Moody's (2010a) and http://www.moodys.com.

[23] Based on http://www.standardandpoors.com and http://www.fitchratings.com. Russia and Indonesia were the only sovereigns that received a nondefault rating from Fitch even though they did not repay their debt.

than nondefaulting sovereigns. During 1924–1925, as remarked previously, defaulting Mexican bonds were rated one notch higher than nondefaulting Polish bonds.

These examples suggest that the credibility of a defaulting country making efforts to ensure a high recovery rate to investors is stronger than that of a still creditworthy country whose willingness to pay is uncertain. The examples clearly support the view that sovereign ratings have, since 1918, measured both a default probability and a recovery rate for lower-rated obligors. S&P ratings are an exception to this trend because for several decades their ratings have strictly reflected the default probability. Fitch began following this procedure in 2005.

## 3.7 Sovereign Recovery Ratings

In 2005, Fitch modified its policy so that ratings would measure the probability of default only. At the same time, Fitch decided to assign Issuer Default Ratings (IDRs) to all the sovereigns it currently rated [24] as well as recovery ratings (RRs) to debt instruments issued by sovereigns with IDRs of B+ and below. It is worth noting that the recovery analysis is performed under a hypothetical assumption that the default scenario has already occurred.

Fitch employs recovery "bands" in its RR approach. Securities rated RR1 have characteristics in line with securities historically recovering 91–100% of current principal and related interest. Likewise, securities rated RR2 (resp., RR3, RR4, RR5, and RR6) have characteristics in line with securities historically recovering 71–90% (resp., 51–70%, 31–50%, 11–30%, and 0–10%) of current principal and related interest. When a security defaults, its issuer will be categorized as D or RD. However, the rating of specific classes of debt securities still ranges from B through C, and nonperforming securities are no longer assigned a specific "default" rating (see Table 3.7).

**Table 3.7** Fitch indicative ratings for distressed and defaulted issues

| Recovery rating | Potential issue rating |
|---|---|
| RR1 | CCC+/B−/B |
| RR2 | CCC/CCC+ |
| RR3 | CCC−/CCC |
| RR4 | CC/CCC− |
| RR5 | C/CC |
| RR6 | C |

*Source*: Fitch (2005b)

---

[24] The IDR, which is equivalent to the issuer credit rating presented previously, is the benchmark "probability of default" rating. The IDR does not distinguish default events according to expected recovery rates.

**Table 3.8** S&P global sovereign recovery rating scale

| Recovery rating | Recovery expectations | Recovery range (%) | Issue rating |
|---|---|---|---|
| 1+ | Full recovery | 100 | +3 notches |
| 1 | Very high recovery | 90–100 | +2 notches |
| 2 | Substantial recovery | 70–90 | +1 notch |
| 3 | Meaningful recovery | 50–70 | 0 notch |
| 4 | Average recovery | 30–50 | 0 notch |
| 5 | Modest recovery | 10–30 | −1 notch |
| 6 | Negligible recovery | 0–10 | −2 notches |

*Sources*: S&P (2007)
*Note*: The issue ratings are determined relative to the issuer credit rating. For example, the bonds of a sovereign issuer rated B+ and with a recovery rating of 2, will be rated one notch higher (i.e., BB−)

Among the factors that affect RRs are collateral, seniority relative to other obligations, FC debt as a percentage of total public debt, proportion of bond debt held by international institutions, debt sustainability, importance of the financial sector, sovereign's willingness to service debt, openness of the economy, GDP per capita, and past debt restructuring practices (Fitch 2005b). This RR methodology has officially made it possible for a defaulting sovereign bond to be rated higher than one that is nondefaulting.

S&P partly adopted the Fitch policy by assigning its first sovereign RRs in December 2006. However, these RRs apply to speculative grade sovereign issuers and not to the actual issues (S&P 2007). The S&P sovereign RR scale consists of seven categories (see Table 3.8).

The S&P sovereign recovery analysis involves the following factors: comparison of stressed debt levels with debt capacities, default and restructuring history, proportion of official bilateral lending, impact of default crisis on the financial system and economic activity in general, recent recovery precedents of other sovereign defaulters, proportion of existing IMF debt, potential for currency depreciation, importance of access to global goods and capital markets, potential for extraordinary assistance, fiscal and external flexibility, exposure of domestic financial sector to sovereign debt, nature of financial inflows, ratio of resident to nonresident debtholders, the possibility of additional debt being added to that of the sovereign, expected postdefault political situation, and bargaining power of the sovereign (S&P 2007).[25]

Unlike its two competitors, Moody's does not assign sovereign RRs. This is consistent with its policy of assigning issuer ratings that reflect both a probability of default and an estimate of financial losses in the event of a default (Moody's 2010b).

---

[25] As of 31 March 2011, S&P assigned a recovery rating to 33 countries; all of them were rated 2, 3, or 4 (http://www.standardandpoors.com).

# References

Eichengreen B., Hausmann R. and Panizza U. (2005), "The Mystery of Original Sin", in Eichengreen B. and Hausmann R. (eds.), *Other People's Money*, Chicago University Press, Chicago.

Fitch (various years), *Fitch Bond Book*.

Fitch IBCA (1998), "Fitch Sovereign Ratings – Rating Methodology".

Fitch Ratings (2002), "Indonesia Upgraded to B, Outlook Stable", 1 August.

Fitch Ratings (2005a), "The Role of Recovery Analysis in Ratings – Enhancing Informational Content and Transparency", 14 February.

Fitch Ratings (2005b), "Sovereign Issuer Default and Recovery Ratings", 14 December.

Fitch Ratings (2008), "Local Currency Debt Markets Emerge from the Shadows", 3 April.

Fitch Ratings (2009), "Definitions of Ratings and Other Scales", March.

Harold G. (1938), *Bond Ratings as an Investment Guide*, Ronald Press Company, New York.

Hausmann R. and Panizza U. (2010), "Redemption or abstinence? Original sin, currency mismatches and counter-cyclical policies in the new millennium", *Working Paper No. 194, Centre for International Development at Harvard University*, January.

Kliger D. and Sarig O. (2000), "The Information Value of Bond Ratings", *Journal of Finance*, Vol. 55, No. 6.

Moody's Investors Service (various years), *Moody's Manual of Investments – American and Foreign Government Securities*.

Moody's Investors Service (various years), "Moody's Investment Letters".

Moody's Investors Service (1999), "Rating Methodology – The Usefulness of Local Currency Ratings in Countries with Low Foreign Currency Country Ceilings", July.

Moody's Investors Service (2001), "Revised Country Ceiling Policy – Rating Methodology", June.

Moody's Investors Service (2004), "Tracing the Origins of 'Investment Grade'", January.

Moody's Investors Service (2008), "A Guide to Moody's Sovereign Ratings", December.

Moody's Investors Service (2010a), "Sovereign Default and Recovery Rates, 1983–2009", April.

Moody's Investors Service (2010b), "Rating Symbols and Definitions", October.

Poor's (various years), *Poor's Volume*.

Poor's (various years), *Poor's Rating Services*.

Standard & Poor's (1979), *Standard & Poor's Ratings Guide 1979*.

Standard & Poor's (2003), "Sovereign Defaults: Heading Lower Into 2004", 18 September.

Standard & Poor's (2005), "Sovereign Foreign and Local Currency Rating Differentials", 19 October.

Standard & Poor's (2007), "Introduction of Sovereign Recovery Ratings", 14 June.

Standard & Poor's (2010a), "Sovereign Rating and Country T&C Assessment Histories", 13 April.

Standard & Poor's (2010b), "Standard & Poor's Ratings Definitions", 3 May.

Standard Statistics (various years), *Standard Bond Books*.

# Chapter 4
# How Are Sovereign Ratings Assigned?

## 4.1 Introduction

This chapter describes the rating process and emphasizes that CRAs have always used an analyst-driven approach to assign sovereign ratings.

The rating process changed radically in January 1968 when S&P decided to charge fees to municipal bond issuers, thus switching from an investor-pay model to an issuer-pay model. Moody's followed S&P's policy and, by July 1974, both agencies were charging for municipal and corporate ratings. Sovereign issuers did not have to pay for their ratings until the early 1990s. This shift in the CRAs' business model, which meant that they stopped publishing unsolicited ratings and instead released their credit opinions with the consent of issuers, naturally affected the rating process. Under the investor-pay model, there was no business relation between the CRAs and the sovereigns that were rated. Hence, the rating process was relatively simple and depended on the internal organization of each agency. Under the current issuer-pay model, however, issuers generally participate in the rating process.

This chapter is organized as follows. Section 4.2 explores the organization of sovereign rating teams and the profile of analysts. Section 4.3 shows how the issuer-pay model has modified sovereign risk assessment. It also highlights the importance of rating committees and the tight relations between issuers and the CRAs' analysts since the early 1990s.

## 4.2 The Sovereign Rating Teams

### 4.2.1 The Interwar Years

Fitch, Moody's, Poor's, and Standard Statistics provided little information on the number and the profile of analysts at work during the interwar years.

*Moody's Manuals* were said to be "prepared with the assistance of a corps of specialists in the various fields, and the services which supplement the volumes [were] conducted by a large staff of experts."[1] In the sovereign rating area, John Moody and Max Winkler played a prominent role. John Moody signed every issue of *Investment Letters* until 1923 and every introduction of the *Manuals* until 1921. Furthermore, he personally supervised all *Manuals* until the late 1920s and kept abreast of the latest news in the sovereign area. In 1921, for example, Moody spent several weeks in England, France, Belgium, and Germany investigating their financial and economic situations.[2] Winkler, a member of Moody's editorial board between 1922 (which saw the creation of a formal rating department, managed by W. Barrett Brown) and 1927, was in charge of foreign government bond ratings. He launched his own manuals in 1928 (*Winkler's Manual of Foreign Corporations*, published by Overseas Statistics) and wrote two books: *Investments of United States Capital in Latin America* (World Peace Foundation Pamphlets, 1929) and *Foreign Bonds, An Autopsy* (Roland Swain Company, 1933). In the latter book, Winkler often refers to his analyses at Moody's. Winkler was also the only senior analyst to have a Ph.D. in economics, as the cover of *Manuals of Government Securities* attested.

The information disclosed by Standard Statistics did not indicate whether it had a specific sovereign rating unit. However, the agency published a list of senior analysts and economists who were part of the rating process.[3] In 1922, Clayton A. Penhale was the senior editor. He became the first president of S&P after Standard Statistics merged with Poor's in 1941. Laurence H. Sloan was managing editor before being appointed vice-president. Sloan wrote several books on corporation profits and stock markets. Standard Statistics had several contributing editors: Eugene E. Agger, Lewis H. Haney, and Carl E. Parry. Agger served as associate professor of economics at Columbia University, and Haney was the director of the New York University Bureau of Business Research. Parry was a professor of economics at Tulane University who subsequently became director of the Division of Security Loans at the Board of Governors of the Federal Reserve System. Standard Statistics also hired consulting economists, including T.E. Gregory and Herbert J. Davenport. Gregory had a Bachelor of Science degree from the London School of Economics; Davenport, professor of economics at Cornell University, was a famous economist who wrote many books and research articles. Standard Statistics had a total staff of nearly 300.[4] However, it is difficult to assess the role played by each staff member in the sovereign rating process.

---

[1] *Moody's Manual* (1926), "Introduction," p. vi.
[2] *Moody's Investment Letter* (1921), "The Foreign Situation," 8 September.
[3] Standard Statistics (1922), *Standard Daily Trade Service*, May.
[4] Standard Statistics (1923), *Standard Daily Trade Service*, August.

Fitch and Poor's seem not to have provided information on the composition of their teams.[5] The four rating agencies all had their headquarters in New York City as well as offices in other American cities.[6] Moody's and Standard Statistics had an office in London, too.

## 4.2.2 The Modern Era

Because of the withdrawal of many sovereign ratings in 1940 through the mid-1980s, sovereign rating activity was moribund during this period. Moody's analysts in charge of corporate and banking ratings supervised the few sovereigns that were still rated.[7] Between 1968 and 1974, S&P suspended its sovereign activity altogether. Fitch gave up rating sovereigns in the 1960s and did not resume until the 1990s.

Following the Venezuelan rating failure of 1983,[8] Moody's sovereign rating activity was broadly reorganized in 1985–1986 under the auspices of Jolene Larson: a sovereign risk unit was established in the latter part of 1985, but it was a component of the bank and finance department. Three senior sovereign analysts were appointed: David Levey, Guillermo Estebañez, and Roger Nye.[9] David Levey was promoted to managing director of the team and then became head and co-head of the sovereign rating unit until 2004. Vincent Truglia, who had been co-head with Levey since 1996, assumed leadership of the team until 2008. Pierre Cailleteau then took over from Truglia as head of the sovereign rating group but resigned in May 2010. Bart Oosterveld (chief credit officer for public sector ratings, which includes sovereign ratings) led the sovereign team on an interim basis until September 2010. Daniel McGovern served as managing director until Bart Oosterveld came back as head of the sovereign risk group in January 2011. Prior to joining Moody's, David Levey had been with Wells Fargo for 2 years as a country risk manager, and Vincent Truglia had worked for the Irving Trust Co./Bank of New York and the Federal Reserve Bank of New York. Pierre Cailleteau had spent several years at the Banque de France, the IMF, and the Crédit Agricole in the 1990s and during the first half of the 2000s. Bert Oosterveld began his career at Moody's.

The recent turnover of the top management at Moody's sovereign rating group contrasts with the relative stability observed at S&P. David Beers (managing director

---

[5] As evidenced by browsing *Poor's Volumes* and *Fitch Bond Books*.
[6] After Poor's went bankrupt and was refinanced by Paul T. Babson, the agency was headquartered in Wellesley (Massachusetts) until its merger with Standard Statistics in 1941.
[7] David Levey (former Managing Director, Sovereign Risk Unit, Moody's Investors Service) in an interview with the author on 16 December 2003 in New York.
[8] Venezuela was rated Aaa by Moody's when it defaulted.
[9] "Moody's Moves into Sovereign Debt Rating," Australian Financial Review, 14 July 1986.

and global head of sovereign and international public finance ratings), John Chambers (deputy head of the sovereign ratings group and later chairman of the sovereign rating committee), Marie Cavanaugh (officer, sovereign rating criteria), Jane Eddy (managing director, Latin America sovereign ratings), and Takahira Ogawa (director, Asia-Pacific sovereign ratings) have held their positions (or nearly equivalent ones) for more than a decade. Several of these senior analysts had experience in the banking industry prior to joining S&P.[10]

The sovereign rating activity of Fitch was boosted after it acquired IBCA and Duff and Phelps in 1997 and 2000, respectively.[11] David Riley has been managing director of the Fitch sovereign and international public finance team since June 2001; he was previously a senior economist at UBS Warburg. Several managing and senior directors worked at Duff and Phelps (Shelley Schetty and Roger Scher) or at IBCA (Paul Rawkins and Richard Fox) before joining Fitch. Most had also been country/sovereign risk analysts in other firms or institutions: Roger Scher at the Federal Reserve, S.G. Warburg, and the US Department of State; Paul Rawkins at Lloyds Bank UK; Richard Fox at Midland Bank; and James McCormack at Export Development Corp. of Canada.[12]

It is worth noting that very few current or former top managers and directors in any rating agency have a Ph.D. in economics. Most have a M.A. in economics from an American, Canadian, or British university.

Moody's sovereign rating group has traditionally been headquartered in New York City, although several senior vice-presidents/regional credit officers as well as vice-presidents/senior credit officers have worked in London, Frankfurt, or Singapore. S&P headquarters in New York City, but David Beers's office is in London. Several S&P managing directors, senior directors, and directors are located in London, Frankfurt, Paris, Toronto, Buenos Aires, Melbourne, or Singapore. Fitch's sovereigns and international public finance team is based in London, but a few managing and senior directors are located in New York City or Hong Kong. Lower-ranking analysts of Fitch, Moody's, and S&P may be based locally and have their office in peripheral countries.

## 4.3 The Sovereign Rating Process

The features of the current rating process, which is based on participation of sovereign borrowers in the CRAs' analyses, took shape in the early 1990s when the investor–pay model gave way to the issuer-pay model in the sovereign rating area.

---

[10] Information collected by the author during the S&P annual meeting in Paris, 24 June 2008.

[11] In August 1996, Fitch, Duff & Phelps, and IBCA rated 1, 8, and 40 countries, respectively (Huhne 1996). In August 2001, Fitch rated 71 sovereigns.

[12] *Fitch Sovereign Brochure* (undated document).

### 4.3.1 Shifting from Unsolicited to Solicited Ratings

During the interwar years, the four rating agencies did not document their rating process. It is therefore impossible to assess the exact role played by the analysts[13] or to determine whether committees were used to assign ratings. Given that CRAs issued unsolicited ratings, it seems that they did not incorporate information provided directly by the foreign governments.

Moody's used data provided by the League of Nations and also relied on its foreign statistical department, which gathered information and statistics from mostly American sources (the State Department, the Department of Commerce, and US embassies). These data were then disseminated through two types of publications. *Moody's Manuals* covered foreign government and municipal securities; analyzed the political, economic, and financial situations of every country; and assigned ratings to their securities. Issued once a year, these manuals consisted of about 1,000 pages in 1918 before reaching more than 3,000 pages in the 1930s. Every week, Moody's also released *Investment Letters*.[14] These contained special articles (devoted to a specific country or group of countries), bulletins of ratings, an annual review and forecast report, and investment recommendations.[15]

Standard Statistics, Fitch, and Poor's did not disclose their information sources. Standard Statistics published its sovereign ratings in its *Standard Bond Books* and provided complementary data in its *Standard Daily Trade Services*. Fitch and Poor's compiled their sovereign risk analyses and ratings in the *Fitch Bond Books* and *Poor's Volumes*, respectively.[16]

The assignment of unsolicited ratings lasted until 1991–1992. In September 1986, shortly after the creation of its sovereign risk unit, Moody's made an announcement in which it explained that it would assign more unsolicited ratings.[17] Although relevant information was publicly available through the IMF, World Bank, and OECD reports and data, rating foreign governments without their participation was not so easy. As a result, Moody's reorganized its rating process by setting up meetings with governments, although no fees were paid. S&P followed Moody's policy and started assigning unsolicited ratings to sovereign borrowers in 1988. Until then, S&P ranked foreign governments that had not requested a rating in terms of six categories ranging from "very strong" to "inadequate."[18]

---

[13] The exception was John Moody, who certainly had a strong influence on the rating process.

[14] *Investment Letters* were renamed *Investment Surveys* in 1931 and *Bond Surveys* in 1936.

[15] Unlike now, Moody's publications then included lists of "attractive" bonds as well as recommendations on whether to sell, buy, or hold securities.

[16] See Flandreau et al. (2010) for an exhaustive presentation of the products offered by the four agencies.

[17] Moody's FC sovereign ratings increased from 11 in 1985 to 34 in 1990.

[18] "US Credit Rating Agency Is Considering Altering the Way It Expresses Its Assessments of Sovereign Borrowers," Financial Times, 8 July 1988.

The implementation of Brady Plan debt restructuring agreements from 1989 combined with the increasing number of countries that needed to borrow on capital markets boosted the demand for sovereign ratings. In 1991 and 1992, sovereigns accepted the policy of paying to be assigned a rating. The most creditworthy governments (e.g., Chile) wanted to demonstrate that their credit standing had recovered from previous financial crises, and middle- and low-income countries preferred a low rating to no rating at all.[19] Sovereign ratings were also appreciated by investors as independent and relevant credit opinions that could differ from those of investment banks.

### 4.3.2 Importance of the Rating Committee

The standardization of the sovereign rating process that began in the early 1990s lies not only on the participation of issuers but also on the conduct of rating committees. Actually, sovereign ratings were assigned and reviewed using a committee process *prior* to the shift from unsolicited to solicited sovereign rating assignments. For instance, Moody's held a committee meeting on 15 August 1986 to reassess the credit risk of Denmark and New Zealand; this followed Moody's decision to refine its sovereign rating scale. However, the current rating process described next is one that involves participation of the issuer.

The rating processes of Fitch, Moody's, and S&P are, in fact, quite similar (see Fitch 2006; Moody's 2004; S&P 2009). The rating process begins with a request for a rating made by the sovereign issuer. Once the terms of payment are made, the issuer is assigned to a lead (or primary) analyst who works with the support of a back-up (or secondary) analyst.[20] The primary analyst is responsible for leading the analysis and organizing a meeting with the issuer.[21] The meeting is an opportunity to discuss with country officials (e.g., the head of state, the prime minister, the minister of finance, the minister of economic affairs, the head of the central bank, top civil servants, trade union leaders). When data collection and analysis have been completed, the primary analyst formulates a rating recommendation for presentation to the committee.

The committee process is intended to limit the influence that any single analyst might have on the agency's rating opinions. The committee size for rating decisions ranges from four to ten analysts and generally includes at least one analyst who is

---

[19] David Levey (former Managing Director, Sovereign Risk Unit, Moody's Investors Service) in an interview with the author on 22 March 2010 in New York.

[20] Since the International Organization of Securities Commissions (IOSCO) code was introduced in 2004, there has been a strict separation between analytical and commercial functions within every rating agency. Thus, analysts are supposed to be shielded from information about the fees being charged for their work (IOSCO 2004).

[21] During the past decade, the number of countries monitored by a given analyst ranged from 8 to 15 (figures based on interviews with various sovereign rating analysts).

## 4.3 The Sovereign Rating Process

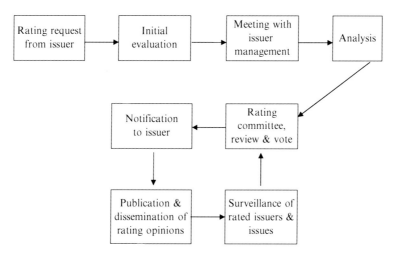

**Fig. 4.1** Standard rating process. *Source*: S&P (2009)

senior director or managing director. The committee discusses the lead analyst's recommendation and the facts supporting that rating. The voting members of the committee, who are senior analysts exclusively, express their views on the recommendation.[22] Each voting member has one vote. Finally, the committee officially assigns the rating.

The issuer is notified of the rating decision and the major considerations supporting it. Fitch and S&P ratings can be appealed prior to their publication if meaningful new information is presented by the issuer. Obviously, this appeal may not alter the rating committee's decision. In contrast, Moody's ratings cannot be appealed. Once the final rating is assigned, the analytic process is complete. The rating decision is then disseminated to the public via the news media and the agency's website.

Sovereign ratings are subsequently monitored on an ongoing basis. Primary analysts are responsible for surveillance of the ratings. They, as well as managing directors and directors, may initiate a rating review whenever they consider that political, economic, fiscal, financial, or any other information is likely to affect the issuer's creditworthiness. Ratings are reviewed at least once a year, which entails another rating process. In principle, watchlist changes, outlook changes, and rating confirmations require evaluation by a rating committee. The main steps of the rating process are summarized in Fig. 4.1.

Some sovereign issuers may refuse to participate in the rating process, in which case there is no communication with the issuer on credit matters. In February 2009,

---

[22] Since lower-ranking analysts can be lead analysts, this rule means that a lead analyst may not be allowed to vote.

Moody's listed three countries as nonparticipating issuers: Bahrain, Saudi Arabia, and Turkmenistan (Moody's 2009). The withdrawal of a sovereign rating may come at the issuer's request (as Mali and the Seychelles demanded from Standard & Poor's in July 2008 and August 2009, respectively). Withdrawal may also occur at the CRA's initiative if it lacks adequate information to maintain the rating (e.g., Moody's decision to withdraw its rating of Moldova in October 2009) or if all the country's traded international bonds have expired (e.g., Fitch's rating withdrawals for Turkmenistan and Gambia in February 2005 and July 2007, respectively). In June 2002, Moody's removed its sovereign rating for Iran because the US administration viewed this rating as being inconsistent with US-led economic sanctions against that country. Fitch removed its ratings for Iran in April 2008 following the maturity and full repayment of the last outstanding Eurobond issued by the Iranian government. Fitch claimed that its rating withdrawal was not the result of economic sanctions or pressure from the US government and did not reflect any developments in the Iranian economy.[23]

## References

Fitch (various years), *Fitch Bond Books*.
Fitch Ratings (undated), "Fitch Sovereign Brochure".
Fitch Ratings (2006), "The Rating Process", July.
Flandreau M., Gaillard N. and Packer F. (2010), "To Err Is Human: Rating Agencies and the Interwar Foreign Government Debt Crisis", *BIS Working Papers No. 335*, December.
Huhne C. (1996), "Rating Sovereign Risk", *Bank of England, Financial Stability Review*, Issue 1, Autumn.
International Organization of Securities Commissions (2004), *Code of Conduct Fundamentals for Credit Rating Agencies*, December.
Moody's Investors Service (various years), "Investment Letters".
Moody's Investors Service (various years), *Manuals of Government Securities*.
Moody's Investors Service (2004), "Guide to Moody's Ratings, Rating Process, and Rating Practices", June.
Moody's Investors Service (2009), "Non-Participating Rated Issuers, February".
Poor's (various years), *Poor's Volumes*.
Standard & Poor's (2009), "Guide to Credit Rating Essentials".
Standard Statistics (various years), *Standard Bond Books*.
Standard Statistics (various years), "Standard Daily Trade Services".

---

[23] See "Fitch Withdraws Iran Rating on Bond Payment," *Reuters*, 24 April 2008.

# Chapter 5
# Moody's Sovereign Ratings: 1918–1939 and 1986–2006 Compared

This chapter analyzes the determinants of sovereign ratings in two different periods. It specifically focuses on ratings issued by Moody's during the interwar years and today (1986–2006), two periods characterized by intense sovereign rating activity. The key finding is that although the regulatory framework and the rating industry are clearly different in the two periods – as the previous chapters showed – the determinants of Moody's sovereign ratings have remained the same.

For the interwar years, I examine foreign government securities, thus excluding from the sample all government-guaranteed bonds, subsovereign bonds (states, counties, cities, etc), bonds issued by countries that were not fully independent at the time of issuance (except Canada), and bonds issued by the government of the United States of America (benchmark). For the modern era, I study sovereign ratings assigned to countries. I also discriminate between sovereign bonds according to their currency of issuance. Putting LC bonds aside, I analyze (a) sovereign securities denominated in USD that were listed on the New York Stock Exchange (NYSE) and/or payable in the United States and (b) sovereign bonds denominated in GBP, listed on the NYSE between 1918 and 1938 (225 foreign government securities in total). For 1986–2006, I focus on sovereign ratings in FC.

This chapter is divided into five sections. Section 5.1 is a review of the literature. Section 5.2 describes Moody's rating policy during the two periods. Section 5.3 presents Moody's official methodologies and Sect. 5.4 analyzes the determinants of sovereign ratings for the periods under consideration. Section 5.5 concludes.

## 5.1 Review of the Literature

This chapter stands at the crossroads of two categories of the literature: empirical studies of the sovereign lending boom and bust in the interwar period, and empirical studies of the determinants of sovereign ratings since the 1990s.

Several research works studied the unprecedented sovereign lending boom on the NYSE in the 1920s and the wave of defaults that followed. Madden et al. (1937),

Lewis (1938, 1945), Borchard (1951), and Wynne (1951) analyze the role of the United States as first creditor from World War I and present a broad overview of the causes and extent of sovereign defaults that surged in 1931. Winkler (1933) and Rippy (1950) insist on the bankers' inability to discriminate among good and bad debtors. More relevantly, Mintz (1951) highlights the decline in the quality of USD foreign government bonds floated in the 1920s: the percentage of securities that lapsed into default in the 1930s, according to their issuance year, was 10% for bonds issued in 1920, 35% for 1925, and more than 80% for 1929. Much later, Eichengreen and Werley (1988) and Eichengreen and Portes (1989), by computing realized rates of return for USD sovereign bonds issued in the 1920s, provide a scale of country creditworthiness. Eastern European and Latin American countries are at the bottom of this scale, whereas Western Europe stands at the top. Finally, Flandreau et al. (2010) study the performance of sovereign ratings during the interwar era and find that they generally did not exhibit forecasting capacities superior to those embedded in available market prices.

The literature dealing with the contemporary sovereign ratings methodology emerges with Cantor and Packer (1996). They find that five variables are likely to explain Moody's and S&P's sovereign ratings issued in September 1995: per capita income, inflation, external debt, and level of economic development and default history. Jüttner and McCarthy (2000) show that Cantor and Packer's model became less accurate after the structural break that was the Asian crisis. After adding five financial sector and monetary variables, Jüttner and McCarthy suggest that the determinants of 1998 ratings are the current account balance, the indicators for economic development and default history, the interest rate differential vis-à-vis the USD, and the range of problematic assets. Nevertheless, two follow-up studies corroborate Cantor and Packer's results. For Afonso (2003), most significant variables for 2002 ratings (per capita income, inflation, and indicators for economic development and default history) were already determinants for Cantor and Packer. Moody's (2004) own study produces a similar finding: two of their four explanatory variables (per capita GDP and external debt) are the same as Cantor and Packer's. The main finding of Moody's is the incorporation of a political variable that significantly improves the model. Focusing on short- and long-run determinants of sovereign ratings, Afonso et al. (2011) find that the level of GDP per capita, real GDP growth, the public debt level, and the government balance have a consistent short-term impact. Government effectiveness, the level of external debt, and external reserves are important long-run determinants. Lastly, Bhatia (2002) has a different approach: he analyzes the evolution of the sovereign rating methodology according to Moody's and S&P's publications: he underlines the structural break of the Asian crisis and the introduction of financial and assets quality criteria by both credit rating agencies after 1998.

## 5.2 Moody's Rating Policy

A common feature of the two periods is the way that Moody's began rating sovereign bonds in 1918 and resumed in 1986. In 1919 and 1920, many sovereign bonds listed in *Moody's Manuals* had not yet been rated: the rating agency explained its

## 5.2 Moody's Rating Policy

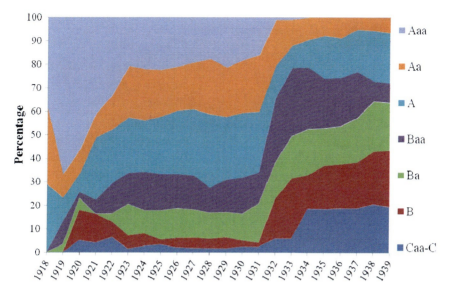

**Fig. 5.1** Distribution of sovereign ratings by categories, 1918–1939. *Note*: All ratings are the ratings listed in *Moody's Manuals* for the year considered. *Sources*: Author's computations based on *Moody's Manuals* (1918–1939)

restraint by citing a lack of information or political and/or financial disturbances.[1] Actually, Moody's had a conservative policy. An examination of the three waves of newly rated bonds (1918, 1919, and 1920) shows that Moody's first rated high-grade sovereign bonds and only later rated riskier and riskier securities (Fig. 5.1): in 1918, the lowest USD bond rating was A; in 1919, it was Ba; and in 1920 Caa. In 1921, all listed sovereign bonds were assigned a rating.[2] The mid-1980s' resumption of rating sovereign bonds followed the same top-down approach. Assignments of low ratings were late: the first B and Caa ratings were not issued until 1989 and 1998 (Fig. 5.2). Second, the proportion of speculative-grade ratings from 1934 to 1939 was greater than for any year in the modern era: more than 65% of sovereign bonds in 1938 vs. a 47.2% high in 1999. This difference is largely due to the massive downgrades that occurred in 1932–1934 (Table 5.1). Third, the number and percentage of countries upgraded in 2002 (including a large proportion of Eastern European countries) were higher than those of countries downgraded in 1997–1998

---

[1] *Moody's Manual of Investments – American and Foreign Government Securities* (1918).

[2] During the following years, Moody's ratings covered not only bonds quoted on the NYSE but also LC and FC securities quoted in Tokyo and on European Stock Exchanges (from the London Stock Exchange to much smaller stock exchanges, such as Belgrade and Kaunas).

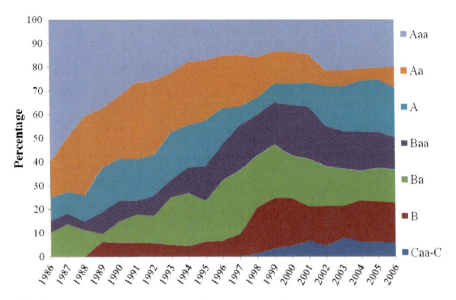

**Fig. 5.2** Distribution of sovereign ratings by categories, 1986–2006. *Note*: All ratings are as of 31 December. *Sources*: Author's computations based on http://www.moodys.com

during the Asian crisis (Table 5.2). These findings tend to minimize the rating impact of this latter crisis. Fourth, examination of ratings during the 4 years prior to the 1931 debt crisis and the Asian crisis (i.e., the periods 1927–1930 and 1993–1996) shows that the percentage of sovereign bonds and countries downgraded never exceeded 10%. This supports the traditional view (Reisen and von Maltzan 1999; Ferri et al. 1999) that ratings have difficulty in anticipating sovereign debt crises and defaults, which echoes Winkler's (1933) and Rippy's (1950) criticism of the bankers' inability to forecast the crisis of 1931, and confirms Flandreau et al.'s (2010) results.

Moody's policy must also be analyzed through the evolution of its ratings. Tables 5.3 and 5.4 show 1-year rating transition rates for 1918–1939 and 1986–2006. For interwar ratings, I take ratings published every year in *Moody's Manuals* between March 1918 and January 1939.[3] I collect all sovereign bonds rated at least 2 consecutive years during this period, resulting in 1,819 overlapping bond-years. Rating withdrawals are the only way a bond can disappear from the sample because defaulting bonds were always assigned a rating. Transition matrices for 1986–2006 are based on 1,180 overlapping country-years. They measure rating changes from December of year $y$ to December of year $y+1$.

---

[3] For the *Manuals* of 1918–1921, publications were irregular (March 1918, February 1920, November 1920, and November 1921). Moody's released its *Manuals* of 1922 and 1923 in August. The *Manuals* were then published in March from 1924 to 1926 and in January from 1927 to 1939.

**Table 5.1** Moody's rating changes, 1919–1939

|      | Number of upgrades | Number of downgrades | Percentage of upgrades | Percentage of downgrades |
|------|------|------|------|------|
| 1919 | 10 | 0 | 41.7 | 0.0 |
| 1920 | 0 | 2 | 0.0 | 6.7 |
| 1921 | 5 | 5 | 12.8 | 12.8 |
| 1922 | 2 | 9 | 4.1 | 18.4 |
| 1923 | 12 | 12 | 19.7 | 19.7 |
| 1924 | 0 | 0 | 0.0 | 0.0 |
| 1925 | 7 | 0 | 9.6 | 0.0 |
| 1926 | 8 | 5 | 8.9 | 5.6 |
| 1927 | 3 | 2 | 3.1 | 2.1 |
| 1928 | 9 | 1 | 8.2 | 0.9 |
| 1929 | 4 | 3 | 3.4 | 2.5 |
| 1930 | 0 | 4 | 0.0 | 3.3 |
| 1931 | 2 | 11 | 1.7 | 9.5 |
| 1932 | 1 | 93 | 0.8 | 77.5 |
| 1933 | 0 | 42 | 0.0 | 35.9 |
| 1934 | 4 | 32 | 3.4 | 27.4 |
| 1935 | 9 | 4 | 7.6 | 3.4 |
| 1936 | 0 | 0 | 0.0 | 0.0 |
| 1937 | 0 | 10 | 0.0 | 8.5 |
| 1938 | 3 | 2 | 2.6 | 1.7 |
| 1939 | 0 | 2 | 0.0 | 1.9 |

*Notes*: All ratings are the ratings listed in *Moody's Manuals* for the year considered. For 1919, the ratings used are those contained in the manual published in February 1920
*Sources*: Author's computations based on *Moody's Manuals* (1918–1939)

**Table 5.2** Moody's rating changes, 1987–2006

|      | Number of upgrades | Number of downgrades | Percentage of upgrades | Percentage of downgrades |
|------|------|------|------|------|
| 1987 | 0 | 1 | 0.0 | 5.0 |
| 1988 | 0 | 0 | 0.0 | 0.0 |
| 1989 | 0 | 5 | 0.0 | 18.5 |
| 1990 | 1 | 4 | 3.1 | 12.5 |
| 1991 | 1 | 3 | 2.9 | 8.8 |
| 1992 | 1 | 2 | 2.9 | 5.9 |
| 1993 | 2 | 2 | 5.7 | 5.7 |
| 1994 | 6 | 4 | 15.0 | 10.0 |
| 1995 | 5 | 3 | 11.1 | 6.7 |
| 1996 | 7 | 1 | 14.9 | 2.1 |
| 1997 | 12 | 6 | 20.3 | 10.2 |
| 1998 | 5 | 11 | 6.8 | 14.9 |
| 1999 | 6 | 4 | 7.3 | 4.9 |
| 2000 | 11 | 3 | 12.4 | 3.4 |
| 2001 | 8 | 3 | 9.0 | 3.4 |
| 2002 | 26 | 4 | 28.9 | 4.4 |
| 2003 | 15 | 7 | 16.9 | 7.9 |
| 2004 | 8 | 4 | 9.0 | 4.5 |
| 2005 | 13 | 3 | 13.4 | 3.1 |
| 2006 | 20 | 2 | 19.8 | 2.0 |

*Sources*: Author's computations based on http://www.moodys.com

**Table 5.3** Moody's 1-year rating transition rates, 1918–1939

| Cohort ratings | Terminal ratings | | | | | | | | |
|---|---|---|---|---|---|---|---|---|---|
| | Aaa | Aa | A | Baa | Ba | B | Caa | Ca | C |
| Aaa | **86.7** | 12.9 | 0.4 | 0.0 | 0.0 | 0.0 | 0.0 | 0.0 | 0.0 |
| Aa | 3.2 | **80.6** | 14.4 | 1.8 | 0.0 | 0.0 | 0.0 | 0.0 | 0.0 |
| A | 0.5 | 2.6 | **81.1** | 13.7 | 0.5 | 1.6 | 0.0 | 0.0 | 0.0 |
| Baa | 0.0 | 0.0 | 9.0 | **76.6** | 11.7 | 2.7 | 0.0 | 0.0 | 0.0 |
| Ba | 0.0 | 0.0 | 0.4 | 3.6 | **82.5** | 11.1 | 2.4 | 0.0 | 0.0 |
| B | 0.0 | 0.0 | 0.0 | 0.5 | 3.4 | **87.8** | 7.8 | 0.5 | 0.0 |
| Caa | 0.0 | 0.0 | 0.0 | 0.0 | 2.1 | 5.2 | **88.5** | 4.2 | 0.0 |
| Ca | 0.0 | 0.0 | 0.0 | 0.0 | 0.0 | 0.0 | 2.0 | **98.0** | 0.0 |
| C | 0.0 | 0.0 | 0.0 | 0.0 | 0.0 | 0.0 | 0.0 | 50.0 | **50.0** |

*Notes*: All ratings are the ratings listed in *Moody's Manuals* for the year considered. For 1919, the ratings used are those contained in the manual published in February 1920
*Sources*: Author's computations based on *Moody's Manuals* (1918–1939)

Comparisons involving Tables 5.3 and 5.4 must be made cautiously, since the rating scales are different (see Chap. 3) and since transition matrices concern bonds for the interwar period and countries for the modern era. Nonetheless, several conclusions can be drawn from these matrices. For both periods, Moody's ratings are particularly stable: respectively 82.6 and 83.3% of rated sovereign bonds and countries did not experience any rating change over the course of each year. Next, investment-grade entities are more stable today, but speculative-grade entities are more stable during the interwar years. Actually, the sovereign debt crisis of 1931 affected investment-grade bonds, whereas the sovereign debt crises of the 1990s hit both speculative- and investment-grade countries (see Appendix 1).

To conclude this section, I provide a summary table of the main characteristics of Moody's sovereign ratings for 1918–1939 and 1986–2006 (Table 5.5).

## 5.3 Moody's Official Methodologies

Moody's official sovereign methodology – that is, the criteria highlighted by the CRA in its publications – turned out to be rather homogenous through the twentieth century. First, Moody's methodology has constantly reflected two risks: the inability to pay and the unwillingness to pay. Second, it has consisted in a list of criteria and/or variables whose weighting has been subjective and unknown.[4] Third, no mathematical formula has been explicitly used to assess sovereign ratings.

In 1919, the main factors listed to assess the risk of sovereign default were the national income, the population changes caused by the war, and the evolution of the

---
[4] *Moody's Manuals* (1924, 1929, and 1937); Moody's (1999, 2006a).

### 5.3 Moody's Official Methodologies

**Table 5.4** Moody's 1-year rating transition rates, 1986–2006

| Cohort ratings | Terminal ratings | | | | | | | | | | | | | | | | | | | | |
|---|---|---|---|---|---|---|---|---|---|---|---|---|---|---|---|---|---|---|---|---|---|
| | Aaa | Aa1 | Aa2 | Aa3 | A1 | A2 | A3 | Baa1 | Baa2 | Baa3 | Ba1 | Ba2 | Ba3 | B1 | B2 | B3 | Caa1 | Caa2 | Caa3 | Ca | C |
| Aaa | **97.9** | 2.1 | 0.0 | 0.0 | 0.0 | 0.0 | 0.0 | 0.0 | 0.0 | 0.0 | 0.0 | 0.0 | 0.0 | 0.0 | 0.0 | 0.0 | 0.0 | 0.0 | 0.0 | 0.0 | 0.0 |
| Aa1 | 11.0 | **79.4** | 8.2 | 1.4 | 0.0 | 0.0 | 0.0 | 0.0 | 0.0 | 0.0 | 0.0 | 0.0 | 0.0 | 0.0 | 0.0 | 0.0 | 0.0 | 0.0 | 0.0 | 0.0 | 0.0 |
| Aa2 | 4.8 | 9.5 | **84.1** | 1.6 | 0.0 | 0.0 | 0.0 | 0.0 | 0.0 | 0.0 | 0.0 | 0.0 | 0.0 | 0.0 | 0.0 | 0.0 | 0.0 | 0.0 | 0.0 | 0.0 | 0.0 |
| Aa3 | 1.9 | 0.0 | 15.4 | **82.7** | 0.0 | 0.0 | 0.0 | 0.0 | 0.0 | 0.0 | 0.0 | 0.0 | 0.0 | 0.0 | 0.0 | 0.0 | 0.0 | 0.0 | 0.0 | 0.0 | 0.0 |
| A1 | 0.0 | 0.0 | 0.0 | 12.3 | **81.6** | 4.1 | 0.0 | 0.0 | 0.0 | 0.0 | 2.0 | 0.0 | 0.0 | 0.0 | 0.0 | 0.0 | 0.0 | 0.0 | 0.0 | 0.0 | 0.0 |
| A2 | 0.0 | 0.0 | 0.0 | 3.2 | 7.9 | **82.5** | 1.6 | 1.6 | 0.0 | 1.6 | 1.6 | 0.0 | 0.0 | 0.0 | 0.0 | 0.0 | 0.0 | 0.0 | 0.0 | 0.0 | 0.0 |
| A3 | 0.0 | 0.0 | 0.0 | 0.0 | 4.6 | 10.6 | **83.3** | 1.5 | 0.0 | 0.0 | 0.0 | 0.0 | 0.0 | 0.0 | 0.0 | 0.0 | 0.0 | 0.0 | 0.0 | 0.0 | 0.0 |
| Baa1 | 0.0 | 0.0 | 0.0 | 0.0 | 3.6 | 5.3 | 12.5 | **75.0** | 0.0 | 1.8 | 0.0 | 1.8 | 0.0 | 0.0 | 0.0 | 0.0 | 0.0 | 0.0 | 0.0 | 0.0 | 0.0 |
| Baa2 | 0.0 | 0.0 | 0.0 | 0.0 | 0.0 | 2.1 | 6.1 | 12.2 | **77.5** | 0.0 | 2.1 | 0.0 | 0.0 | 0.0 | 0.0 | 0.0 | 0.0 | 0.0 | 0.0 | 0.0 | 0.0 |
| Baa3 | 0.0 | 0.0 | 0.0 | 0.0 | 0.0 | 0.0 | 1.4 | 5.4 | 11.0 | **75.3** | 1.4 | 2.7 | 1.4 | 0.0 | 0.0 | 1.4 | 0.0 | 0.0 | 0.0 | 0.0 | 0.0 |
| Ba1 | 0.0 | 0.0 | 0.0 | 0.0 | 0.0 | 0.0 | 0.0 | 1.1 | 2.2 | 11.0 | **80.2** | 3.3 | 0.0 | 0.0 | 1.1 | 1.1 | 0.0 | 0.0 | 0.0 | 0.0 | 0.0 |
| Ba2 | 0.0 | 0.0 | 0.0 | 0.0 | 0.0 | 0.0 | 0.0 | 1.6 | 0.0 | 4.9 | 12.9 | **70.9** | 1.6 | 1.6 | 4.9 | 1.6 | 0.0 | 0.0 | 0.0 | 0.0 | 0.0 |
| Ba3 | 0.0 | 0.0 | 0.0 | 0.0 | 0.0 | 0.0 | 0.0 | 0.0 | 0.0 | 0.0 | 3.9 | 9.8 | **70.6** | 9.8 | 2.0 | 3.9 | 0.0 | 0.0 | 0.0 | 0.0 | 0.0 |
| B1 | 0.0 | 0.0 | 0.0 | 0.0 | 0.0 | 0.0 | 0.0 | 0.0 | 0.0 | 0.0 | 0.0 | 3.2 | 9.7 | **74.2** | 8.9 | 3.6 | 0.0 | 0.0 | 0.0 | 0.0 | 0.0 |
| B2 | 0.0 | 0.0 | 0.0 | 0.0 | 0.0 | 0.0 | 0.0 | 0.0 | 0.0 | 0.0 | 0.0 | 0.0 | 0.0 | 12.7 | **74.5** | 5.5 | 5.5 | 0.0 | 1.8 | 1.6 | 0.0 |
| B3 | 0.0 | 0.0 | 0.0 | 0.0 | 0.0 | 0.0 | 0.0 | 0.0 | 0.0 | 0.0 | 0.0 | 0.0 | 2.9 | 6.0 | 17.6 | **61.8** | 8.8 | 0.0 | 2.9 | 0.0 | 0.0 |
| Caa1 | 0.0 | 0.0 | 0.0 | 0.0 | 0.0 | 0.0 | 0.0 | 0.0 | 0.0 | 0.0 | 0.0 | 0.0 | 0.0 | 0.0 | 7.4 | 7.4 | **77.8** | 3.7 | 0.0 | 3.7 | 0.0 |
| Caa2 | 0.0 | 0.0 | 0.0 | 0.0 | 0.0 | 0.0 | 0.0 | 0.0 | 0.0 | 0.0 | 0.0 | 0.0 | 0.0 | 0.0 | 0.0 | 0.0 | 25.0 | **75.0** | 0.0 | 0.0 | 0.0 |
| Caa3 | 0.0 | 0.0 | 0.0 | 0.0 | 0.0 | 0.0 | 0.0 | 0.0 | 0.0 | 0.0 | 0.0 | 0.0 | 0.0 | 0.0 | 0.0 | 0.0 | 0.0 | 50.0 | **50.0** | 0.0 | 0.0 |
| Ca | 0.0 | 0.0 | 0.0 | 0.0 | 0.0 | 0.0 | 0.0 | 0.0 | 0.0 | 0.0 | 0.0 | 0.0 | 0.0 | 0.0 | 0.0 | 0.0 | 50 | 0.0 | 0.0 | **50.0** | 0.0 |
| C | 0.0 | 0.0 | 0.0 | 0.0 | 0.0 | 0.0 | 0.0 | 0.0 | 0.0 | 0.0 | 0.0 | 0.0 | 0.0 | 0.0 | 0.0 | 0.0 | 0.0 | 0.0 | 0.0 | 0.0 | **0.0** |

*Note*: All ratings are as of 31 December
*Sources*: Author's computations based on http://www.moodys.com

**Table 5.5** Characteristics of Moody's sovereign ratings: 1918–1939 vs. today

| | Interwar years | Modern era |
|---|---|---|
| Regulation of the activity | No | Yes: *NRSRO* status from 1975, *Credit Rating Agency Reform Act of 2006* and *Dodd-Frank Act of 2010* |
| Use of ratings for financial regulatory purposes | Not until September 1931 | Increasing use by the SEC throughout the 1990s and 2000s |
| Moody's competitors in the sovereign rating area | None until 1922, 1 from 1922 to 1924 (Poor's), and 3 thereafter (Poor's, Standard Statistics, and Fitch) | 4 from 1986 to 1997 (S&P, Fitch, IBCA, and Duff & Phelps), 3 from 1997 to 2000 (S&P, Fitch, and Duff & Phelps), and 2 since 2000 (S&P and Fitch) |
| Moody's publications | 2 types: "Manuals" and "Investment Letters" | At least 10 types: "Manuals," "Rating News," "Special Comments," "Special Reports," "Rating Methodology" reports, "Rating Lists," "Credit Opinions," "Country Statistics," "Country Analyses," and "Country Credit Statistical Handbooks" |
| Investment recommendations | Yes | No |
| Sources of revenues | Sales of "Manuals" and "Investment Letters" to investors | Fees charged to issuers |
| Moody's rating scale | 9 Rating categories | 21 Rating categories |
| Moody's rating measure | Default probability + recovery rate | Default probability + recovery rate |
| Number of offices | 2 in 1918 and 8 from 1929 to 1939 | 29 in 2007 |
| Number of top senior sovereign rating analysts | 1 (+John Moody until 1929) | 3 in 1986 and 12 in 2006 |
| "Big boss" of Moody's sovereign rating department | John Moody (1918–1922) and Max Winkler (1922–1927) | Jolene Larson (1986–1990), David Levey (1990–2004), Vincent Truglia (2004–2008), Pierre Cailleteau (2008–2010), and Bert Oosterveld (since 2010) |
| Existence of a specific sovereign rating department | Only a global rating department from 1922 | Creation of a specific sovereign risk unit in late 1985 |
| Type of entities rated | Bonds | Bonds and countries |
| Number of entities rated (for 1918–1939, bonds in USD and GBP, listed on the NYSE; for 1986–2006, countries with a FC rating) | 24 in 1918, 123 in 1929, and 108 in 1939 | 20 in 1986, 59 in 1996, and 101 in 2006 |
| Annual percentage of upgrades (average) | 6 | 10 |
| Annual percentage of downgrades (average) | 11 | 7 |
| Percentage of ratings unchanged | 83 | 83 |

5.3 Moody's Official Methodologies

**Table 5.6** List of the 25 criteria highlighted by Moody's in 1924

| Criteria | Quantitative criterion | Qualitative criterion | Direct availability | Indirect availability | Lack of information |
|---|---|---|---|---|---|
| 1. Legality and validity of issue | | x | | x | |
| 2. Tax exemptions in the country of issue | | x | x | | x |
| 3. International alliances | | x | x | x | |
| 4. Racial characteristics of population | x | x | x | | |
| 5. Educational standards | x | x | | | x |
| 6. Occupational statistics | x | x | x | | |
| 7. Institutional and political stability | | x | x | | |
| 8. Risk of debt repudiation | | x | x | x | |
| 9. Natural resources | x | x | x | | |
| 10. Per capita wealth | x | | x | | |
| 11. Ratio of national debt to national wealth | x | | x | | |
| 12. Ratio of annual debt charges to annual revenues | x | | x | x | |
| 13. Rates of growth in debt and wealth | x | | x | x | |
| 14. Importance of state-owned industries | x | x | x | x | |
| 15. Monetary system | x | x | x | | |
| 16. Existence of sinking funds | | x | x | | x |
| 17. Past record | | x | x | x | |
| 18. Promptness of interest payments | | x | x | | |
| 19. Bonds payable in gold or in bills | x | x | x | | |
| 20. Exchange rates | x | | x | | |
| 21. Government revenues, expenses and taxation | x | | x | | |
| 22. Visible foreign trade | x | | x | | |
| 23. Blind items of exchange | x | | x | x | |
| 24. Currency system | x | x | x | | |
| 25. Degree of industrialization | x | x | x | | |

*Sources*: Author's classification based on *Moody's Manual* (1924)

"earning power of peoples."[5] Moody's objective was to know to what extent yearly savings and incomes were large enough to balance increasing public debts. In 1924, its methodological framework became more exhaustive and provided a list of 25 criteria. Table 5.6 lists these criteria, indicating whether each was a qualitative or a

---
[5] *Moody's Investment Letter* (1919), "The Credit of Foreign Governments," 3 April.

Table 5.7 The eight broad categories of variables for 1924

| | |
|---|---|
| Industrialization | Occupational statistics |
| | Importance of state-owned industries |
| | Degree of industrialization |
| Institutional stability | International alliances |
| | Institutional and political stability |
| Default history | Risk of debt repudiation |
| | Past record |
| | Promptness of interest payments |
| Monetary stability | Monetary system |
| | Bonds payable in gold or in bills |
| | Exchange rates |
| | Currency system |
| Foreign trade | Visible foreign trade |
| | Blind items of exchange |
| Fiscal balance | Government revenues, expenses and taxation |
| Per capita wealth | Per capita wealth |
| Debt burden | Ratio of national debt to national wealth |
| | Ratio of annual debt charges to annual revenues |
| | Rates of growth in debt and wealth |

*Sources*: Author's classification based on *Moody's Manual* (1924)

quantitative criterion, as well as whether the information was available in *Moody's Manuals* or *Investment Letters* (i.e., directly available), available elsewhere, or not available.

I group these 25 criteria of 1924 into eight broad categories (Table 5.7), as Moody's does in its 2006 methodology (Table 5.8). Criteria 6, 14, and 25 reflect a country's degree of industrialization. Variables 3 and 7 are indicators for its institutional, political, and geopolitical stability. The "track record" of a country includes criteria 8, 17, and 18; monetary stability is represented by variables 15, 19, 20, and 24. Foreign trade data are available through criteria 22 and 23. Fiscal balance and wealth per capita refer to criteria 21 and 10, respectively. Criteria 11, 12, and 13 represent the debt burden relative to wealth or revenue. As for other criteria, I can make several observations. The criterion "legality and validity of issue" is irrelevant because Moody's never detected a bond whose issue was illegal. Moody's often presented "racial characteristics" criterion as a proxy for national wealth; I thus do not consider it a proper criterion. Criteria 2, 5, and 16 must also be discarded owing to insufficient information.

This classification into eight categories enables an empirical analysis of Moody's methodology in order to reveal the actual determinants of sovereign ratings.

## 5.3 Moody's Official Methodologies

**Table 5.8** List of the 46 criteria highlighted by Moody's in 2006

| | |
|---|---|
| Economic structure and performance | Nominal GDP (US$ bil.) |
| | Population (mil.) |
| | GDP per capita (US$) |
| | GDP per capita (PPP basis, US$) |
| | Nominal GDP (% change, local currency) |
| | Real GDP (% change) |
| | Inflation (CPI, % change Dec/Dec) |
| | Gross investment/GDP |
| | Gross domestic saving/GDP |
| | Nominal exports of G & S (% change, US$ basis) |
| | Nominal imports of G & S (% change, US$ basis) |
| | Openness of the economy |
| Government finance | Gen. gov. revenue/GDP |
| | Gen. gov. expenditures/GDP |
| | Gen. gov. financial balance/GDP |
| | Gen. gov. primary balance/GDP |
| | Gen. gov. debt (US$ bil.) |
| | Gen. gov. debt/GDP |
| | Gen. gov. debt/Gen. gov. revenue |
| | Gen. gov. int. pymt/Gen. gov. revenue |
| | Gen. gov. FC and FC-indexed debt/Gen. gov. debt |
| External payments and debt | Nominal exchange rate (local currency per US$, Dec) |
| | Real eff. exchange rate (% change) |
| | Current account balance (US$ bil.) |
| | Current account balance/GDP |
| | External debt (US$ bil.) |
| | Short-term external debt/Total external debt |
| | External debt/GDP |
| | External debt/CA receipts |
| | Interest paid on external debt (US$ bil.) |
| | Amortization paid on external debt (US$ bil.) |
| | Net foreign direct investment/GDP |
| | Official forex reserves (US$ bil.) |
| | Net foreign assets of domestic banks (US$ bil.) |
| Monetary, external vulnerability and liquidity indicators | M2 (% change Dec/Dec) |
| | Short-term nominal interest rate (% per annum, 31 Dec) |
| | Domestic credit (% change Dec/Dec) |
| | Domestic credit/GDP |
| | M2/Official forex reserves |
| | Total external debt/Official forex reserves |
| | Debt service ratio |
| | External vulnerability indicator |
| | Liquidity ratio |
| | Total liab. due BIS banks/Total assets held in BIS banks |
| | "Dollarization" ratio |
| | "Dollarization" vulnerability indicator |

*Source*: Moody's (2006a)

## 5.4 Empirical Analysis of the Determinants of Moody's Sovereign Ratings

To assess the determinants of Moody's sovereign ratings during the interwar years, I successively use OLS and ordered probit regression analyses for the years 1925 and 1929. I first test the eight explanatory variables highlighted by Cantor and Packer (Table 5.9). Seven of the eight variables they used refer to the same criteria I detected for Moody's methodology in 1924 (Table 5.7): the only difference is that Cantor and Packer tested GDP growth, whereas I identified an institutional stability variable.

As in Cantor and Packer's model, the dependent variable is the country's average rating – that is, the mean of the numerical values of all ratings assigned by Moody's in its 1925 and 1929 *Manuals* to USD and GBP government bonds issued or listed on the NYSE.[6] For example, when the four USD Argentine bonds are rated Aa (i.e., 8), the Argentine rating is 8. The sample consists of 37 countries for 1925 and 43 countries for 1929. The description of the eight variables for 1925 and 1929 is provided in Table 5.10 (information about sources can be found in Appendix 2). Tables 5.11 and 5.12 present correlation coefficients for 1925 and 1929, respectively.

Table 5.13 provides a comparison between my regressions [4] and [7] for 1925 and 1929 and Cantor and Packer's regression for ratings issued by Moody's in

**Table 5.9** Description of the eight independent variables used by Cantor and Packer (1996)

| Variable name | Definition | Unit of measurement |
|---|---|---|
| Per capita income | GNP per capita, 1994 | Dollars |
| Growth | Average annual real GDP growth on a year-to-year basis, 1991–1994 | Percent |
| Inflation | Average annual CPI, 1992–1994 | Percent |
| Fiscal balance | Average annual central government budget surplus relative to GDP, 1992–1994 | Percent |
| External balance | Average annual current account surplus relative to GDP, 1992–1994 | Percent |
| External debt | Foreign currency debt relative to exports, 1994 | Percent |
| Development indicator | IMF classification as an industrialized country, September 1995 | Indicator variable: 1 = industrialized country and 0 = otherwise |
| Default history | Default on foreign currency debt since 1970 | Indicator variable: 1 = default and 0 = no default |

*Note*: Per capita income and inflation have been transformed to logarithms

---

[6] Ratings are transformed numerically as follows: Aaa = 9, Aa = 8, A = 7, Baa = 6, Ba = 5, B = 4, Caa = 3, Ca = 2 and C = 1. This linear transformation is used by Cantor and Packer (1996) and Moody's (2004).

## 5.4 Empirical Analysis of the Determinants of Moody's Sovereign Ratings

**Table 5.10** Description of the eight independent variables used for 1925 (and for 1929 in *parentheses*)

| Variable name | Symbol | Definition | Unit of measurement |
|---|---|---|---|
| Per capita income | PCI | Wealth per capita, 1921 (1925) | Dollars |
| Growth | GRO | Average annual real GDP growth on a year-to-year basis, 1921–1923 (1925–1927) | Percent |
| Inflation | INF | Average annual consumer price rate, 1921–1923 (1925–1927) | Percent |
| Fiscal balance | FB | Average annual central gov. budget surplus relative to gross wealth, 1921–1923 (1925–1927) | Percent |
| External balance | EB | Average annual trade surplus relative to gross wealth, 1921–1923 (1925–1927) | Percent |
| External debt | FCDX | Foreign currency debt relative to exports, 1923 (1927) | Percent |
| Development indicator | DI | Moody's classification as a "manufacturing country," 1925 (1929) | Indicator variable: 1 = manufacturing country and 0 = otherwise |
| Default history | DH | Default on foreign currency debt since 1900 (since 1904) | Indicator variable: 1 = default and 0 = no default |

*Note*: Per capita income and inflation have been transformed to logarithms

**Table 5.11** Correlation coefficients for 1925 ($N=37$)

|  | PCI | GRO | INF | FB | EB | FCDX | DI | DH | INST |
|---|---|---|---|---|---|---|---|---|---|
| PCI | 1 | – | – | – | – | – | – | – | – |
| GRO | 0.30 | 1 | – | – | – | – | – | – | – |
| INF | −0.07 | −0.19 | 1 | – | – | – | – | – | – |
| FB | 0.00 | 0.22 | −0.28 | 1 | – | – | – | – | – |
| EB | −0.10 | 0.01 | −0.04 | 0.04 | 1 | – | – | – | – |
| FCDX | −0.01 | −0.28 | 0.43 | 0.05 | 0.01 | 1 | – | – | – |
| DI | 0.49 | −0.06 | 0.11 | 0.06 | −0.12 | −0.05 | 1 | – | – |
| DH | −0.46 | −0.13 | 0.15 | 0.11 | 0.21 | 0.13 | −0.26 | 1 | – |
| INST | 0.54 | 0.31 | −0.42 | 0.02 | −0.22 | −0.39 | 0.35 | −0.20 | 1 |

**Table 5.12** Correlation coefficients for 1929 ($N=43$)

|  | PCI | GRO | INF | FB | EB | FCDX | DI | DH | INST |
|---|---|---|---|---|---|---|---|---|---|
| PCI | 1 | – | – | – | – | – | – | – | – |
| GRO | 0.25 | 1 | – | – | – | – | – | – | – |
| INF | −0.21 | −0.25 | 1 | – | – | – | – | – | – |
| FB | −0.09 | −0.01 | 0.00 | 1 | – | – | – | – | – |
| EB | −0.14 | −0.07 | 0.02 | 0.02 | 1 | – | – | – | – |
| FCDX | −0.12 | −0.06 | 0.08 | 0.04 | −0.09 | 1 | – | – | – |
| DI | 0.46 | 0.10 | 0.16 | −0.17 | −0.15 | −0.06 | 1 | – | – |
| DH | −0.47 | −0.05 | 0.28 | −0.17 | 0.21 | 0.23 | −0.25 | 1 | – |
| INST | 0.55 | 0.23 | −0.28 | −0.08 | −0.01 | −0.30 | 0.31 | −0.19 | 1 |

Table 5.13 OLS regression results

| Regressions | [1] | [2] | [3] | [4] | [5] | [6] | [7] | [8] | [9] | [10] | [11] |
|---|---|---|---|---|---|---|---|---|---|---|---|
| Date of ratings | September 1995 | July 2003 | | January 1925 | | | January 1929 | | | December 2006 | |
| No. countries | 49 | 67 | | 37 | | | 43 | | | 95 | |
| Intercept | 3.408 (1.379) | 14.910 (16.481) | 12.780 (15.047) | 0.582 (0.350) | −0.292 (0.169) | 1.360 (1.065) | −0.788 (0.638) | −0.107 (0.081) | 1.029 (0.911) | −20.099 (4.939) | 15.378 (13.722) |
| Per capita income | **1.027** **(4.041)** | **0.485** **(8.118)** | **0.205** **(2.852)** | **1.926** **(2.852)** | **2.369** **(3.590)** | 0.801 (1.439) | **2.339** **(5.425)** | **2.675** **(5.872)** | **1.776** **(4.087)** | **3.825** **(10.203)** | |
| Growth | 0.130 (1.545) | **0.419** **(4.019)** | **0.304** **(3.404)** | 0.083 (0.959) | | | 0.031 (0.883) | | | 0.008 (0.638) | |
| Inflation | **−0.630** **(2.701)** | | | **−0.306** **(2.534)** | | | **−0.044** **(2.669)** | | | **−0.199** **(3.049)** | **−0.327** **(3.993)** |
| Fiscal balance | 0.049 (0.818) | | | −0.006 (0.808) | 0.003 (0.371) | 0.002 (0.289) | −0.242 (4.015) | −0.254 (3.852) | −0.258 (4.730) | −0.075 (1.174) | −0.015 (0.175) |
| External balance | 0.006 (0.535) | | | −0.294 (3.412) | −0.282 (3.044) | −0.188 (2.733) | −0.327 (4.985) | −0.326 (4.529) | −0.334 (5.597) | 0.052 (1.759) | **0.134** **(3.510)** |
| External debt | **−0.015** **(5.365)** | **−0.898** **(3.273)** | **−0.749** **(3.261)** | **−0.001** **(3.851)** | **−0.002** **(5.932)** | **−0.001** **(4.573)** | **−0.002** **(6.582)** | **−0.002** **(6.070)** | **−0.002** **(5.667)** | | |
| General debt | | | | | | | | | | −0.005 (2.509) | −0.009 (3.103) |
| Development indicator | **2.957** **(4.175)** | | | 0.545 (1.026) | 0.720 (0.138) | −0.123 (0.325) | 0.130 (0.333) | −0.215 (0.531) | −0.341 (1.013) | | |
| Default history | **−1.463** **(2.097)** | | | **−0.852** **(2.312)** | **−0.987** **(2.510)** | **−1.289** **(4.476)** | −0.468 (1.680) | **−0.624** **(2.124)** | **−0.786** **(3.185)** | −2.035 (3.433) | |

|  | [1] | [2] | [3] | [4] | [5] | [6] | [7] | [8] | [9] | [10] | [11] |
|---|---|---|---|---|---|---|---|---|---|---|---|
| Governance effectiveness |  | **2.971** (5.399) |  |  |  |  |  |  |  |  |  |
| Institutional indicator |  |  |  |  |  | **1.132** (5.390) |  |  |  |  |  |
| Governance indicator |  |  |  |  |  |  |  |  | **0.650** (4.174) |  | **3.461** (7.515) |
| Adjusted $R^2$ | 0.905 | 0.671 | 0.776 | 0.762 | 0.723 | 0.857 | 0.841 | 0.808 | 0.868 | 0.835 | 0.710 |
| Standard error | 1.325 | 2.273 | 1.889 | 0.870 | 0.938 | 0.674 | 0.672 | 0.740 | 0.613 | 2.149 | 2.852 |

*Notes*: Absolute *t*-statistics are in *parentheses*. Coefficients with the expected sign and significant *t*-statistics (at the 5% level) are in **bold**. Regression [1] is Cantor and Packer's results for 1995 Moody's ratings. Regressions [2] and [3] are Moody's results for 2003 ratings (Moody's 2004). Considering the very high correlation between "development indicator" and "per capita income" for 2006, the former variable is not tested in regression [10]. Considering the very high correlation between "per capita income," "development indicator," and "default history" variables on the one hand, and "governance indicator" on the other hand, the first three variables are not tested in regression [11]

September 1995 (regression [1]). My findings show that determinants of Moody's ratings in the 1920s are the same as those of 1995: per capita income, inflation, external debt, and the indicator for default history. Wealth growth is never significant, while fiscal balance and trade balance either do not have the anticipated sign or are not significant. The main difference between the three regressions appears with the variable "indicator for economic development": it is significant in Cantor and Packer's model, but not in the regressions for 1925 and 1929.

In order to refine my model, I only keep the variables that were actually available for Moody's in 1925 and 1929. Consequently, wealth growth and inflation are dropped.[7] Regressions [5] and [8] are run with the six variables available in the 1920s. Results confirm the importance of three determinants: per capita income, external debt, and the indicator for default history are all significant and have the expected sign.

Observe that Moody's explicitly affirmed that the higher the wealth per capita, the more creditworthy the country.[8] When I compute average wealth per capita for 1921 and for each rating category, I note that this variable is positively correlated to ratings: $1,188 for countries rated Aaa, $1,135 for Aa, $770 for A, $381 for Baa, $465 for Ba, and $456 for B and lower. As for the fiscal balance, no relationship is observable. This result is not surprising given that among high-rated countries there were substantial deficits in France and Belgium, balanced budgets in the Scandinavian states, and a surplus in the United Kingdom, whose fiscal policy was the most drastic. Similarly, the irrelevance of the trade balance variable was expected because most Western European countries possessed structural deficits (up to 3.5% for Netherlands and 5.7% for Norway), whereas countries with medium-grade ratings (Baa and Ba) had, on average, positive trade balances for the 1921–1923 period. The significance of the external debt to exports ratio is worth underlining because it demonstrates to what extent a country's borrowing ability depends on its trade openness and export volume. In 1933, Moody's affirmed that "probably the most effective way of ranking the debtor nations would be to compare the net foreign indebtedness with the gross proceeds from exports and other sources of foreign funds."[9] The insignificance of the indicator for economic development can be explained by the fact that few countries were classified as "manufacturing countries" (only Belgium, France, Germany, Switzerland, the United Kingdom, and the United States), while several "non-manufacturing countries" (Canada, Denmark, Netherlands, Norway, and Sweden) were rated Aaa. Lastly, the indicator for default history on which Moody's insisted in its *Manuals* and *Investment Letters* (naming it "the good faith," "the reputation," or "the honor of nations") was a robust discriminating variable throughout all rating categories: no

---

[7] These two series of data were collected from Maddison (2003), Mitchell (1992, 1993), and Oxford Latin American Economic History database (http://oxlad.qeh.ox.ac.uk).

[8] *Moody's Investment Letter* (1923), "The Wealth and Credit of Foreign Nations," 2 August.

[9] *Moody's Investment Survey* (1933), "Foreign Bonds – Position and Prospects," 7 September.

### 5.4 Empirical Analysis of the Determinants of Moody's Sovereign Ratings

country rated Aaa or Aa had defaulted since 1900, whereas all countries rated B or below had defaulted during 1900–1925.[10]

Nevertheless, the in-depth examination of regressions [5] and [8] shows that three countries (Ecuador, Mexico, and Poland) are clearly outliers: their ratings are lower than their respective fitted ratings yielded by the model. These countries share the prominent characteristic of having faced recurrent political disturbances, as Moody's stressed.

Poland: "Political conditions are still to a certain extent uncertain, and it is largely for this reason that I do not feel that for the time being a decidedly optimistic view is justified regarding this type of obligations."[11]

Mexico: "Government foundations are quite important. If, for example, every official in Great Britain suddenly perished, a whole new government would be established the next day by virtue of the British universal conceptions of common law and constitutional rights. If, on the other hand, officialdom in Mexico perished, government itself would almost perish with it."[12]

Ecuador: Moody's uses the annual report published by the Ecuadorian Ministry of Finance in 1923 to highlight the "internal revolutions in the past that tended greatly to exhaust the National Treasury and increase the Public Debt" and "the effects of the war, felt particularly in the decrease of the import and export trade."[13]

These comments led me to consider that Moody's might have decided to discriminate even more against these countries in light of an institutional stability variable. This variable was not taken into account by Cantor and Packer, but was listed in the 1924 Moody's methodology. Hence, I ran a third series of regressions with an "institutional indicator," a scoring composed of three factors: the "political stability and absence of violence/terrorism," the "rule of law," and the "age of the country" (Table 5.14).[14] I obtain a final scoring of 0, 1, 2, or 3 (the higher the score, the better the institutions). As regressions [6] and [9] show, this "institutional indicator" significantly improves the explanatory power of the model for 1925 and 1929.

Two series of results are added in Table 5.13 for Moody's ratings issued in July 2003 and December 2006. The first ones (regressions [2] and [3]) come from Moody's (2004) and the second ones are my results (regressions [10] and [11]).[15] For ratings issued in 2006, I use Cantor and Packer's variables plus a governance indicator, which is an average of the six governance indicators used by Kaufmann et al. (2005). Tables 5.15 and 5.16, respectively, provide the description of these nine variables and correlation coefficients. Governance indicators for the 95 countries in

---

[10] Author's calculations.

[11] *Moody's Investment Letter* (1925), "The Rehabilitation of Poland," 26 February.

[12] *Moody's Manual* (1925), "The Art of Investing in Public Securities," p. xvi.

[13] *Moody's Manual* (1924) "Republic of Ecuador," p. 390.

[14] These three factors were regularly highlighted by Moody's in the 1920s. They capture the institutional quality of the countries at that time.

[15] As previously, ratings are transformed numerically: Aaa = 20, Aa1 = 19, Aa2 = 18,…, Caa3 = 2, Ca = 1, C = 0.

**Table 5.14** "Institutional indicator" scorings (INST) for 1925 and 1929 ($N_{1925} = 37$ and $N_{1929} = 43$)

| Country | Institutional indicator | Country | Institutional indicator |
|---|---|---|---|
| Argentina | 3 | Guatemala | 1 |
| Australia | 3 | Haiti | 2 |
| Austria | 2 | Hungary | 2 |
| Belgium | 3 | Irish Free State | 2 |
| Bolivia | 2 | Italy | 1 |
| Brazil | 3 | Japan | 3 |
| Bulgaria | 2 | Mexico | 1 |
| Canada | 3 | Netherlands | 3 |
| Chile | 2 | Nicaragua | 1 |
| China | 1 | Norway | 2 |
| Colombia | 3 | Panama | 1 |
| Costa Rica | 3 | Peru | 2 |
| Cuba | 2 | Poland | 1 |
| Czechoslovakia | 2 | Romania | 2 |
| Denmark | 3 | Russia | 1 |
| Dominican Republic | 2 | Salvador | 3 |
| Ecuador | 1 | Sweden | 3 |
| Estonia | 2 | Switzerland | 3 |
| Finland | 2 | United Kingdom | 3 |
| France | 3 | Uruguay | 3 |
| Germany | 2 | Yugoslavia | 2 |
| Greece | 1 | | |

*Notes*: For the interwar years, it is impossible to use the "governance effectiveness" index implemented by Kaufmann et al. (2005), as Moody's (2004) did, because of the lack of data concerning four of the six criteria used ("voice and accountability," "government effectiveness," "regulatory quality," and "control of corruption"). As a result, I create an "institutional indicator" that aggregates the scorings of three dummy variables: (a) value 1 if the country was created before 1900 (value 0 otherwise); (b) value 1 if there is the rule of law (value 0 otherwise); and (c) value 1 if there is no risk of coup, war, anarchy or foreign intervention (value 0 otherwise)
The assessment of the value of each dummy variable is based on Moody's analyses contained in *Manuals* and *Investment Letters*
The 37 countries of the 1925 sample are all included in the 1929 sample. The six additional countries for 1929 are Australia, Bulgaria, Costa Rica, Estonia, Guatemala, and the Irish Free State. The countries included in the two samples have the same "institutional indicator" for 1925 and 1929

the sample are compiled in Table 5.17 (the higher the score, the better the governance). Moody's results for 2003 and my results for 2006 support the view that the determinants of sovereign ratings have not fundamentally changed since Cantor and Packer's paper, but these results also highlight the crucial importance now, as in the 1920s, of institutional and political variables.

The last step of my empirical analysis consists of replicating OLS regressions [4] through [11] using a multinomial ordered probit model. This model is more appropriate when dealing with qualitative ordinal dependent variables, such as ratings. Ordered probit results (Table 5.18) corroborate OLS results: GDP per capita, FC debt to exports ratio, the indicator for default history, and the institutional indicator

## 5.4 Empirical Analysis of the Determinants of Moody's Sovereign Ratings

**Table 5.15** Description of the nine independent variables for 2006

| Variable name | Symbol | Definition | Unit of measurement |
|---|---|---|---|
| Per capita income | PCI | GDP per capita PPP, 2004 | Dollars |
| Growth | GRO | Average annual real GDP growth on a year-to-year basis, 2002–2005 | Percent |
| Inflation | INF | Average annual CPI, 2003–2005 | Percent |
| Fiscal balance | FB | Average annual general government financial surplus relative to GDP, 2003–2005 | Percent |
| External balance | EB | Average annual current account surplus relative to GDP, 2003–2005 | Percent |
| General debt | GDGR | General government debt relative to general government revenue, 2005 | Percent |
| Development indicator | DI | Moody's classification as an industrial country, May 2006 | Indicator variable: 1 = industrial country and 0 = otherwise |
| Default history | DH | Default on foreign currency debt since 1981 | Indicator variable: 1 = default and 0 = no default |
| Governance indicator | GOV | Average of the six indicators implemented by Kaufmann et al. (2005), May 2005 | Index |

*Note*: Per capita income has been transformed to logarithms

**Table 5.16** Correlation coefficients for 2006 ($N=95$)

|  | PCI | GRO | INF | FB | EB | GDGR | DI | DH | GOV |
|---|---|---|---|---|---|---|---|---|---|
| PCI | 1 | – | – | – | – | – | – | – | – |
| GRO | −0.34 | 1 | – | – | – | – | – | – | – |
| INF | −0.45 | 0.18 | 1 | – | – | – | – | – | – |
| FB | 0.23 | 0.29 | −0.06 | 1 | – | – | – | – | – |
| EB | 0.27 | 0.16 | 0.00 | 0.59 | 1 | – | – | – | – |
| GDGR | −0.33 | −0.20 | 0.07 | −0.55 | −0.24 | 1 | – | – | – |
| DI | 0.79 | −0.46 | −0.38 | 0.04 | 0.10 | −0.13 | 1 | – | – |
| DH | −0.56 | 0.11 | 0.53 | −0.17 | −0.13 | 0.18 | −0.47 | 1 | – |
| GOV | 0.76 | −0.34 | −0.50 | 0.06 | 0.01 | −0.28 | 0.68 | −0.54 | 1 |

explain 90% of Moody's sovereign ratings for the interwar period. All these variables were included in the official methodology (Table 5.6). For ratings issued in December 2006, inflation, general debt ratio, and default history remain important determinants, but GDP per capita and the governance indicator have, by far, the strongest explanatory power.

**Table 5.17** Governance index for 2006 ($N=95$)

| Country | Governance effectiveness index | Country | Governance effectiveness index |
|---|---|---|---|
| Argentina | −0.3397 | Lithuania | 0.7729 |
| Australia | 1.6400 | Luxembourg | 1.8850 |
| Austria | 1.5753 | Malaysia | 0.3766 |
| Bahamas | 1.1282 | Malta | 1.2531 |
| Bahrain | 0.3755 | Mauritius | 0.6592 |
| Barbados | 1.1325 | Mexico | 0.0383 |
| Belgium | 1.3750 | Moldova | −0.6363 |
| Belize | 0.3698 | Mongolia | −0.0351 |
| Bolivia | −0.4284 | Morocco | −0.1887 |
| Bosnia and Herzegovina | −0.5818 | Netherlands | 1.6944 |
| Botswana | 0.8001 | New Zealand | 1.8531 |
| Brazil | 0.0092 | Nicaragua | −0.3224 |
| Bulgaria | 0.2072 | Norway | 1.7369 |
| Canada | 1.6311 | Oman | 0.4918 |
| Chile | 1.2456 | Pakistan | −1.0255 |
| China | −0.4889 | Panama | 0.1602 |
| Colombia | −0.5528 | Papua New Guinea | −0.7237 |
| Costa Rica | 0.7657 | Paraguay | −0.7840 |
| Croatia | 0.2434 | Peru | −0.3503 |
| Cyprus | 0.8748 | Philippines | −0.4098 |
| Czech Republic | 0.7446 | Poland | 0.5423 |
| Denmark | 1.8302 | Portugal | 1.1375 |
| Dominican Republic | −0.2512 | Qatar | 0.3635 |
| Ecuador | −0.6525 | Romania | −0.0085 |
| Egypt | −0.4615 | Russia | −0.6344 |
| Estonia | 1.0621 | Salvador | −0.0609 |
| Fiji Islands | −0.1676 | Saudi Arabia | −0.3794 |
| Finland | 1.9171 | Singapore | 1.6205 |
| France | 1.1475 | Slovakia | 0.7399 |
| Germany | 1.4196 | Slovenia | 0.9852 |
| Greece | 0.7222 | South Africa | 0.4310 |
| Guatemala | −0.6450 | South Korea | 0.6112 |
| Honduras | −0.5084 | Spain | 1.1173 |
| Hong Kong | 1.3107 | Sweden | 1.7343 |
| Hungary | 0.9021 | Switzerland | 1.8114 |
| Iceland | 1.9371 | Taiwan | 0.8303 |
| India | −0.2624 | Thailand | 0.0276 |
| Indonesia | −0.7340 | Trinidad and Tobago | 0.2990 |
| Ireland | 1.4761 | Tunisia | −0.0118 |
| Israel | 0.4451 | Turkey | −0.1671 |
| Italy | 0.7200 | Ukraine | −0.6265 |
| Jamaica | −0.0518 | United Arab Emirates | 0.6900 |
| Japan | 1.1319 | United Kingdom | 1.5629 |
| Jordan | 0.0345 | USA | 1.3526 |
| Kazakhstan | −0.8186 | Uruguay | 0.5387 |
| Kuwait | 0.3039 | Venezuela | −0.9683 |
| Latvia | 0.7086 | Vietnam | −0.5980 |
| Lebanon | −0.5463 | | |

*Note*: This governance index is the average of the six indicators used by Kaufmann et al. (2005)

### 5.4 Empirical Analysis of the Determinants of Moody's Sovereign Ratings

**Table 5.18** Ordered probit regression results

| Regressions | [1] | [2] | [3] | [4] | [5] | [6] | [7] | [8] |
|---|---|---|---|---|---|---|---|---|
| Date of ratings | January 1925 | | | January 1929 | | | December 2006 | |
| No. countries | 37 | | | 43 | | | 95 | |
| Intercept | −4.673 (0.792) | −4.518 (1.003) | −4.629 (1.571) | −5.626 (1.936) | −5.647 (2.068) | −4.878 (1.590) | −11.157 (5.031) | 4.487 (7.283) |
| Per capita income | **3.347 (3.454)** | **3.286 (3.812)** | **2.104 (2.200)** | **5.026 (4.222)** | **4.741 (4.444)** | **3.990 (3.519)** | **1.902 (7.981)** | |
| Growth | 0.630 (0.496) | | | 0.037 (0.590) | | | 0.012 (0.189) | −0.084 (1.436) |
| Inflation | **−0.532 (2.993)** | | | **−0.097 (2.994)** | | | **−0.091 (2.829)** | **−0.104 (3.365)** |
| Fiscal balance | −0.009 (0.841) | 0.004 (0.425) | 0.003 (0.319) | −0.422 (3.423) | −0.372 (3.243) | −0.508 (3.708) | −0.047 (1.456) | −0.004 (0.117) |
| External balance | −0.521 (3.495) | −0.406 (3.088) | −0.429 (2.824) | −0.665 (4.276) | −0.530 (3.976) | −0.677 (4.384) | **0.031 (2.068)** | **0.055 (3.559)** |
| External debt | **−0.002 (2.462)** | **−0.002 (3.268)** | **−0.002 (2.306)** | **−0.005 (3.731)** | **−0.004 (3.710)** | **−0.004 (3.123)** | | |
| General debt | | | | | | | **−0.003 (2.537)** | **−0.003 (2.688)** |
| Development indicator | 0.789 (1.061) | 0.025 (0.038) | −0.519 (0.737) | 0.673 (0.819) | −0.341 (0.501) | −0.779 (1.072) | | |
| Default history | **−1.158 (2.223)** | **−1.233 (2.463)** | **−2.220 (3.604)** | −0.749 (1.485) | **−0.973 (2.082)** | **−1.526 (2.908)** | **−0.938 (3.132)** | |
| Institutional indicator | | | **2.015 (3.995)** | | | **1.231 (3.467)** | | |
| Governance indicator | | | | | | | | 1.372 (6.746) |
| Pseudo $R^2$ | 0.893 | 0.831 | 0.941 | 0.945 | 0.904 | 0.951 | 0.873 | 0.755 |

*Notes*: Absolute *t*-statistics are in *parentheses*. Coefficients with the expected sign and significant *t*-statistics (at the 5% level) are in **bold**. The means of some numerical values of ratings are rounded off to fit the ordered probit model. Considering the very high correlation between "development indicator" and "per capita income" for 2006, the former variable is not tested in regression [7]. Considering the very high correlation between "per capita income," "development indicator," and "default history" variables on the one hand, and "governance indicator" on the other hand, the first three variables are not tested in regression [8]

## 5.5 Concluding Remarks

This chapter compares Moody's sovereign rating business and methodology for the interwar period and for 1986–2006. Although the current business conditions, organization, and rating process differ substantially from what they were in the 1920s and 1930s, I note unexpected and astonishing similarities with regard to the methodological framework. In both periods, Moody's official methodology is to list a series of economic, financial, and political variables without providing any macroeconomic formula. More essentially, Moody's sovereign ratings, for both periods, have been explained by a limited number of macroeconomic and institutional variables: GDP per capita, FC debt to exports ratio, default history, and institutional stability. These findings lead me to conclude that Moody's sovereign risk perception tends to be "timeless" notwithstanding official methodological changes in the aftermath of the Asian crisis.

## References

Afonso A. (2003), "Understanding the Determinants of Sovereign Debt Ratings: Evidence for the Two Leading Agencies", *Journal of Finance and Economics*, Vol.27, No.1.

Afonso A., Gomes P. and Rother P. (2011), "Short- and Long-Run Determinants of Sovereign Debt Credit Ratings", *International Journal of Finance and Economics*, Vol.16, Issue 1.

Bhatia A. (2002), "Sovereign Credit Ratings Methodology: An Evaluation", *IMF Working Paper, WP/02/170*.

Borchard E. (1951), *State Insolvency and Foreign Bondholders – Volume I*, Yale University Press, New Haven.

Cantor R. and Packer F. (1996), "Determinants and Impact of Sovereign Credit Ratings", *Federal Reserve Bank of New York, Economic Policy Review*, October.

Corporation of Foreign Bondholders (various issues), *Annual Report*, London.

Eichengreen B. and Portes R. (1989), "Settling Defaults in the Era of Bond Finance", *World Bank Economic Review*, Vol.3, No.2.

Eichengreen B. and Werley C. (1988), "How the Bondholders Fared: Realized Rates of Return on Foreign Dollar Bonds Floated in the 1920s", *University of California at Berkeley, Economic Working Paper 8869*.

Ferri G., Liu L.-G. and Stiglitz J. (1999), "The Procyclical Role of Rating Agencies: Evidence from the East Asian Crisis", *Economic Notes, Banca Monte dei Paschi di Siena SpA*, No.3.

Flandreau M., Gaillard N. and Packer F. (2010), "To Err Is Human: Rating Agencies and the Interwar Foreign Government Debt Crisis", *BIS Working Papers No. 335*, December.

Jüttner J.D. and McCarthy J. (2000), "Modelling a Rating Crisis", *Macquarie University, Unpublished manuscript*, Sydney.

Kaufmann D., Kraay A. and Mastruzzi M. (2005), "Governance Matters IV: Governance Indicators for 1996–2004", World Bank.

League of Nations (1925), *Memorandum on Currency and Central Banks 1913–1924*, Geneva.

League of Nations (1932), *Statistical year-book of the League of Nations*, Geneva.

Lewis C. (1938), *America's Stake in International Investments*, Brookings Institution, Washington.

Lewis C. (1945), *Debtor and Creditor Countries: 1938, 1944*, Brookings Institution, Washington.

Madden J., Nadler M. and Sauvain H. (1937), *America's Experience as a Creditor Nation*, Prentice-Hall Inc, New York.

# References

Maddison A. (2003), *L'Economie mondiale, Une perspective millénaire*, Etudes du Centre de Développement, OCDE.

Mintz I. (1951), *Deterioration in the Quality of Foreign Bonds Issued in the United States 1920–30*, NBER, Cambridge.

Mitchell B. R. (1992), *International Historical Statistics – Europe, 1750–1988*, MacMillan Publishers, Basingstoke.

Mitchell B. R. (1993), *International Historical Statistics – The Americas, 1750–1988*, MacMillan Publishers, Basingstoke.

Moody's Investors Service (various issues), *Manual of Government Securities*.

Moody's Investors Service (various issues), *Investment Letters*.

Moody's Investors Service (various issues), *Investment Surveys*.

Moody's Investors Service (1999), *Moody's Sovereign Ratings: A Ratings Guide*, March.

Moody's Investors Service (2004), *A Quantitative Model for Foreign Currency Government Bond Ratings*, February.

Moody's Investors Service (2006a), *Moody's Statistical Handbook – Country Credit*, May.

Moody's Investors Service (2006b), *Sovereign Ratings Summary*, December.

Moody's Investors Service (2007), *Sovereign Default and Recovery Rates, 1983–2006*, June.

Mulhall M. G. (1896), *Industries and Wealth of Nations*, Longmans, Green and Co., London.

Reisen H. and von Maltzan J. (1999), "Boom and Bust and Sovereign Ratings", *OECD Development Centre, Technical Papers No.148*.

Rippy J. F. (1950), "A Bond-Selling Extravaganza of the 1920's", *Journal of Business of the University of Chicago*, Vol.23, No.4.

Standard & Poor's (2004), *Sovereign Defaults Set to Fall Again in 2005*, 28 September.

Winkler M. (1933), *Foreign Bonds – An Autopsy*, Roland Swain Company, Philadelphia.

Wynne W. (1951), *State Insolvency and Foreign Bondholders – Volume II*, Yale University Press, New Haven.

# Chapter 6
# Sovereign Rating Methodologies: From Theory to Practice

This chapter opens the "black box" of leading CRAs' sovereign rating methodologies. Because only Moody's provided details about its rating criteria during the interwar years (see Chap. 5), the scope of this analysis is restricted to the "modern era" – that is, the period 1986–2010.

Section 6.1 shows that the criteria listed by Fitch, Moody's, and S&P in their official methodologies are broadly similar. Section 6.2 reminds that sovereign ratings can be explained by a small set of variables. However, the increasing number of low-income countries that are assigned a rating and the economic success of major emerging countries since the mid-2000s have led agencies to take more variables into account when issuing sovereign credit opinions. Section 6.3 examines the split ratings across CRAs and explains these disagreements by inferring from the agencies' reports. This section also investigates to what extent the recent entry of new CRAs in the sovereign rating business may modify risk assessment.

## 6.1 Evolution and Comparison of Official Rating Criteria

Fitch, Moody's, and S&P official sovereign rating methodologies have evolved since the 1990s. The three CRAs have made efforts to improve the transparency of their analytical process, update their rating criteria, and formalize the conceptual framework of their methodologies. However, the use of both qualitative and quantitative variables, the combination of top-down and bottom-up approaches, and peer-to-peer comparison have remained prominent features of sovereign risk assessment through the last 2 decades.

## 6.1.1 Common and Unchanged Methods for Assessing Sovereign Risk

Fitch, Moody's, and S&P ratings have always been the result of qualitative and quantitative analyses. As emphasized in Chap. 5, qualitative factors (e.g., political stability, reliability of institutions, and degree of consensus on major economic policy issues) have been decisive in assessing the sovereign's willingness and ability to pay. Section 5.4 details how uncertainties about the political situation may jeopardize the credit standing of a country. Quantitative data (e.g., ratio of public debt to government revenue and GDP per capita) are useful because they enable rating analysts to measure sovereign risk more objectively and efficiently.

Rating agencies have also traditionally combined bottom-up and top-down approaches to assign ratings. The bottom-up approach, which is the core of the analytical framework, focuses on the credit fundamentals of each sovereign (Fitch 2002, 2010c; Moody's 2002a, 2008b; S&P 1997a, b, 2010). It is complemented by the top-down analysis, the objective of which is to assess the impact of regional or worldwide events on the creditworthiness of a sovereign or group of sovereigns – for example, membership in the European Monetary Union (EMU) or the 2007–2008 financial crisis.

Comparison with peers is the third key element of sovereign rating methodologies. The country analyses of Fitch, Moody's, and S&P often include comparisons between the rated country and its peer group (i.e., other sovereigns that are in the same broad rating category). The three CRAs also publish specific reports that contain comparative statistics for rated sovereigns (see e.g., Fitch 2010d; Moody's 2009b; S&P 2006a). These publications facilitate comparisons among peer groups of similarly rated countries and help establish the relative performance of each country.

## 6.1.2 More Crises Lead to Expanded Criteria

Until the Asian crisis, the rating agencies' sovereign risk assessment was largely influenced by three strands of the economic literature.[1] The first one studies the reputation of sovereign borrowers. The theoretical works of Eaton and Gersovitz (1981), who claim that sovereigns repay because otherwise they would develop a reputation for defaulting and thereby lose access to international capital markets, and of Bulow and Rogoff (1989), whose diverging analysis is based on the notion that lending to small countries should not be without the direct sanctions available to creditors, both supported the CRAs' view that default history was a key variable when assigning ratings. The second influential strand of the economic literature focuses on currency

---

[1] The conclusions reported here are drawn from interviews with several senior rating analysts.

crises. Krugman (1979) and Flood and Garber (1984) explain why countries may be unable to fight against speculative attacks on their currency when reserves are not sufficient. Obstfeld (1994) argues that currency crises may be a self-fulfilling prophecy. These works echo the agencies' tendency to overweight variables such as GDP growth rate and foreign exchange reserves (Moody's 1994a; S&P 1992). The third strand analyzes the debt overhang problem. Krugman (1988), Sachs (1989), and Borensztein (1990) argue that accumulated external debt creates an obstacle to future investment and growth. These studies convinced CRAs that debt ratios were the most prominent financial variables to take into account in the short and medium term (Moody's 1990, 1991, 1994b; S&P 1994a, 1995).

S&P (1997b) provides an exhaustive analytical framework as of April 1997 – that is, 3 months prior to the onset of the Asian crisis. The agency highlights eight major criteria: political stability, economic structure, economic growth, budgetary flexibility, public debt, price stability, balance of payments, and external debt. Yet S&P like Moody's and Fitch IBCA, paid too little attention to contingent liability, private-sector external debt, and short-term debt. These were the roots of the difficulties experienced by Indonesia, South Korea, Malaysia, and Thailand.

In a remarkable mea culpa, Fitch IBCA (1998) owns up to its mistakes and lists the new criteria that need to be taken into account. Fitch IBCA admits that short-term debt created a key vulnerability for any sovereign and recognizes that total external debt, and not just public external debt, matters. The agency also concludes that exchange rates must be sustainable.

Fitch, Moody's, and S&P updated their sovereign rating methodologies by 2002. Fitch (2002) publishes a list of 14 major criteria: (a) demographic, educational, and structural factors; (b) labor market analysis; (c) structure of output and trade; (d) dynamism of the private sector; (e) balance of supply and demand; (f) balance of payments; (g) analysis of medium-term growth constraints; (h) macroeconomic policy; (i) trade and foreign investment policy; (j) analysis of the banking and financial sector; (k) focus on external assets; (l) focus on external liabilities; (m) political and institutional system; and (n) international position. Like Moody's (see Sect. 5.3), Fitch does not provide information about the weighting of its criteria and variables. However, Fitch does indicate that its sovereign rating model generates a score calibrated to its FC ratings (Fitch 2007, 2010c). The S&P methodology is quite similar: each country is ranked on a scale from 1 (the highest score) to 6 (the lowest) for each analytical category (S&P 1998).[2] The number of these categories expanded from eight in 1997–1998 to ten in 2002. It was reduced to nine in 2006 (see Table 6.1) and has not changed since then.

Bhatia (2002) studies S&P's methodology update in the aftermath of the Asian crisis.[3] He highlights that S&P began to attach greater importance to quantification

---

[2] There is, however, no exact formula that combines the scores to determine ratings. As a result, we cannot consider S&P's methodology to be much more "formalized" than that of Fitch and Moody's at the time.

[3] Bhatia's analysis is particularly relevant because he was at S&P until the early 2000s prior to joining the International Monetary Fund.

Table 6.1 S&P sovereign rating criteria in 1997, 2002, and 2008

| April 1997 | April 2002 | May 2008 |
|---|---|---|
| Political stability | Political stability | Political risk |
| Economic prospects I: structure | Economic prospects I: structure | Economic structure |
| Economic prospects II: growth | Economic prospects II: growth | Economic growth prospects |
| Fiscal flexibility I: budgetary flexibility | Fiscal flexibility I: revenue, expenditure, and balance performance | Fiscal flexibility |
| Fiscal flexibility II: public debt | Fiscal flexibility II: debt and interest burdens | General government debt burden |
| Price stability | Fiscal flexibility III: off-budget and contingent liabilities | Offshore and contingent liabilities |
| External flexibility I: balance of payments flexibility | Monetary stability | Monetary flexibility |
| External flexibility II: external debt | External flexibility I: liquidity | External liquidity |
|  | External flexibility II: public-sector net external debt | External debt burden |
|  | External flexibility III: bank and private-sector net external debt |  |

*Sources*: S&P (1997b, 2002, 2008a)

of off-budget and contingent liabilities, adequacy of reserves, and size of private debt. Moody's enhanced methodology in the 2000s was in line with the Fitch and S&P updates (Fitch 2002, 2007, 2010c; Moody's 2002a, 2003d, 2009b; S&P 2002, 2008a).

After the Argentine default in 2001, rating agencies were obliged to revise their sovereign risk assessment in dollarized countries. They had previously tended to view dollarization as a factor that was likely to strengthen sovereign creditworthiness (Duff and Phelps 1999) or at least to support the ratings of corporates and financial institutions in dollarized countries (S&P 1997c). But Fitch, Moody's, and S&P have employed since 2001 more cautious rating policies as regards dollarized economies. Moody's introduced a "dollarization" vulnerability indicator in its handbooks (Moody's 2003d).[4] Globally, banking systems' high level of dollarization, particularly in Central America, has been regarded as a potential systemic risk and constrained sovereign ratings of most countries in the region (Fitch 2004; Moody's 2003a; S&P 2006b). In addition to the ongoing updates that increased the number of criteria under consideration, CRAs have improved the transparency of their rating process and enhanced their methodologies. These efforts have led to attempts to model sovereign risk.

---

[4] This indicator represents the ratio of FC deposits in domestic banks to the sum of official foreign exchange reserves and foreign assets of domestic banks.

## 6.1.3 Modeling Sovereign Risk

Fitch, Moody's, and S&P came under intense criticism after the collapse of Enron in December 2001.[5] Their methodologies were considered opaque, inaccurate, and outdated. In January 2003, the U.S. Securities and Exchange Commission (SEC) published a report on the role and function of rating agencies in the operation of the securities markets in response to the congressional directive contained in the Sarbanes–Oxley Act of 2002 (SEC 2003). The report stressed the importance of greater transparency in the rating process. In September of that year, International Organization of Securities Commissions (IOSCO) released a statement of principles regarding the activities of CRAs (IOSCO 2003). One of these principles was that rating agencies should "adopt and implement written procedures and methodologies to ensure that the opinions they issue are based on a fair and thorough analysis of all relevant information available to the CRA, and that CRA analysts perform their duties with integrity. CRA rating methodologies should be rigorous, systematic, and CRA ratings should be subject to some form of validation based on historical experience." Another principle was that rating agencies should "make disclosure and transparency an objective in their ratings activities." For instance, "CRAs should publish sufficient information about their procedures and methodologies so that outside parties can understand how a rating was arrived at by the CRA." In December 2004, IOSCO published a detailed code of conduct giving guidance on implementing its principles (IOSCO 2004).

Although aimed at corporate ratings, these principles were implemented in the sovereign rating area in two ways: through the development of (a) quantitative models and (b) "conceptual" methodological frameworks.

Moody's was the only CRA to reveal its sovereign rating methodologies by publishing quantitative models for both LC and FC ratings (Moody's 2003c, 2004). The objective of these two studies[6] was to identify the few criteria that (roughly) determine sovereign ratings. Four key variables explained more than 80% of both LC and FC sovereign ratings: ratio of general government debt to general government revenue, GDP per capita, real GDP growth, and government effectiveness (as indexed by the World Bank). The quantitative model resulted in few outliers: less than 20% of the predicted ratings deviated by more than two notches from Moody's actual ratings.

Moody's explained the rating gaps that did result as follows. Countries for which the predicted ratings were higher included countries that had just defaulted (Argentina and Uruguay) or had been near to default (Brazil and Turkey). Sovereigns for which the actual ratings were higher were countries with favorable debt dynamics (Italy), positive debt management (Colombia and Egypt), or low debt burden (Peru and Kazakhstan). Moody's quantitative models have not been subsequently

---

[5] Enron was still rated in investment grade by Fitch, Moody's, and S&P several days prior to its bankruptcy on 2 December 2001.

[6] The three authors were David Levey, Luis Ernesto Martínez-Alas, and Vincent Truglia.

updated, and no other major rating agencies have chosen to implement their own sovereign risk models.

In September 2008, however, Moody's published a report whose purpose was to explain how the agency determined sovereign ratings in terms of both LC and FC (Moody's 2008b). This methodology provided a conceptual framework based on a three-step approach that produced a narrow rating range.[7]

The first step determines the economic resiliency of the country. The degree of resiliency depends on the country's economic strength (Factor 1) and its institutional strength (Factor 2). Economic strength is based mainly on GDP per capita, diversification and size of the economy, and long-term economic trends. Institutional strength results from quality of governance, respect for property rights, and the transparency, efficiency, and predictability of government action. Factors 1 and 2 are classified on a five-point scale: very high, high, moderate, low, or very low. Combining these two factors' scores yields the economic resiliency score on the same five-point scale.

The second step consists of analyzing the financial strength of the government (Factor 3) and its "susceptibility to event risk" (Factor 4). Financial strength is measured as the government's ability to mobilize resources to repay its debt. This measurement involves assessing the sustainability of public debt and the country's ability to raise taxes and access foreign currency. Evaluating susceptibility to event risk focuses on "the risk of a direct and immediate threat to debt repayment, and, for countries higher in the rating scale, the risk of a sudden multi-notch downgrade." Factors 3 and 4 are also classified on a five-point scale ranging from very high to very low. Combining the scores of these two factors produces the financial robustness score, which is classified on the same five-point scale.

The third step involves comparing the country's economic resiliency to its financial robustness. This results in the identification of a rating range, as shown in Table 6.2. Determination of the final rating is based on the peer comparison and weighting additional factors.

This framework of Moody's is more "conceptual" than previous versions, but the agency's methodology remains fundamentally an analyst-driven one: the evaluation of countries (along Factors 1–4) in terms of the five categories (from very high to very low) is ultimately based on the individual judgments of rating analysts.

In November 2010, S&P proposed an updated sovereign rating methodology and requested comments from market participants (S&P 2010). This framework, too, incorporates a multi-step analytical process. First, S&P groups the major criteria listed in its 2008 methodology into five broad categories, which are assigned a score on a six-point scale ranging from 1 (the strongest) to 6 (the weakest); see Table 6.3.

Second, the five scores are grouped into two profiles. The political and economic scores are combined to form the political and economic profile, while the external,

---

[7] This methodological approach was initiated by Pierre Cailleteau, Guido Cipriani, Kristin Lindow, and Thomas J. Byrne.

6.1 Evolution and Comparison of Official Rating Criteria

**Table 6.2** Moody's sovereign rating road map

| | Economic resiliency | | | | |
|---|---|---|---|---|---|
| | Very high | High | Moderate | Low | Very low |
| Aaa | ■ | | | | |
| Aa1 | ▓ | | | | |
| Aa2 | ▒ | ■ | | | |
| Aa3 | ░ | ▓ | | | |
| A1 | | ▒ | ■ | | |
| A2 | | ░ | ▓ | | |
| A3 | | | ▒ | | |
| Baa1 | | | ░ | ■ | |
| Baa2 | | | ░ | ▓ | |
| Baa3 | | | | ▒ | |
| Ba1 | | | ░ | ░ | ■ |
| Ba2 | | | | | ▓ |
| Ba3 | | | | ░ | ▒ |
| B1 | | | | ░ | ░ |
| B2 | | | | | ░ |
| B3 | | | | | ░ |
| Caa | | | | | ░ |
| C | | | | | |

Legend: financial robustness

■ Very high   ▓ High   ▒ Moderate   ░ Low   　 Very low

*Source*: Moody's (2008b)

**Table 6.3** S&P's five key rating factors

| Factors assessed | Score assigned on a six-point scale |
|---|---|
| Institutional effectiveness and political risks | Political score |
| Economic structure and growth prospects | Economic score |
| External liquidity and international investment position | External score |
| Fiscal flexibility and fiscal performance combined with debt burden | Fiscal score |
| Funding and monetary flexibility | Monetary score |

*Source*: S&P (2010)

fiscal, and monetary scores are combined to form the flexibility and performance profile. These two profiles are based on 11- and 9-point scales, respectively. Finally, the two profiles are combined to yield an "indicative" sovereign rating level (Table 6.4). Exceptional adjustments may be made prior to assigning the final FC rating. The S&P procedure then assigns the LC rating, which is often higher than the FC rating because the CRA views countries as having more fiscal and monetary flexibility with respect to local currency obligations. Figure 6.1 illustrates S&P's analytical process.

**Table 6.4** S&P sovereign rating indicative level

| | Political and economic profile | | | | | | | | |
|---|---|---|---|---|---|---|---|---|---|
| | Superior | Extremely strong | Very strong | Strong | Moderately strong | Intermediate | Moderately weak | Weak | Very weak | Extremely weak | Risky |
| Extremely strong | AAA | AAA | AA+ | AA | AA− | A+ | A | N.A. | N.A. | N.A. |
| Very strong | AAA | AAA | AA | AA− | A+ | A | A− | BBB+ | N.A. | N.A. |
| Strong | AAA | AA+ | AA | AA− | A | A− | BBB+ | BBB | BBB− | N.A. |
| Moderately strong | AA+ | AA | AA− | A+ | A− | BBB | BBB− | BB+ | BB | BB+ |
| Intermediate | AA | AA− | A+ | A | BBB+ | BBB− | BB+ | BB | BB− | B+ |
| Moderately weak | AA− | A+ | A | A− | BBB | BB+ | BB | BB− | B+ | B |
| Weak | A | A− | BBB+ | BBB | BB+ | BB | BB− | B+ | B | B− |
| Very weak | N.A. | BBB | BBB− | BB+ | BB | BB− | B+ | B | B | B− |
| Extremely weak | N.A. | BB | BB− | B+ | B | B− | B− | B− | CCC/CC | CCC/CC | CCC/CC |

N.A. Not applicable
*Source*: S&P (2010)

## 6.1 Evolution and Comparison of Official Rating Criteria

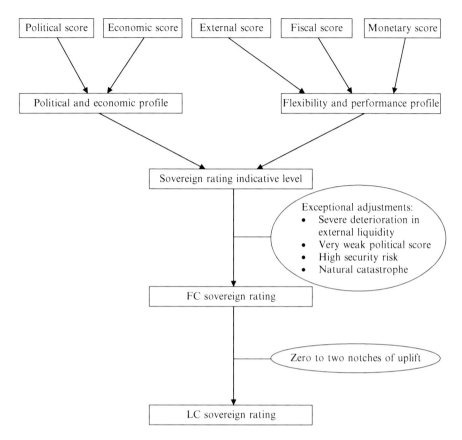

**Fig. 6.1** S&P sovereign rating methodology (*Source*: S&P 2010)

Moody's 2008 analytical framework and S&P's proposed 2010 methodology have common features: both involve a multi-step process, employ a relatively conceptual approach, and combine features of a country's political and economic structure to develop a financial profile upon which the rating is based. One major difference is that, unlike S&P, Moody's does not assign speculative-grade rating to countries with an above-average economic resiliency score. This may mean that Moody's tends to place much weight on political and economic criteria. Fitch has not implemented a similar analytical framework for rating sovereigns (Fitch 2010c). However, it uses essentially the same criteria as Moody's and S&P.

The efforts made by rating agencies to disclose their methodologies have promoted transparency and should enable investors and regulators to judge the adequacy and relevance of sovereign ratings. From this viewpoint, the agencies' recent publications are a welcome complement to academic research on the determinants of sovereign ratings.

## 6.2 Determinants of Sovereign Ratings

As Chap. 5 shows, several research papers studied the determinants of sovereign ratings and demonstrated that a small number of variables can explain a large percentage of CRAs' credit opinions. But the increase in low- and middle-income countries that have been assigned a rating since the late 1990s has underscored the significance of additional determinants.

### 6.2.1 Conventional Determinants

Table 6.5 summarizes the main findings of some empirical research that addresses the determinants of both developed and developing countries' sovereign ratings.

Whether using OLS or ordered probit models for cross-sectional or panel data, these authors find that the robust determinants of the sovereign ratings issued between 1981 and 2006 are GDP per capita; ratio of public debt to exports, revenue, or GDP; inflation; government effectiveness indicators; and the indicator for default history. These empirical studies also establish that the named variables correspond to the political, economic, and financial criteria highlighted in the reports of Fitch, S&P, and Moody's, confirming the transparency of the rating agency methodologies.

Clearly, the most relevant issue here is the extent to which the key determinants of sovereign ratings actually differ across rating categories.

### 6.2.2 Determinants Specific to Low- and Middle-Income Countries

Over the past two decades, more and more low- and middle-income countries have managed to gain access to capital markets and hence obtain a credit rating from Fitch, Moody's, or S&P.[8] As a result, the proportion of high-income countries in the total number of sovereigns rated has decreased dramatically since the early 1990s. For S&P, this percentage fell from 80% in January 1990 to 42% in January 2010.[9] As stated in Sect. 6.1, this evolution has led rating agencies to take more and more criteria into account when assessing sovereign risk. Recent empirical studies that focus on the determinants of emerging countries' ratings show that external reserves and workers' remittances are key variables.[10]

---

[8] See Chap. 1 for the various reasons behind the expansion of sovereign rating in the 1990s–2000s.

[9] Author's computations based on World Bank analytical classifications and http://www.standardandpoors.com.

[10] For the rest of this section, the expression "emerging countries" refers to "low- and middle-income countries" because there was no high-income country among the emerging economies under study (with the exception of Israel and South Korea in Eliasson 2002).

6.2 Determinants of Sovereign Ratings

**Table 6.5** Main studies on the determinants of sovereign ratings

| References | Model | Data | Years | CRAs | Main determinants |
|---|---|---|---|---|---|
| Cantor and Packer (1996) | OLS | Cross-section; 45 countries | 1995 | Moody's and S&P | GNP per capita, GDP growth, inflation, FC debt-to-exports ratio, indicator for economic development, and indicator for default history |
| Hu et al. (2002) | Ordered probit | Panel; 92 countries | 1981–1998 | S&P | Debt service to exports, debt to GNP, reserves to debt, and reserves-to-imports ratios, GNP growth, inflation, indicators for default history, regional dummies, and non-industrial countries dummy |
| Afonso (2003) | OLS | Cross-section; 81 countries | 2001 | Moody's and S&P | Per capita income, GDP growth, inflation, current account surplus, government budget surplus, debt-to-exports ratio, indicator for economic development, and indicator for default history |
| Alexe et al. (2003) | OLS | Cross-section; 68 countries | 1998 | S&P | GDP per capita, debt-to-GDP ratio, domestic credit-to-GDP ratio, government efficiency, and political stability |
| Canuto et al. (2004) | OLS | Panel; 66 countries | 1998–2002 | Fitch, Moody's, and S&P | GDP per capita, GDP growth, inflation, government debt-to-receipts ratio, government budget surplus, trade-to-GDP ratio, debt-to-exports ratio, indicator for economic development, and indicator for default history |
| Borio and Packer (2004) | OLS | Panel; 52 countries | 1996–2003 | Moody's and S&P | GDP per capita, GDP growth, inflation, years since FC default, public debt-to-GDP ratio, external debt-to-exports ratio, corruption perception index, and political risk score |
| Afonso et al. (2011) | Ordered probit | Panel; 130 countries | 1995–2005 | Fitch, Moody's, and S&P | GDP per capita, GDP growth, government debt-to-GDP ratio, external debt-to-exports ratio, reserves, government effectiveness indicators, and indicator for default history |
| Gaillard (2011) | OLS and ordered probit | Cross-section; 95 countries | 2006 | Moody's | GDP per capita, inflation, current account surplus, public debt-to-revenue ratio, government effectiveness indicators, and indicator for default history |

*Note*: Gaillard (2011) refers to the findings reported in Chap. 5

**Table 6.6** Reserves and ratings of the BRIC countries, 2005 and 2009

|  | Reserves including gold (USD billion) | | Fitch ratings | | Moody's ratings | | S&P ratings | |
|---|---|---|---|---|---|---|---|---|
|  | 2005 | 2009 | 2005 | 2009 | 2005 | 2009 | 2005 | 2009 |
| China | 828.8 | 2,453.2 | A– | A+ | A2 | A1 | BBB+ | A+ |
| Russia | 182.3 | 439.1 | BBB– | BBB | Baa3 | Baa1 | BBB– | BBB |
| India | 144.2 | 272.2 | BB+ | BBB– | Baa3 | Baa3 | BB+ | BBB– |
| Brazil | 53.8 | 238.5 | BB– | BBB– | B1 | Ba1 | BB– | BBB– |

*Note*: Ratings are as of 30 June
*Sources*: Fitch (2005, 2010c) for reserves data; http://www.fitchratings.com, http://www.moodys.com, and http://www.standardandpoors.com

Eliasson (2002) analyzes the determinants of sovereign ratings assigned by S&P to 38 emerging countries during the period 1990–1999. Eliasson's findings corroborate Cantor and Packer's (1996) results, but she determines that the ratio of short-term debt to reserves is also an important explanatory variable that should be added to the traditional determinants. Afonso et al. (2011) find that the reserves-to-imports ratio is a significant variable, too – particularly for Fitch and S&P. Even more interesting is that external reserves turn out to have a higher explanatory power in the later period of their study (i.e., 2001–2005). Because their research includes both developed and developing countries, these results suggest that the size of a country's external reserves is now an influential factor in CRAs' credit opinions.

Table 6.6 lists the 2005 and 2009 reserves and ratings of the countries holding the most foreign reserves among the low- and middle-income economies: Brazil, Russia, India, and China (the so-called BRIC countries). One may suppose that their growing foreign reserves have contributed to the upward trend of these countries' ratings.[11] Various agency reports support this view (see Fitch 2010a; Moody's 2007a, 2008a; S&P 2008b, 2009c).

Workers' remittances are a second significant determinant of sovereign ratings for low-income countries. As of 1 July 2010, 22 of the 140 countries that were assigned a rating by at least one of the three major agencies had a ratio of workers' remittances to GDP that exceeded 7%. When one considers that half of these countries were not yet rated in 2000, it is easier to understand why remittances have only recently become a decisive criterion; see Table 6.7.

Ratha (2005) shows that large and stable remittance flows can improve the creditworthiness of low-income economies. In analyzing the period 1993–2006, Avendaño et al. (2011) find that rating agencies take remittance flows into account when rating small, low-income economies. The remittance dependence of Central America was confirmed during the recent economic crisis: five of the six rated countries with the highest remittances-to-GDP ratios in the Latin American and Caribbean region (i.e., Jamaica, El Salvador, Guatemala, Honduras, and the

---

[11] Between June 2005 and June 2009 the four countries were upgraded, on average, by 3, 1.3, 0.7, and 2 notches, respectively (author's computations).

6.2 Determinants of Sovereign Ratings

**Table 6.7** Rated countries most dependent on remittances

| Country | Workers' remittances and compensation of employees received as percentage of GDP | | | Date of first FC rating assignment (CRA) |
|---|---|---|---|---|
| | 2000 | 2004 | 2008 | |
| Moldova | 13.9 | 27.1 | 31.4 | 14 January 1997 (Moody's) |
| Lesotho | 32.2 | 27.5 | 27.0 | 2 September 2002 (Fitch) |
| Lebanon | 9.2 | 25.7 | 24.5 | 26 February 1997 (Fitch, Moody's, and S&P) |
| Honduras | 6.8 | 13.4 | 21.5 | 29 September 1998 (Moody's) |
| Jordan | 21.8 | 20.4 | 17.9 | 27 October 1995 (Moody's and S&P) |
| El Salvador | 13.4 | 16.2 | 17.2 | 26 August 1996 (S&P) |
| Jamaica | 9.9 | 16.0 | 14.9 | 30 March 1998 (Moody's) |
| Bosnia | 30.1 | 20.7 | 14.8 | 29 March 2004 (Moody's) |
| Nicaragua | 8.1 | 11.6 | 12.4 | 27 March 1998 (Moody's) |
| Albania | 16.2 | 15.5 | 12.2 | 29 June 2007 (Moody's) |
| Guatemala | 3.1 | 11.0 | 11.4 | 8 July 1997 (Moody's) |
| Bangladesh | 4.2 | 6.3 | 11.3 | 5 April 2010 (S&P) |
| Philippines | 9.2 | 13.2 | 11.2 | 1 July 1993 (Moody's) |
| Serbia | 12.6 | 16.8 | 11.1 | 1 November 2004 (S&P) |
| Cape Verde | 16.4 | 12.3 | 9.7 | 15 August 2003 (Fitch) |
| Senegal | 5.0 | 7.9 | 9.7 | 18 December 2000 (S&P) |
| Armenia | 4.6 | 12.1 | 8.9 | 24 May 2006 (Fitch) |
| Gambia | 3.3 | 15.5 | 8.2 | 11 November 2002 (Fitch) |
| Vietnam | N.A. | 7.0 | 7.9 | 28 May 2002 (S&P) |
| Dominican R. | 7.7 | 11.3 | 7.8 | 13 February 1997 (S&P) |
| Morocco | 5.8 | 7.4 | 7.8 | 2 March 1998 (Moody's and S&P) |
| Sri Lanka | 7.1 | 7.7 | 7.3 | 8 December 2005 (Fitch and S&P) |

*Notes*: Gambia's sole rating, which was issued by Fitch, was withdrawn in July 2007. Data on Vietnam are not available for 2000
*Sources*: WDI/GDF, http://www.fitchratings.com, http://www.moodys.com, and http://www.standardandpoors.com

Dominican Republic) were downgraded or had their outlooks revised from positive to stable or from stable to negative between September 2008 and September 2009.

In conclusion, one must concede that the key determinants of sovereign ratings have remained the same since the interwar years. However, the easier access of low- and middle-income countries to capital markets since the 1990s has led CRAs to take new variables into account (e.g., foreign reserves and the remittances-to-GDP ratio) when they rate these economies. Moreover, no empirical study has shown that the determinants of credit opinions differ significantly from one agency to another. This is consistent with our observation that the official criteria highlighted by Fitch, Moody's, and S&P are much the same. The next section goes beyond this overall similarity in sovereign rating methodologies to explore the commonalities and differences across the rating agencies.

## 6.3 Rating Gaps Across Agencies

This section investigates rating gaps (i.e., divergences of opinion) among CRAs by examining split sovereign ratings.[12]

### 6.3.1 Split Ratings Among Fitch, Moody's, and S&P

A basic measurement of the relationship between different agencies' sovereign ratings consists of computing Spearman correlation coefficients. Pairwise correlations for the three CRA pairs are provided in Table 6.8. The correlations range from 0.957 to 0.993, strongly suggesting that Fitch, Moody's, and S&P have converging views on the rank ordering of relative sovereign risks.

However, Spearman correlations imperfectly capture the disagreements across rating agencies. Hence, the sharper analysis afforded by an examination of split ratings is needed. Toward this end, three databases are built to compare Fitch and Moody's ratings (sample 1), Fitch and S&P ratings (sample 2), and Moody's and S&P ratings (sample 3). Each sample consists of quarterly observations (on the first day of January, April, July, and October) of the FC sovereign ratings assigned by Fitch and Moody's, by Fitch and S&P, and by Moody's and S&P (for samples 1, 2, and 3, respectively). For instance, an observation in sample 1 is the Fitch–Moody's ratings pair for a given country at a given date. The starting date of samples 1 and 2 is 1 July 2000 (i.e., the first quarter following the merger of Fitch IBCA and Duff & Phelps on 19 May 2000). The starting date of sample 3 is 1 October 1986 (i.e., the first quarter following the refinement of Moody's sovereign rating scale that occurred on 15 August 1986). The end date of all three samples is 1 January 2011.

The last step of building the three databases is to transform the Fitch, Moody's, and S&P rating scales into a unified 21-point numerical scale (see Table 6.9) so that the ratings gap within each pair could be measured.

**Table 6.8** Spearman correlation coefficients

|  | 1992 | 1995 | 1998 | 2001 | 2004 | 2007 | 2010 |
|---|---|---|---|---|---|---|---|
| Fitch–Moody's | N.R. | N.R. | N.R. | 0.986 | 0.977 | 0.981 | 0.990 |
| Fitch–S&P | N.R. | N.R. | N.R. | 0.986 | 0.991 | 0.993 | 0.989 |
| Moody's–S&P | 0.957 | 0.979 | 0.964 | 0.983 | 0.971 | 0.979 | 0.987 |

*Notes*: Based on ratings as of 1 January. The computations are not adjusted for outlooks and creditwatches. *N.R.* denotes Not Relevant because Fitch rated too few sovereigns until the late 1990s
*Sources*: Author's computations based on http://www.fitchratings.com, http://www.moodys.com, and http://www.standardandpoors.com

---

[12] A *split rating* occurs when at least two rating agencies disagree on the rating of a particular issuer.

## 6.3 Rating Gaps Across Agencies

**Table 6.9** Numerical transformation of ratings

| Fitch | Moody's | S&P | Numerical scale |
|---|---|---|---|
| AAA | Aaa | AAA | 20 |
| AA+ | Aa1 | AA+ | 19 |
| AA | Aa2 | AA | 18 |
| AA− | Aa3 | AA− | 17 |
| A+ | A1 | A+ | 16 |
| A | A2 | A | 15 |
| A− | A3 | A− | 14 |
| BBB+ | Baa1 | BBB+ | 13 |
| BBB | Baa2 | BBB | 12 |
| BBB− | Baa3 | BBB− | 11 |
| BB+ | Ba1 | BB+ | 10 |
| BB | Ba2 | BB | 9 |
| BB− | Ba3 | BB− | 8 |
| B+ | B1 | B+ | 7 |
| B | B2 | B | 6 |
| B− | B3 | B− | 5 |
| CCC+ | Caa1 | CCC+ | 4 |
| CCC | Caa2 | CCC | 3 |
| CCC− | Caa3 | CCC− | 2 |
| CC/C | Ca | CC | 1 |
| DDD/DD/D−RD/D | C | SD/D | 0 |

*Note*: Fitch default rating categories were DDD, DD, and D until 2005 and were RD and D thereafter (see Chap. 3)

Table 6.10 documents the frequency and the magnitude of agreements and disagreements in the ratings assigned by Fitch, Moody's, and S&P. There are 289 series of pairs resulting in 13,032 observations.[13]

The disagreements across leading agencies account for fewer than half of all observations, but comparisons differ significantly depending on whether it is the Fitch–Moody's, Fitch–S&P, or Moody's–S&Ps pair being evaluated.

Fitch and S&P have the highest frequency of identical ratings, 64.45% vs. only 51.36% for Moody's–S&P pairs and 50.51% for Fitch–Moody's pairs. A close examination of split ratings between Moody's and the other two CRAs shows that the percentage of higher Moody's ratings is greater than the percentage of higher Fitch and S&P ratings (29.69% vs. 19.80% and 25.05% vs. 23.59%, respectively). The percentage of higher Fitch ratings is greater only for split ratings between Fitch and S&P (20.45% vs. 15.10%). These results are summed up in the mean differences between the three CRAs' ratings. Moody's ratings are, on average, higher than Fitch and S&P ratings by 0.17 and 0.05 notch, respectively. In contrast, S&P is the most conservative firm: on average, its ratings are lower than those of Fitch by 0.04 notch.

Issuers rated by both Fitch and Moody's differ by up to five notches. Split ratings with six- and seven-notch differentials are observed for Moody's–S&P pairs and Fitch–S&P pairs, respectively. However, 90.63 and 97.93% of all pairs are within

---

[13] A *series* of pairs includes all pairs of ratings observed for one country that is rated by two agencies simultaneously.

**Table 6.10** Agreements and disagreements across leading agencies

|  | Fitch–Moody's (sample 1) | Fitch–S&P (sample 2) | Moody's–S&P (sample 3) |
|---|---|---|---|
| Period under consideration | 2000:07–2011:01 | 2000:07–2011:01 | 1986:10–2011:01 |
| Number of series of pairs | 87 | 100 | 102 |
| Number of observations | 3,318 | 3,550 | 6,164 |
| Number of identical ratings | 1,676 | 2,288 | 3,166 |
| Number of split ratings | 1,642 | 1,262 | 2,998 |
| Mean absolute difference (notches) | 0.17 | 0.04 | 0.05 |
| Identical ratings (%) | 50.51 | 64.45 | 51.36 |
| Fitch rating 1 notch higher (%) | 15.64 | 18.56 | N.A. |
| Fitch rating 2 notches higher (%) | 3.44 | 1.49 | N.A. |
| Fitch rating 3 notches higher (%) | 0.69 | 0.23 | N.A. |
| Fitch rating 4 notches higher (%) | 0.03 | 0.03 | N.A. |
| Fitch rating 5 notches higher (%) | 0.00 | 0.11 | N.A. |
| Fitch rating 6 notches higher (%) | 0.00 | 0.03 | N.A. |
| Fitch rating 7 notches higher (%) | 0.00 | 0.00 | N.A. |
| Moody's rating 1 notch higher (%) | 22.66 | N.A. | 18.53 |
| Moody's rating 2 notches higher (%) | 4.31 | N.A. | 4.93 |
| Moody's rating 3 notches higher (%) | 1.15 | N.A. | 0.89 |
| Moody's rating 4 notches higher (%) | 0.87 | N.A. | 0.49 |
| Moody's rating 5 notches higher (%) | 0.69 | N.A. | 0.19 |
| Moody's rating 6 notches higher (%) | 0.00 | N.A. | 0.02 |
| Moody's rating 7 notches higher (%) | 0.00 | N.A. | 0.00 |
| S&P rating 1 notch higher (%) | N.A. | 13.30 | 18.45 |
| S&P rating 2 notches higher (%) | N.A. | 1.15 | 4.80 |
| S&P rating 3 notches higher (%) | N.A. | 0.00 | 0.31 |
| S&P rating 4 notches higher (%) | N.A. | 0.03 | 0.03 |
| S&P rating 5 notches higher (%) | N.A. | 0.28 | 0.00 |
| S&P rating 6 notches higher (%) | N.A. | 0.14 | 0.00 |
| S&P rating 7 notches higher (%) | N.A. | 0.20 | 0.00 |

*N.A.* not applicable
*Sources*: Author's computations

(respectively) one notch and two notches. Results are not homogeneous across the three samples: 88.34 (98.07%), 88.82 (96.56%), and 96.31% (98.96%) of Moody's–S&P, Fitch–Moody's, and Fitch–S&P pairs are within one notch (two notches), respectively. These figures support the view that Fitch and S&P ratings are highly correlated, whereas split ratings between Moody's and its two competitors are more frequent.

The 270 more-than-two-notch split ratings (or "large split ratings" hereafter) account for a small fraction of observations (3.44, 1.04, and 1.93% of samples 1, 2, and 3, respectively). However, they require further attention given their evidencing significant disagreements across agencies.[14] Table 6.11 lists countries with

---

[14] This affirmation is based on interviews and discussions held with several senior rating analysts. Further support is given by Moody's quantitative models (Moody's 2003c, 2004), which regard as outliers any ratings that deviate from the models' predictions by more than two notches.

## 6.3 Rating Gaps Across Agencies

**Table 6.11** Countries with large split ratings

| | Fitch–Moody's | Fitch–S&P | Moody's–S&P |
|---|---|---|---|
| Countries for which Fitch rating is higher (no. of obs.) | Bahrain (3), Ecuador (1), Hong Kong (10), Kuwait (4), Moldova (1), Romania (1), and Saudi Arabia (4) | Cameroon (1), Dominican Rep. (6), Indonesia (3), Portugal (2), and Russia (2) | N.A. |
| Countries for which Moody's rating is higher (no. of obs.) | Argentina (28), Czech Rep. (2), Dominican Rep. (1), Estonia (5), Hungary (4), Iceland (24), Latvia (4), Moldova (5), Slovakia (1), Turkmenistan (15), and Uruguay (1) | N.A. | Belize (2), China (1), Dominican Rep. (7), Fiji (9), Greece (1), Hungary (2), Iceland (24), India (1), Indonesia (3), Japan (18), Latvia (2), Lithuania (1), Pakistan (4), Paraguay (6), Portugal (1), Russia (9), South Korea (1), Ukraine (1), and Venezuela (5) |
| Countries for which S&P rating is higher (no. of obs.) | N.A. | Argentina (21), Dominican Rep. (1), and Ecuador (1) | Bahrain (5), Barbados (1), Ecuador (3), Indonesia (1), Peru (1), Romania (1), and Saudi Arabia (9) |

*N.A.* not applicable
*Sources*: Author's classifications

more-than-two-notch split ratings and the number of events for each sovereign. A thorough analysis of the sovereign rating methodologies and reports released by the three agencies allows one to explain most of these large split ratings.

A substantial portion (39.3%) of all large split ratings involves countries that are on the verge of default, are in default, or have just recovered from default. In most cases, such distressed countries are rated B3 or Caa1 by Moody's, but are assigned a more-than-two-notch lower rating by Fitch and S&P. The ratings assigned to Argentina, Belize, the Dominican Republic, Indonesia, Moldova, Pakistan, Paraguay, Russia, and Uruguay exemplify such split ratings. In a few cases, Moody's assigns Caa3 or Ca ratings to countries (e.g., Ecuador and Moldova) that have just finished restructuring their debt and hence are rated three or four notches higher by Fitch and S&P (B– or CCC+).[15] This type of large split ratings reflects Moody's policy to overweight willingness to pay and to incorporate recovery rates into low ratings (see Chap. 3), so it does not indicate any major disagreement between Moody's and its two competitors.[16] The large split ratings between Fitch and S&P can be classified into two categories. Most of the more-than-two-notch lower Fitch ratings are concentrated in Argentina, which was rated in the default category (DDD and RD) for 5 years, while its S&P ratings were in the B category.[17] Nevertheless, S&P normally assigns much lower ratings (typically in the SD and CCC categories) to defaulting sovereigns (e.g., Cameroon, the Dominican Republic, Indonesia, and Russia).[18] Other large split ratings may last only a few weeks and are the result of slightly different timing for movement in to and out of the default rating category.

Of all large split ratings, 7.8% are observed when an agency has just started rating a country that is already rated by the other agency. These split ratings concern Bahrain, Barbados, India, Peru, and Saudi Arabia for Fitch–Moody's or Moody's–S&P pairs. In each case, Moody's is the initial rater and also is the agency that first modifies its rating so that the gap between its own credit opinion and that of Fitch or S&P is reduced.[19] In all cases except for India, Moody's has the lower initial rating prior to upgrading it. These findings suggest that assigning a first-ever rating is difficult, and the CRAs' lack of experience until the early 2000s is likely to lead to divergent risk assessments, as Cantor and Packer (1995) emphasize. One may also suppose that this type of split ratings encourages the initial rater to converge toward the subsequent raters' views.

A third type of large split ratings are temporary (i.e., they do not last for more than two consecutive quarters). They occur for both investment- and speculative-grade countries and result from different timings of rating changes. For instance,

---

[15] See Moody's (2009a).

[16] This argument is distinct from that developed by Beattie and Searle (1992a) and Cantor and Packer (1997), who find that split corporate ratings may reflect differences in rating scales.

[17] Unlike S&P, Fitch did not upgrade Argentina from default until the country completed restructuring more than 90% of its defaulted bonds in June 2010 (Fitch 2009b, 2010b).

[18] Cameroon was in default only on its LC debt when the split rating was observed; its LC and FC ratings were both at CCC.

[19] It is interesting that these are all two-notch rating changes.

## 6.3 Rating Gaps Across Agencies

South Korea, Lithuania, Ukraine, and Portugal each have one large split rating resulting from an S&P downgrade to a rating three or four notches below that of Moody's or Fitch. S&P was always the quickest to lower by several notches the rating of these countries when they were in financial distress (South Korea in December 1997, Lithuania and Ukraine from October 2008 to March 2009, Portugal in April 2010). However, the split ratings were short-lived : Fitch and Moody's downgraded those countries within 8 months.[20] Symmetrically, several upgrades lead to large split ratings. Moody's three-notch upgrades of the Czech Republic and Slovakia in November 2002 caused the large Fitch–Moody's split ratings observed. Similarly, the S&P and Fitch upgrades of Romania in September 2003 and November 2004 (respectively) resulted in the three-notch S&P–Moody's and Fitch–Moody's split ratings noted for this sovereign.

Other large split ratings can be explained on a region-by-region or country-by-country basis. For instance, there is one large split rating observed for China that results from a lower S&P rating and a higher Moody's rating. Actually, this particular split rating reflects two more prominent facts: S&P has never rated China above Moody's level; and there is a two-notch gap for half of the sample period. Until the two ratings began to converge in 2004–2005, this rating differential was seemingly driven by S&P's lack of confidence in China's banking sector (S&P 2003).[21] This explanation is in line with Morgan (2002), who finds that the frequent split ratings in the banking sector are caused by the greater opaqueness of banks as compared to other types of debt issuers. The reasoning also complements the study of Livingston et al. (2007), which concludes that there is a causal link between asset opaqueness and split corporate ratings.

The three-notch gap between Fitch and Moody's ratings of Hong Kong (which accounted for 3.7% of all large split ratings) lasted for more than 2 years (from June 2001 through October 2003). The rationale for Fitch rating Hong Kong higher may be related to its growing international reserves and Fitch's belief that the "one country, two systems" policy implemented by the Chinese government would enable Hong Kong to have a "remarkable degree of autonomy, both economically and politically" (Fitch 2001b). Yet Moody's had a quite divergent view, reporting that the economies and financial markets of Hong Kong and the rest of China were increasingly integrated (Moody's 2001a).

The more-than-two-notch split ratings of Bahrain, Kuwait, and Saudi Arabia (amounting to 9.3% of all observations) stem from lower Moody's ratings and higher Fitch and S&P ratings issued between 2001 and 2005. More globally, for these three countries, Moody's ratings are lower (resp. higher) than Fitch and S&P during 68% (resp. 2.3%) of the sample periods. This conservatism of Moody's

---

[20] There is one exception: 2 months after the multi-notch downgrade, S&P upgraded South Korea by three notches.

[21] At the time, many alarming reports highlighted the large stock of nonperforming loans (NPLs) in China. In 2006, for example, Ernst & Young estimated China's NPL liability at USD 911 billion (Ernst & Young 2006).

mostly reflects its perception of persistent geopolitical risk (see Moody's 1997, 2003b, e, 2007b).

The Moody's rating of Greece exceeded by more than two notches the S&P rating on several occasions in 1999, 2009, and 2010. However, these large split ratings were of short duration. A close examination of Moody's–S&P pairs does reveal that the latter agency has never assigned a higher rating to this country. Greece received its highest Moody's rating in November 2002; the upgrade to A1 from A2 was underpinned by high GDP growth, lower annual budget deficits, and a drop in the debt-to-GDP ratio to 105.3% in 2002 from 108.7% in 1995 (Moody's 2002b).

Turkmenistan is a puzzling split-rated country. Although Fitch and Moody's concurred in identifying the rating constraints as the country's opaque institutional structure and lack of reliable economic information, the former agency rated Turkmenistan four notches lower than did the latter (CCC– vs. B2) from May 2001 through February 2005 (Fitch 2001a; Moody's 2001b, 2005).[22] One could well argue that this differential is due only to Fitch's more intransigent view.

Moody's and S&P had a diverging risk assessment of Fiji that culminated with a large split rating from March 2007 through April 2009. In the wake of the political unrest in late 2006 and early 2007, S&P several times downgraded the rating of Fiji (S&P 2007, 2009b). Meanwhile, Moody's rating remained the same, which caused a three-notch split rating. Moody's was less concerned than S&P was about the economic and political position of Fiji, and Moody's affirmed that the effects of the December 2006 coup on government finance were not threatening in light of the country's low level of required external debt servicing (Moody's 2006).

The more-than-two-notch split rating between Moody's and S&P with regard to Venezuela was the first large split rating in the "modern era" to exceed a year in duration (February 1996–June 1997). S&P lowered Venezuela's rating several times between 1994 and 1996, bringing its credit opinion three notches below that of Moody's. Not surprisingly, the rationale for the S&P downgrades (dwindling international reserves, mismanagement of the banking system, oil price volatility, and political uncertainties) was the same as given for Moody's subsequent three-notch downgrade, which occurred in 1998 (see, resp., S&P 1994b; Moody's 1998). This finding may reflect two distinct assessments of sovereign risk: the first consists of adjusting more frequently to economic and financial news and the second is based on a "through the cycle" rating system.[23]

The remaining large split ratings are all characterized by higher Moody's ratings and driven by Moody's revision of its "country ceiling" policy in 2001 (see Chap. 3). This update resulted in a wave of upgrades of FC ratings: within 1 month (from 20 October to 12 November 2002), Moody's raised by two or three notches the FC country ceilings and the FC ratings of the following 12 sovereigns on the grounds that they had become increasingly less likely to impose debt moratoria as a policy tool: Australia, Czech Republic, Estonia, Hungary, Iceland, Japan, Latvia, Lithuania, New Zealand, Poland, Slovakia, and Slovenia. These multi-notch upgrades had two

---

[22] Fitch withdrew its rating of Turkmenistan in February 2005.

[23] Chapter 8 explores this assumption.

## 6.3 Rating Gaps Across Agencies

**Table 6.12** Rating gaps between Moody's and Fitch and between Moody's and S&P (1 January 2003–1 January 2011)

|  | Moody's vs. Fitch | | | | Moody's vs. S&P | | | |
|---|---|---|---|---|---|---|---|---|
|  | Estonia | Hungary | Iceland | Latvia | Hungary | Iceland | Japan | Latvia |
| Identical ratings (%) | 0.00 | 3.03 | 3.03 | 0.00 | 3.03 | 15.15 | 21.21 | 0.00 |
| Moody's rating 1 notch higher (%) | 57.58 | 21.21 | 12.12 | 57.58 | 0.00 | 0.00 | 0.00 | 39.39 |
| Moody's rating 2 notches higher (%) | 27.27 | 63.64 | 12.12 | 30.30 | 90.91 | 12.12 | 24.24 | 54.55 |
| Moody's rating 3 notches higher (%) | 15.15 | 12.12 | 54.55 | 12.12 | 6.06 | 21.21 | 54.55 | 6.06 |
| Moody's rating 4 notches higher (%) | 0.00 | 0.00 | 15.15 | 0.00 | 0.00 | 48.48 | 0.00 | 0.00 |
| Moody's rating 5 notches higher (%) | 0.00 | 0.00 | 3.03 | 0.00 | 0.00 | 3.03 | 0.00 | 0.00 |

*Sources*: Author's computations

main consequences. First, from 1 January 2003 to 1 January 2011, the Moody's ratings of these 12 countries were equal to or higher than the Fitch and S&P ratings during 98.9% of the time.[24] Second, during the same period, eight of these sovereigns had large split ratings: Czech Republic, Estonia, Hungary, Iceland, Japan, Latvia, Lithuania, and Slovakia. The cases of three of these split-rated countries have already been discussed, but the others require further comment. Table 6.12 presents the rating differentials between Moody's and Fitch for Estonia, Hungary, Iceland, and Latvia, as well as those between Moody's and S&P for Hungary, Iceland, Japan, and Latvia, for the period from 1 January 2003 to 1 January 2011.[25]

The largest split ratings concern Japan and Iceland, whose more-than-two-notch split occurred during 2003–2007 and 2003–2008, respectively. It is worth noting that the five-notch split ratings are observed in September–October 2008, as Fitch and S&P were more prompt in downgrading Iceland. The other large split ratings are mainly concentrated in 2006 and 2009, when Fitch and S&P downgraded Hungary and Latvia prior to Moody's doing so. Since late 2008, the ratings assigned by Moody's, Fitch, and S&P have converged, essentially owing to the massive downgrades by Moody's. It turns out that the most striking large split ratings stem from Moody's update of its country ceiling policy and its conviction that lower transfer and convertibility risk should lead to multi-notch upgrades.

In order to detect the possible significant disagreements between two CRAs that never led to more-than-two-notch split ratings, it is helpful to examine the mean differences of the 289 series of pairs. The mean differences that exceed 1.5 notches (called "significant average split ratings" hereafter) are reported in Table 6.13.

---

[24] The Fitch ratings of Slovenia and Hungary were above those of Moody's for 14 and 17 days, respectively. The S&P ratings of Slovenia and Lithuania were above those of Moody's for 71 and 280 days, respectively.

[25] No large split rating is observed for Moody's–Fitch pairs involving Japan and for Moody's–S&P pairs involving Estonia.

Table 6.13 Significant average split ratings

| | Fitch vs. Moody's (sample 1) | | Fitch vs. S&P (sample 2) | | Moody's vs. S&P sample 3 | |
|---|---|---|---|---|---|---|
| | Country | Gap (notches) | Country | Gap (notches) | Country | Gap (notches) |
| Countries with a higher Fitch rating | None | N.A. | None | N.A. | N.A. | N.A. |
| Countries with a higher Moody's rating | Turkmenistan<br>Argentina<br>Iceland | 3.37<br>3.00<br>2.12 | N.A. | N.A. | Fiji | 2.44 |
| Countries with a higher S&P rating | N.A. | N.A. | Argentina<br>Aruba | 2.81<br>2.00 | Saudi Arabia | 1.53 |

*N.A.* not applicable
*Sources*: Author's computations

All the countries with significant average split ratings have been investigated previously except for Aruba. This overseas territory of the Netherlands has been rated A− by S&P and BBB (i.e., two notches below) by Fitch since the first Fitch–S&P pair was formed. The two agencies emphasize the same strengths and weaknesses, but S&P seems to be more impressed with Aruba's stable political system and constitutional status (Fitch 2009a; S&P 2009a).

Many lessons can be drawn from this in-depth analysis of split ratings. First, there is consensus in the way Fitch, Moody's, and S&P assess sovereign risk. Among the 13,032 Fitch–Moody's, Fitch–S&P, and Moody's–S&P pairs examined, 54.7% are identical and fewer than 2.1% differ by more than two notches. Fitch and S&P are the two CRAs that agree most frequently, whereas Moody's ratings tend to be slightly less correlated to those of its competitors. Second, the frequency of split ratings is lower for high-income countries (ranging from 30.75% for Fitch–S&P pairs to 34.84% for Fitch–Moody's pairs) than for low- and middle-income countries (from 37.84% for Fitch–S&P pairs to 58.41% for Moody's–S&P pairs).[26] Moreover, the percentage of more-than-two-notch split ratings among high-income countries is very low (ranging from 0% for Fitch–S&P pairs to 3.31% for Fitch–Moody's pairs). These findings are consistent with Al-Sakka and ap Gwilym's (2010) analysis of split sovereign ratings in 49 emerging countries from January 2000 to January 2008. Third, most of the large split ratings are due to (a) distinct policies when assigning ratings to defaulting sovereigns and (b) differing weighting criteria. In particular, the idiosyncratic rating policy of Moody's (whose low ratings measure both a default probability and a recovery rate and country ceiling practice resulted in a wave of upgrades in 2002) is a major factor in the occurrence of large split ratings. These results shed new light on the reasons for the few disagreements in the sovereign rating area.

In fact, the widespread agreement across the three leading CRAs mirrors sovereign rating methodologies that are quite similar. It is now relevant to consider the extent to which smaller agencies that have recently entered the sovereign rating business may have more diverging views.

### 6.3.2 *Split Ratings Between Leading Agencies and Smaller Non-U.S. Firms*

The Credit Rating Agency Reform Act of 2006 was enacted to improve ratings quality for the protection of investors and in the public interest by fostering accountability, transparency, and competition in the credit rating agency industry. This legislation led the SEC to grant Nationally Recognized Statistical Rating Organization (NRSRO) registration to more and more firms. As of 1 January 2011, ten rating agencies were granted registration as NRSROs vs. only three (Fitch, Moody's, and

---

[26] Here a *high-income* country is a sovereign that was continuously in the World Bank high-income category from 1986 to 2010 (World Bank 2010).

S&P) in 2001.[27] Three of the newly registered agencies are non-U.S. firms that assign credit opinions to sovereigns: Dominion Bond Rating Service (DBRS), Japan Credit Rating Agency (JCR), and Rating & Investment Information (R&I). Another non-U.S. agency, Dagong International Credit Rating Company (Dagong), failed to comply with the federal securities laws and regulations applicable to NRSROs, but nonetheless rated 64 countries by the end of 2010.[28]

The sovereign rating methodologies published by the four small non-U.S. firms ("the followers" hereafter) are much like those of the big three CRAs ("the leaders"): they affirm that their ratings are based on a quantitative and a qualitative analysis and derived from a list of economic, financial, and political criteria (Dagong 2010b; DBRS 2006a; JCR n.d.; R&I 2009). Moreover, their rating scales are the same, enabling comparison between followers' and leaders' ratings.

The rest of this section compares the sovereign ratings issued by these four followers to those of the leaders as of 1 January 2011. The comparison will consist of computing the frequencies of agreements and disagreements between each follower and each leader (see Tables 6.14 and 6.15).

Dagong is the follower that disagrees most frequently by far with the three leaders: 73.1% of pairs are split ratings vs. 41.0, 46.2, and 47.1% for (respectively) DBRS, JCR, and R&I. The degree of agreement between these three followers and the three leaders is even stronger than that observed across Fitch, Moody's, and S&P (see Table 6.10).

For the pairs formed with DBRS, JCR, and R&I ratings, there are only four more-than-two-notch split ratings. For each one, the higher rating is that of the follower. This suggests that DBRS, JCR, and R&I are reluctant to rate much lower than Fitch, Moody's, or S&P. One can verify that DBRS credit opinions are highly correlated with those of the three leaders by observing that the number of higher DBRS ratings is nearly equal to the number of lower ones. In contrast, higher R&I and JCR ratings are (respectively) 2.25 and 7 times more frequent than lower ones. Note that half of the sovereigns that are assigned a more-than-one-notch higher rating by one of the two Japanese CRAs are Asian countries.[29] More remarkably, 9 of the 12 Asian countries rated by JCR and/or R&I (namely, India, Indonesia, Japan, Malaysia, Philippines, South Korea, Taiwan, Thailand, and Vietnam) have an average JCR–R&I rating higher than the average Fitch–Moody's–S&P rating.[30]

---

[27] See SEC (2011) for a recent overview of the NRSROs.

[28] DBRS, established in 1976, is headquartered in Toronto; it did not issue sovereign ratings until 2006 (DBRS 2006b). JCR was founded in 1985 and began assigning ratings to countries in 1987. R&I was established in April 1998 following the merger of Japanese Bond Rating Institute and Nippon Investor Service; its sovereign rating activity started the same year. Both JCR and R&I are headquartered in Tokyo. Dagong, a Beijing-based agency, was formed in 1994; it boosted its sovereign rating coverage in 2010.

[29] Asian countries account for less than 26% of the JCR and R&I sovereign rating coverage.

[30] The three exceptions are Singapore (rated AAA by the five agencies), Hong Kong (rated at the same level by JCR, R&I, Fitch, and Moody's but one notch higher by S&P), and China (rated A+ by R&I and Fitch, but AA– by Moody's and S&P).

## 6.3 Rating Gaps Across Agencies

**Table 6.14** Agreements and disagreements: the leaders vs. Dagong and Dominion Bond Rating Service (DBRS)

| As of 1 January 2011 | Dagong vs. Fitch | Dagong vs. Moody's | Dagong vs. S&P | DBRS vs. Fitch | DBRS vs. Moody's | DBRS vs. S&P |
|---|---|---|---|---|---|---|
| Number of observations | 60 | 61 | 61 | 13 | 13 | 13 |
| Identical ratings (%) | 28.33 | 19.67 | 32.79 | 53.85 | 46.15 | 76.92 |
| Follower's rating 1 notch higher (%) | 20.00 | 18.03 | 9.84 | 15.38 | 7.69 | 15.38 |
| Follower's rating 2 notches higher (%) | 6.67 | 6.56 | 9.84 | 0.00 | 0.00 | 0.00 |
| Follower's rating 3 notches higher (%) | 5.00 | 4.92 | 6.56 | 7.69 | 7.69 | 0.00 |
| Follower's rating 4 notches higher (%) | 1.67 | 1.64 | 0.00 | 0.00 | 0.00 | 0.00 |
| Follower's rating 5 notches higher (%) | 0.00 | 0.00 | 0.00 | 0.00 | 0.00 | 0.00 |
| Follower's rating 6 notches higher (%) | 0.00 | 0.00 | 0.00 | 0.00 | 0.00 | 0.00 |
| Leader's rating 1 notch higher (%) | 18.33 | 29.51 | 22.95 | 15.38 | 30.77 | 7.69 |
| Leader's rating 2 notches higher (%) | 10.00 | 6.56 | 6.56 | 7.69 | 7.69 | 0.00 |
| Leader's rating 3 notches higher (%) | 6.67 | 6.56 | 9.84 | 0.00 | 0.00 | 0.00 |
| Leader's rating 4 notches higher (%) | 3.33 | 4.92 | 1.64 | 0.00 | 0.00 | 0.00 |
| Leader's rating 5 notches higher (%) | 0.00 | 0.00 | 0.00 | 0.00 | 0.00 | 0.00 |
| Leader's rating 6 notches higher (%) | 0.00 | 1.64 | 0.00 | 0.00 | 0.00 | 0.00 |

*Sources*: Author's computations

**Table 6.15** Agreements and disagreements: the leaders vs. Japan Credit Rating Agency (JCR) and Rating & Investment Information (R&I)

| As of 1 January 2011 | JCR vs. Fitch | JCR vs. Moody's | JCR vs. S&P | R&I vs. Fitch | R&I vs. Moody's | R&I vs. S&P |
|---|---|---|---|---|---|---|
| Number of observations | 35 | 34 | 35 | 46 | 46 | 46 |
| Identical ratings (%) | 51.43 | 55.88 | 54.29 | 60.87 | 52.17 | 45.65 |
| Follower's rating 1 notch higher (%) | 25.71 | 20.59 | 17.14 | 17.39 | 13.04 | 23.91 |
| Follower's rating 2 notches higher (%) | 17.14 | 11.76 | 22.86 | 15.22 | 10.87 | 15.22 |
| Follower's rating 3 notches higher (%) | 0.00 | 2.94 | 2.86 | 0.00 | 2.17 | 0.00 |
| Follower's rating 4 notches higher (%) | 0.00 | 0.00 | 0.00 | 0.00 | 0.00 | 0.00 |
| Follower's rating 5 notches higher (%) | 0.00 | 0.00 | 0.00 | 0.00 | 0.00 | 0.00 |
| Follower's rating 6 notches higher (%) | 0.00 | 0.00 | 0.00 | 0.00 | 0.00 | 0.00 |
| Leader's rating 1 notch higher (%) | 5.71 | 8.82 | 2.86 | 6.52 | 21.74 | 13.04 |
| Leader's rating 2 notches higher (%) | 0.00 | 0.00 | 0.00 | 0.00 | 0.00 | 2.17 |
| Leader's rating 3 notches higher (%) | 0.00 | 0.00 | 0.00 | 0.00 | 0.00 | 0.00 |
| Leader's rating 4 notches higher (%) | 0.00 | 0.00 | 0.00 | 0.00 | 0.00 | 0.00 |
| Leader's rating 5 notches higher (%) | 0.00 | 0.00 | 0.00 | 0.00 | 0.00 | 0.00 |
| Leader's rating 6 notches higher (%) | 0.00 | 0.00 | 0.00 | 0.00 | 0.00 | 0.00 |

*Sources*: Author's computations

6.3 Rating Gaps Across Agencies

**Table 6.16** Large split ratings: Dagong vs. Fitch, Moody's, and S&P

|  | Dagong vs. Fitch | Dagong vs. Moody's | Dagong vs. S&P |
|---|---|---|---|
| Countries with a higher Dagong rating | Brazil, China, Russia, and Venezuela | Brazil, China, Morocco, and Venezuela | Brazil, China, Nigeria, and Russia |
| Countries with a higher leader's rating | Belgium, France, Italy, Spain, United Kingdom, and United States | Belgium, France, Iceland, Italy, Spain, United Arab Emirates, United Kingdom, and United States | Belgium, France, Iceland, Ireland, Spain, United Kingdom, and United States |

*Sources*: Author's computations

These findings support the view that Japanese agencies may be more indulgent, particularly when rating Asian governments, in ways that do not reflect JCR's and R&I's official methodologies.[31]

The split ratings between Dagong and the three leaders require a detailed analysis. The more-than-two-notch split ratings account for 18.1% of all observations, thus revealing numerous significant disagreements. Table 6.16 presents the countries with large split ratings between Dagong and Fitch, Moody's, and S&P.

Countries with a more-than-two-notch higher leader's rating outnumber those with a more-than-two-notch higher Dagong rating by a factor of 2. This finding suggests that Dagong is more conservative than its competitors, which is consistent with the observation that the average ratings assigned by Fitch, S&P, and Moody's are (respectively) 0.17, 0.23, and 0.39 notch higher than the Dagong average rating.

Next, the countries that are rated more severely by Dagong are industrial countries, except for the United Arab Emirates. In fact, Dagong has an uncompromising view on traditionally top-rated sovereigns: 8 of the 14 countries rated AAA by Fitch, Moody's, and S&P jointly are rated in the AA or even A categories by Dagong. From this perspective, the United States is the most affected country (it is rated A+). The sovereigns with a higher Dagong credit opinion are mainly large or medium-sized emerging countries. China, Russia, Brazil, Morocco, Nigeria, and Venezuela are rated, respectively, AAA, A+, A, BBB+, BB+, and BB+ by Dagong.

Dagong's rationale for this specific risk assessment is its belief that sovereign creditworthiness is at stake if the growth rate of government debt exceeds that of the economic output and that of fiscal revenue (Dagong 2010a). Most industrial countries failed to follow this rule, and were therefore assigned lower ratings by the Chinese CRA. Conversely, most emerging countries have their ratings enhanced because of their high GDP growth rate and their stable ratio of government debt to GDP.

---

[31] These results complement Beattie and Searle's (1992b) and Shin and Moore's (2003) studies, which show that agencies tend to rate issuers from their home country more leniently.

It is safe to say that most small, non-U.S. agencies (e.g., DBRS, JCR, and R&I) and leading agencies have converging views when it comes to assessing sovereign ratings. In contrast, Dagong often disagrees with Fitch, Moody's, and S&P. This firm has a unique profile: unlike its competitors, it only recently entered the sovereign rating business, it is headquartered in an emerging country, and its ratings are unsolicited. Dagong has also developed an offensive rhetoric against the big three CRAs, stating that "the current credit rating standard is the root cause of damages to international credit relations" (Dagong n.d.). One may suppose that the numerous disagreements between Dagong and the three leading agencies are closely related to the Chinese firm's desire to break the Western CRA monopoly.

The general conclusions of this chapter are as follows. First, Fitch, Moody's, and S&P have similar rating methodologies. Second, their sovereign ratings can be explained by the same set of political, economic, and financial variables. Third, the extent of agreement across leading agencies is high. Fourth, the qualitative and judgmental aspects of sovereign risk analysis explain most split ratings identified between 1986 and 2011. Fifth, Dagong is the sole new entrant to issue divergent ratings.

Now that the black box of sovereign ratings has been opened, it is time to assess the CRAs' performance in terms of accurate sovereign credit ratings.

## References

Afonso A. (2003), "Understanding the Determinants of Sovereign Debt Ratings: Evidence for the Two Leading Agencies", *Journal of Economics and Finance*, Vol. 27 (1).

Afonso A., Gomes P. and Rother P. (2011), "Short- and Long-Run Determinants of Sovereign Debt Credit Ratings", *International Journal of Finance and Economics*, Vol. 16, Issue 1.

Al-Sakka R. and ap Gwilym O. (2010), "Split Sovereign Ratings and Rating Migrations in Emerging Economies", *Emerging Markets Review*, Vol. 11.

Alexe S., Hammer P., Kogan A. and Lejeune M. (2003), "A Non-Recursive Regression Model for Country Risk Rating", *Rutcor Research Report 9, Rutgers Center for Operational Research*, March.

Avendaño R., Gaillard N. and Nieto-Parra S. (2011), "Are Working Remittances Relevant for Credit Rating Agencies?", *Review of Development Finance*, Vol. 1, Issue 1, January-March.

Beattie V. and Searle S. (1992a), "Bond Ratings and Inter-Rater Agreement", *Journal of International Securities Markets*, Summer.

Beattie V. and Searle S. (1992b), "Credit Rating Agencies: the Relationship between Rater Agreement and Issuer-Rater Characteristics", *Journal of International Securities Markets*, Winter.

Bhatia A. (2002), "Sovereign Credit Ratings Methodology: An Evaluation", *IMF Working Paper, WP/02/170*, Washington, D.C.

Borensztein E. (1990), "Debt Overhang, Credit Rationing, and Investment", *Journal of Development Economics*, Vol. 32.

Borio C. and Packer F. (2004), "Assessing New Perspectives on Country Risk", *BIS Quarterly Review*, December.

Bulow J. and Rogoff K. (1989), "Sovereign Debt: Is to Forgive to Forget?", *American Economic Review*, Vol. 79 (1).

# References

Cantor R. and Packer F. (1995), "Sovereign Credit Ratings", *Current Issues in Economics and Finance*, Vol. 1, No.3, Federal Reserve Bank of New York, June.

Cantor R. and Packer F. (1996), "Determinants and Impact of Sovereign Credit Ratings", *Economic Policy Review*, Federal Reserve Bank of New York, October.

Cantor R. and Packer F. (1997), "Differences of Opinion and Selection Bias in the Credit Rating Industry", *Journal of Banking and Finance*, Vol. 21.

Canuto O., Santos P. and Porto P. (2004), "Macroeconomics and Sovereign Risk Ratings", January, *mimeo*.

Dagong International Credit Rating Company (n.d.), "Building a New Sovereign Rating Standard".

Dagong International Credit Rating Company (2010a), "Sovereign Credit Rating Report of 50 Countries in 2010", July.

Dagong International Credit Rating Company (2010b), "Sovereign Rating Methodology", August.

DBRS (2006a), "Methodology – Sovereign Ratings", February.

DBRS (2006b), "DBRS Launches Sovereign Ratings Operations", 22 March.

Duff & Phelps Credit Rating Co. (1999), "Argentine Dollarization Could Begin to Pave Way To Investment Grade Rating", 4 February.

Eaton J. and Gersovitz M (1981), "Debt with Potential Repudiation: Theoretical and Empirical Analysis", *Review of Economic Studies*, Vol. 48 (2).

Eliasson A. (2002), "Sovereign Credit Ratings", *Research Notes in Economics & Statistics No.02-1*, Deutsche Bank Research.

Ernst & Young (2006), *Global Nonperforming Loan Report 2006*, May.

Fitch IBCA (1998), "After Asia: Some Lessons of the Crisis", 13 January.

Fitch Ratings (2001a), "Turkmenistan's Sovereign Ratings Downgraded", 18 May.

Fitch Ratings (2001b), "Fitch Upgrades Hong Kong's Foreign Currency Rating", 25 June.

Fitch Ratings (2002), "Fitch Sovereign Ratings – Rating Methodology".

Fitch Ratings (2004), "A Review of Central American Banking Systems", 29 March.

Fitch Ratings (2005), "Sovereign Data Comparator", December.

Fitch Ratings (2007), "Sovereign Rating Methodology", 12 October.

Fitch Ratings (2009a), "Aruba", 10 August.

Fitch Ratings (2009b), "Argentina: Rapprochement with Creditors and Sovereign Ratings", 19 November.

Fitch Ratings (2010a), "China", 15 January.

Fitch Ratings (2010b), "Fitch Lifts Argentina out of Default to 'B'; Outlook Stable", 12 July.

Fitch Ratings (2010c), "Sovereign Rating Methodology", 16 August.

Fitch Ratings (2010d), "Sovereign Data Comparator", December.

Flood R. and Garber P. (1984), "Collapsing Exchange-Rate Regimes: Some Linear Examples", *Journal of International Economics*, Vol. 17 (1–2).

Hu Y.-T., Kiesel R. and Perraudin W. (2002), "The Estimation of Transition Matrices for Sovereign Credit Ratings", *Journal of Banking & Finance*, Vol. 26 (7).

International Organization of Securities Commissions (2003), *IOSCO Statement of Principles Regarding the Activities of Credit Rating Agencies*, September.

International Organization of Securities Commissions (2004), *Code of Conduct Fundamentals for Credit Rating Agencies*, December.

Japan Credit Rating Agency (n.d.), "JCRs Sovereign Rating Methodology: Multi-Stage Evaluation System".

Krugman P. (1979), "A Model of Balance of Payments Crises", *Journal of Money, Credit, and Banking*, Vol. 11.

Krugman P. (1988), "Financing vs. Forgiving a Debt Overhang: Some Analytical Notes", *Journal of Development Economics*, Vol. 29.

Livingston M., Naranjo, A. and Zhou, L. (2007), "Asset Opaqueness and Split Bond Ratings", *Financial Management*, Vol. 36 (3).

Moody's Investors Service (1990), "Government of Malaysia", *Moody's Bond Survey*, 26 March.

Moody's Investors Service (1991), "India", *Moody's Bond Survey*, 15 July.

Moody's Investors Service (1994a), "Taiwan", *Moody's Bond Survey*, 11 April.
Moody's Investors Service (1994b), "Republic of South Africa", *Moody's Bond Survey*, 10 October.
Moody's Investors Service (1997), "Offshore Banking Centers and Country Risk", December.
Moody's Investors Service (1998), "Moody's Downgrades Venezuela's Country Ceiling for Foreign Currency Debt to B2; The Country Ceiling for Foreign Currency Deposits to Caa1; and the Government of Venezuela's Domestic Currency Debt to Caa1", 3 September.
Moody's Investors Service (2001a), "Bank & Sovereign Credit Comments", June.
Moody's Investors Service (2001b), "Turkmenistan: Global Credit Research", August.
Moody's Investors Service (2002a), "Sovereign Rating History", January.
Moody's Investors Service (2002b), "Moody's Upgrades Greece to A1 from A2", 4 November.
Moody's Investors Service (2003a), "Sovereign Rating Methodology: the Implications of Highly Dollarized Banking Systems for Sovereign Credit Risk", March.
Moody's Investors Service (2003b), "Moody's Reports Saudi Arabia's Baa2 Ratings and Stable Outlook Reflect Size of Oil Reserves and Diminished Risk in Wake of Iraq War", 4 August.
Moody's Investors Service (2003c), "A Quantitative Model for Local Currency Government Bond Ratings", September.
Moody's Investors Service (2003d), "Moody's Statistical Handbook – Country Credit", November.
Moody's Investors Service (2003e), "Moody's Upgrades Bahrain's Ratings to Baa1 as War in Iraq Has Little Impact and Reforms Continue", 11 December.
Moody's Investors Service (2004), "A Quantitative Model for Foreign Currency Government Bond Ratings", February.
Moody's Investors Service (2005), "Credit Opinion: Turkmenistan, Government of", 16 November.
Moody's Investors Service (2006), "Moody's Changes Fiji Government's Outlook to Negative", 6 December.
Moody's Investors Service (2007a), "Moody's Upgrades China's Ratings", 27 July.
Moody's Investors Service (2007b), "Moody's Explains Why Wealthiest Gulf States Are Not Rated Aaa", 7 November.
Moody's Investors Service (2008a), "Moody's Upgrades Russia's Government Ratings to Baa1 with a Positive Outlook", 16 July.
Moody's Investors Service (2008b), "Sovereign Bond Ratings", September.
Moody's Investors Service (2009a), "Moody's Assigns Caa3 Rating to Ecuador's Bonds Post-Default", 24 September.
Moody's Investors Service (2009b), "Moody's Statistical Handbook – Country Credit", November.
Morgan D. P. (2002), "Rating Banks: Risk and Uncertainty in an Opaque Industry", *American Economic Review*, Vol. 92.
Obstfeld M. (1994), "The Logic of Currency Crises", *Cahiers Economiques et Monétaires*, Vol. 43.
Ratha D. (2005), *Leveraging Remittances for International Capital Market Access*, November 18, World Bank, Washington, D.C.
Rating and Investment Information (2009), "R&I's Analytical Approach to Sovereigns", 8 April.
Sachs J. (1989), "The Debt Overhang of Developing Countries", in *Debt, Stabilization and Development: Essays in Memory of Carlos Diaz Alejandro*, ed. By Calvo G. et al., Oxford: Basil Blackwell.
Securities and Exchange Commission (2003), *Report on the Role and Function of Credit Rating Agencies in the Operation of the Securities Markets*, January.
Securities and Exchange Commission (2011), *Annual Report on Nationally Recognized Statistical Rating Organizations*, January.
Shin Y. and Moore W. (2003), "Explaining Credit Rating Differences between Japanese and US Agencies", *Review of Financial Economics*, Issue 12.
Standard & Poor's (1992), "Thailand's Ratings Affirmed, Off Creditwatch", *CreditWeek*, 14 December.

# References

Standard & Poor's (1994a), "Rep. of Korea's Implied Long-Term Rating Affirmed", *CreditWeek,* 3 January.
Standard & Poor's (1994b), "Venezuela's Ratings Cut to 'B+', Neg.; Off Watch", *CreditWeek,* 1 August.
Standard & Poor's (1995), "Republic of Paraguay Assigned Ratings", *CreditWeek,* 30 October.
Standard & Poor's (1997a), "Understanding Sovereign Risk", 1 January.
Standard & Poor's (1997b), "Sovereign Credit Ratings: A Primer", April.
Standard & Poor's (1997c), "Less Credit Risk for Borrowers in 'Dollarized' Economies", 30 April.
Standard & Poor's (1998), "Sovereign Credit Ratings: A Primer", December.
Standard & Poor's (2002), "Sovereign Credit Ratings: A Primer", April.
Standard & Poor's (2003), "Asia-Pacific Banking Outlook 2004".
Standard & Poor's (2006a), "Sovereign Risk Indicators", 25 May.
Standard & Poor's (2006b), "Asia and Latin America: A Tale of Two Emerging Markets", 6 September.
Standard & Poor's (2007), "Asia-Pacific Markets Outlook 2007: Conditions Will Be Favorable, But Some Threats Loom", 3 January.
Standard & Poor's (2008a), "Sovereign Credit Ratings: A Primer", May.
Standard & Poor's (2008b), "Federative Republic of Brazil", 26 August.
Standard & Poor's (2009a), "Aruba", 28 May.
Standard & Poor's (2009b), "Fiji Islands (Republic of)", 16 December.
Standard & Poor's (2009c), "India (Republic of)", 30 December.
Standard & Poor's (2010), "Sovereign Government Rating Methodology and Assumptions", 26 November.
World Bank (2010), *World Bank Analytical Classifications.*

# Chapter 7
# Consistency and Performance of Sovereign Ratings During the Interwar Years

This chapter provides a comparison of sovereign ratings issued by Fitch, Moody's, Poor's, and Standard Statistics during the interwar years. The objective is to assess the quality of ratings assigned by these four CRAs by focusing on their ability to anticipate defaults.

Section 7.1 presents a short review of the literature. Section 7.2 analyzes rating changes by the four CRAs by studying 1-year migration rates and comparing the timing and the scope of upgrades and downgrades. It shows that the four agencies failed to anticipate the sovereign debt crisis that broke out in January 1931. However, the cumulative default rates computed in Sect. 7.3 support the view that the four agencies successfully discriminated among foreign government bonds. Section 7.4 concludes that two distinct rating policies emerged during the interwar years: the first policy was more reactive and accurate in the short term; the second policy was based on more stable ratings and turned out to perform better in the medium and long term.

## 7.1 Review of the Literature

This chapter makes a contribution to the literature on the interwar sovereign debt crisis. Winkler (1933) and Rippy (1950) examine excessive lending to foreign governments in the 1920s. Mintz (1951) analyzes the deterioration in the quality of foreign government bonds issued in the second half of the 1920s. Eichengreen and Portes (1986) and Eichengreen and Werley (1988) shed new light on this topic by showing that, despite the wave of sovereign defaults during 1931–1934, foreign dollar bonds issued in the 1920s yielded positive rates of return. More recently, Flandreau et al. (2010) investigate the performances of interwar sovereign ratings. They find that rating agencies did not exhibit forecasting capacities superior to those embedded in available market prices.

This chapter also provides a complementary perspective to the research works that study credit ratings in the interwar years. In the first book to focus on CRAs, Harold (1938) focuses on the increasing role played by rating agencies, highlighting the use of credit ratings for regulatory purposes. Although Palyi (1938) concedes that the data compilation by the rating agencies was remarkable, he emphasizes their lack of transparency. Lastly, mention the monumental studies carried out by Hickman (1958, 1960). The author scrutinizes industrial, public utility, and railroad bonds issued on the NYSE for the period 1900–1944, providing much statistical data on issuance volumes, default rates, expected yields, and effective yields by year, maturity, sector, and rating. To measure the default probability, Hickman uses the ratings issued by the four CRAs: Fitch, Moody's, Poor's, and Standard Statistics. His main conclusion is as follows: if all bond issues had been pooled into a single portfolio held from offering to extinguishment or 1944, then the portfolio would have suffered no loss in current dollars.

## 7.2 Analysis of Rating Changes

This section compares the four CRAs in terms of the frequency and scope of rating changes (upgrades or downgrades) that occurred during the interwar period, analyzing rating migration rates with a 1-year horizon. My analysis employs a unique sample of sovereign bonds for a single period in order to enable a strict comparison of the four CRAs.

The period under study begins in 1924 – that is, the first year that all four CRAs issued sovereign ratings. The last year of the period is 1939. The sample gathers all bonds in USD and in GBP quoted on the NYSE and rated in at least two consecutive years by the four CRAs during 1924–1939: this results in 135 sovereign securities (see Appendix 3).

The method of computing migration rates is the same as that applied in Chapter 5 to compare Moody's rating changes (1918–1939 vs. 1986–2006). The ratings used are those published by each agency's manual every year. Tables 7.1–7.4 display transition matrices for the four agencies.

Observe first that the stability of the Moody's, Poor's, and Standard Statistics ratings contrasts with the greater mobility of the Fitch ratings, particularly for the BBB–B classes. The weighted average percentages of unchanged ratings reach 83.2% for Moody's, 81.8% for Poor's, and 79.6% for Standard Statistics but only 69.8% for Fitch.

Second, looking at the scope of downgrades is instructive: Moody's never downgraded bonds by more than three notches within a year, whereas Poor's downgraded seven bonds by four notches. The most severe downgrades came from Standard Statistics and Fitch: the former downgraded nineteen securities by four notches; the latter, fifteen bonds by four notches and six bonds by five notches. An in-depth analysis shows that the most severe downgrades affected Chile: all of Moody's three-notch downgrades, all of Poor's four-notch downgrades, all of Fitch five-notch

## 7.2 Analysis of Rating Changes

**Table 7.1** Fitch average 1-year rating migration rates, 1924–1939

|     | AAA   | AA    | A     | BBB   | BB    | B     | CCC   | CC    | C     | DDD   | DD   | D     |
|-----|-------|-------|-------|-------|-------|-------|-------|-------|-------|-------|------|-------|
| AAA | **79.47** | 7.95  | 11.92 | 0.66  | 0.00  | 0.00  | 0.00  | 0.00  | 0.00  | 0.00  | 0.00 | 0.00  |
| AA  | 10.39 | **72.08** | 10.39 | 7.14  | 0.00  | 0.00  | 0.00  | 0.00  | 0.00  | 0.00  | 0.00 | 0.00  |
| A   | 1.37  | 8.56  | **69.18** | 14.38 | 4.11  | 0.69  | 1.71  | 0.00  | 0.00  | 0.00  | 0.00 | 0.00  |
| BBB | 0.00  | 0.00  | 21.36 | **52.28** | 17.27 | 1.36  | 0.91  | 4.09  | 2.73  | 0.00  | 0.00 | 0.00  |
| BB  | 0.00  | 0.00  | 0.00  | 25.36 | **56.53** | 10.87 | 3.62  | 3.62  | 0.00  | 0.00  | 0.00 | 0.00  |
| B   | 0.00  | 0.00  | 0.00  | 0.00  | 33.33 | **53.34** | 0.00  | 6.67  | 4.44  | 2.22  | 0.00 | 0.00  |
| CCC | 0.00  | 0.00  | 0.00  | 0.00  | 0.00  | 8.06  | **75.81** | 8.06  | 3.23  | 4.84  | 0.00 | 0.00  |
| CC  | 0.00  | 0.00  | 0.00  | 0.00  | 0.00  | 0.00  | 5.56  | **80.55** | 9.72  | 4.17  | 0.00 | 0.00  |
| C   | 0.00  | 0.00  | 0.00  | 0.00  | 0.00  | 1.16  | 1.16  | 1.16  | **96.52** | 0.00  | 0.00 | 0.00  |
| DDD | 0.00  | 0.00  | 0.00  | 0.00  | 0.00  | 0.00  | 0.00  | 0.00  | 5.17  | **94.83** | 0.00 | 0.00  |
| DD  | 0.00  | 0.00  | 0.00  | 0.00  | 0.00  | 0.00  | 0.00  | 0.00  | 0.00  | 0.00  | **0.00** | 0.00  |
| D   | 0.00  | 0.00  | 0.00  | 0.00  | 0.00  | 0.00  | 0.00  | 0.00  | 0.00  | 50.00 | 0.00 | **50.00** |

*Sources*: Author's computations based on *Fitch Bond Books*

**Table 7.2** Moody's average 1-year rating migration rates, 1924–1939

|     | Aaa   | Aa    | A     | Baa   | Ba    | B     | Caa   | Ca    | C     |
|-----|-------|-------|-------|-------|-------|-------|-------|-------|-------|
| Aaa | **85.71** | 13.64 | 0.65  | 0.00  | 0.00  | 0.00  | 0.00  | 0.00  | 0.00  |
| Aa  | 0.89  | **82.15** | 14.73 | 2.23  | 0.00  | 0.00  | 0.00  | 0.00  | 0.00  |
| A   | 0.00  | 2.03  | **81.36** | 13.90 | 0.68  | 2.03  | 0.00  | 0.00  | 0.00  |
| Baa | 0.00  | 0.00  | 5.79  | **78.09** | 13.64 | 2.48  | 0.00  | 0.00  | 0.00  |
| Ba  | 0.00  | 0.00  | 0.00  | 4.97  | **80.13** | 13.66 | 1.24  | 0.00  | 0.00  |
| B   | 0.00  | 0.00  | 0.00  | 0.00  | 1.32  | **88.09** | 9.93  | 0.66  | 0.00  |
| Caa | 0.00  | 0.00  | 0.00  | 0.00  | 0.00  | 1.27  | **97.46** | 1.27  | 0.00  |
| Ca  | 0.00  | 0.00  | 0.00  | 0.00  | 0.00  | 0.00  | 0.00  | **100.00** | 0.00  |
| C   | 0.00  | 0.00  | 0.00  | 0.00  | 0.00  | 0.00  | 0.00  | 50.00 | **50.00** |

*Sources*: Author's computations based on *Moody's Manuals*

**Table 7.3** Poor's average 1-year rating migration rates, 1924–1939

|       | A****  | A***  | A**    | A*    | A     | B**   | B*    | B     | C**   | C*    | C     |
|-------|--------|-------|--------|-------|-------|-------|-------|-------|-------|-------|-------|
| A**** | **90.79** | 6.58  | 2.63   | 0.00  | 0.00  | 0.00  | 0.00  | 0.00  | 0.00  | 0.00  | 0.00  |
| A***  | 0.00   | **0.00** | 100.00 | 0.00  | 0.00  | 0.00  | 0.00  | 0.00  | 0.00  | 0.00  | 0.00  |
| A**   | 1.87   | 0.00  | **83.18** | 14.95 | 0.00  | 0.00  | 0.00  | 0.00  | 0.00  | 0.00  | 0.00  |
| A*    | 0.00   | 0.00  | 0.75   | **84.32** | 14.93 | 0.00  | 0.00  | 0.00  | 0.00  | 0.00  | 0.00  |
| A     | 0.00   | 0.00  | 0.00   | 1.65  | **83.13** | 11.11 | 0.82  | 0.41  | 2.88  | 0.00  | 0.00  |
| B**   | 0.00   | 0.00  | 0.00   | 0.00  | 3.56  | **76.43** | 14.67 | 3.56  | 1.78  | 0.00  | 0.00  |
| B*    | 0.00   | 0.00  | 0.00   | 0.00  | 0.00  | 13.30 | **66.48** | 18.09 | 0.53  | 1.60  | 0.00  |
| B     | 0.00   | 0.00  | 0.00   | 0.00  | 0.00  | 0.00  | 2.07  | **84.14** | 13.79 | 0.00  | 0.00  |
| C**   | 0.00   | 0.00  | 0.00   | 0.00  | 0.00  | 0.00  | 0.00  | 0.00  | **81.11** | 18.89 | 0.00  |
| C*    | 0.00   | 0.00  | 0.00   | 0.00  | 0.00  | 0.00  | 0.00  | 0.00  | 0.00  | **96.52** | 3.48  |
| C     | 0.00   | 0.00  | 0.00   | 0.00  | 0.00  | 0.00  | 0.00  | 0.00  | 0.00  | 0.00  | **100.00** |

*Sources*: Author's computations based on *Poor's Volumes*

**Table 7.4** Standard Statistics average 1-year rating migration rates, 1924–1939

|    | A1+   | A1    | A     | B1+   | B1    | B     | C1+   | C1    | C     | D1+   | D1    | D      | E      |
|----|-------|-------|-------|-------|-------|-------|-------|-------|-------|-------|-------|--------|--------|
| A1+ | 92.18 | 0.00  | 7.26  | 0.00  | 0.56  | 0.00  | 0.00  | 0.00  | 0.00  | 0.00  | 0.00  | 0.00   | 0.00   |
| A1  | 0.59  | 85.21 | 8.88  | 4.14  | 1.18  | 0.00  | 0.00  | 0.00  | 0.00  | 0.00  | 0.00  | 0.00   | 0.00   |
| A   | 0.38  | 2.64  | 81.50 | 6.04  | 6.42  | 0.38  | 2.64  | 0.00  | 0.00  | 0.00  | 0.00  | 0.00   | 0.00   |
| B1+ | 0.00  | 0.00  | 11.25 | 71.25 | 8.12  | 3.75  | 4.38  | 1.25  | 0.00  | 0.00  | 0.00  | 0.00   | 0.00   |
| B1  | 0.00  | 0.57  | 0.57  | 12.00 | 70.29 | 6.86  | 5.71  | 4.00  | 0.00  | 0.00  | 0.00  | 0.00   | 0.00   |
| B   | 0.00  | 0.00  | 0.00  | 2.56  | 6.41  | 65.39 | 11.54 | 10.26 | 2.56  | 1.28  | 0.00  | 0.00   | 0.00   |
| C1+ | 0.00  | 0.00  | 0.00  | 0.00  | 0.00  | 7.55  | 73.59 | 3.77  | 3.77  | 3.77  | 7.55  | 0.00   | 0.00   |
| C1  | 0.00  | 0.00  | 0.00  | 0.00  | 0.00  | 2.27  | 15.91 | 72.73 | 2.27  | 0.00  | 6.82  | 0.00   | 0.00   |
| C   | 0.00  | 0.00  | 0.00  | 0.00  | 0.00  | 0.00  | 3.45  | 0.00  | 75.86 | 3.45  | 10.34 | 6.90   | 0.00   |
| D1+ | 0.00  | 0.00  | 0.00  | 0.00  | 0.00  | 25.00 | 0.00  | 0.00  | 0.00  | 75.00 | 0.00  | 0.00   | 0.00   |
| D1  | 0.00  | 0.00  | 0.00  | 0.00  | 0.00  | 0.00  | 0.00  | 0.00  | 8.33  | 0.00  | 91.67 | 0.00   | 0.00   |
| D   | 0.00  | 0.00  | 0.00  | 0.00  | 0.00  | 0.00  | 0.00  | 0.00  | 0.00  | 0.00  | 0.00  | 100.00 | 0.00   |
| E   | 0.00  | 0.00  | 0.00  | 0.00  | 0.00  | 0.00  | 0.00  | 0.00  | 0.00  | 0.00  | 0.00  | 0.00   | 100.00 |

*Sources*: Author's computations based on *Standard Bond Books*

## 7.2 Analysis of Rating Changes

downgrades, and nearly three fourths of Standard Statistics four-notch downgrades. With respect to upgrades, the results for the four CRAs are fairly homogeneous: Moody's never upgraded by more than one notch, and two-notch and three-notch upgrades by Fitch, Poor's, and Standard Statistics were rare.

It is worth emphasizing that, for all four CRAs, the number of downgrades greatly exceeded the number of upgrades. Nevertheless, the ratio of upgrades to downgrades varies considerably: from 0.70 for Fitch to 0.45 for Standard Statistics, 0.22 for Poor's, and 0.19 for Moody's. These figures indicate that the period 1924–1939 was characterized by a significant deterioration in the quality of sovereign bonds.[1]

Behind these ratios there are two distinct rating policies. Upgrades by Moody's and Poor's were much less frequent (35 and 43, respectively) than upgrades by Standard Statistics and Fitch (82 and 159, respectively). This explains the greater volatility of Standard Statistics and Fitch ratings, since the number of downgrades differed little across the four agencies (from a minimum of 181 for Standard Statistics up to a maximum of 227 for Fitch).

The next informative aspect of rating changes is their timing. Table 7.5 presents the relevant data by year and CRA. The data portrayed in Table 7.5 support six general comments as follows.

First, the overall low number of downgrades between 1928 and 1930 indicates that none of the four agencies managed to anticipate the sovereign defaults that occurred in 1931. Second, Fitch downgrades were more numerous than those of its three competitors for 1925–1930 – a period characterized by a sharp deterioration in the quality of sovereign bonds issued (Mintz 1951).[2] Third, Fitch reacted quickly to the first sovereign defaults in January 1931 by downgrading 60% of the affected bonds over the following weeks. The scope of these downgrades was much greater than that for Poor's (33%), Standard Statistics (30.5%), and Moody's (11%). These observations show that Fitch was the most procyclical agency of the interwar period. Fourth, the scope of the downgrades occurring in 1932, once the seriousness of the sovereign debt crisis became obvious, was extensive for all four CRAs. Fitch was particularly prompt to cut ratings, but the percentage of downgrades was also high for Moody's (84.5%), which may have been compensating for the paucity of changed ratings during 1931. This leads one to conclude that the procyclicality of ratings was acute and unquestionable during the crisis years. Fifth, the upgrades of 1934 and 1935 – which concerned mainly Argentinean, Australian, and Finnish bonds – were decided by all agencies except Moody's, whose ratings remained stable. Sixth, a study of the ratings during 1934–1939 reveals two diverging perceptions of sovereign risk. Moody's and Poor's downgraded three times as often as they upgraded, whereas Fitch and Standard Statistics upgraded more often than they downgraded (ratios as high as 2.6 and 1.3, respectively).

---

[1] This deterioration was particularly pronounced because downgrades were far more severe than upgrades (many four- and five-notch downgrades versus only one four-notch and two three-notch upgrades).

[2] The measure used is the percentage of defaulting foreign government bonds (by year of issuance) on the NYSE. From less than 30% in 1924, the default rate soared to 65% in 1927 and to more than 85% in 1929.

Table 7.5 Percentages of annual rating changes for the four CRAs, 1925–1939

| | Fitch UP | Moody's UP | Poor's UP | Standard Statistics UP | Fitch DN | Moody's DN | Poor's DN | Standard Statistics DN |
|---|---|---|---|---|---|---|---|---|
| 1925 | 20.75 | 9.80 | 2.13 | 9.09 | 41.51 | 0.00 | 4.26 | 4.55 |
| 1926 | 25.00 | 9.23 | 1.47 | 1.54 | 1.56 | 4.62 | 0.00 | 1.54 |
| 1927 | 17.91 | 2.74 | 2.74 | 0.00 | 0.00 | 1.37 | 0.00 | 0.00 |
| 1928 | 4.94 | 3.80 | 12.50 | 2.74 | 0.00 | 1.27 | 0.00 | 1.37 |
| 1929 | 16.67 | 4.35 | 0.00 | 5.88 | 4.17 | 3.26 | 0.96 | 1.18 |
| 1930 | 23.76 | 0.00 | 0.00 | 1.89 | 0.00 | 3.88 | 4.85 | 4.72 |
| 1931 | 0.00 | 0.99 | 1.98 | 3.81 | 60.00 | 10.89 | 32.67 | 30.48 |
| 1932 | 0.00 | 0.97 | 0.95 | 0.00 | 93.07 | 84.47 | 49.52 | 50.47 |
| 1933 | 2.88 | 0.00 | 0.00 | 0.00 | 17.31 | 38.83 | 21.15 | 33.01 |
| 1934 | 18.63 | 2.94 | 3.96 | 20.59 | 6.86 | 26.47 | 23.76 | 9.80 |
| 1935 | 21.65 | 8.82 | 21.05 | 13.40 | 2.06 | 3.92 | 11.58 | 10.31 |
| 1936 | 16.48 | 0.00 | 0.00 | 11.46 | 3.30 | 0.00 | 7.53 | 1.04 |
| 1937 | 15.29 | 0.00 | 2.20 | 0.00 | 12.94 | 6.45 | 6.59 | 7.53 |
| 1938 | 5.63 | 1.18 | 0.00 | 4.82 | 7.04 | 0.00 | 15.12 | 6.02 |
| 1939 | 1.52 | 0.00 | 0.00 | 17.44 | 0.00 | 2.33 | 23.26 | 20.93 |

*UP* upgrades; *DN* downgrades
*Sources*: Based on Flandreau et al. (2010)

These comments support the view that two types of rating policy were operative during the interwar years. The one employed by Fitch (and, to a lesser extent, by Standard Statistics) placed more emphasis on reactivity, which led to greater volatility and procyclicality. The other policy, as implemented by Moody's and Poor's, consisted in rating through the cycle, which implied a greater rating stability. It is now time to assess whether these two rating policies performed differently in terms of ability to discriminate among sovereign bonds.

## 7.3 Analysis of Average Cumulative Default Rates

The quality of ratings issued by the four CRAs during the interwar period can be measured by computing their average cumulative default rates at different horizons (see Moody's 1995). For each rating category, the cumulative default rate in year $t$ is the probability of defaulting during any year before or during year $t$. The most accurate ratings are those for which these default rates are the lowest.

The calculation of the average cumulative default rate for rating class $i$, $\overline{D_i}(T)$, is derived from the weighted average marginal default rates, $\overline{d_i}(t)$, calculated from all the available cohort marginal default rates in the reference sample:

$$\overline{D_i}(T) = 1 - \prod_{t=1}^{T} [1 - \overline{d_i}(t)]$$

where

$$\overline{d_i}(t) = \frac{\sum_{y \in Y} x_i^y(t)}{\sum_{y \in Y} n_i^y(t)}$$

$x_i^y(t)$ = number of defaults x holding rating i on cohort date y that occur in the time interval t; $n_i^y(t)$ = number of issue n holding rating i on cohort date y that survived at the start of time t.

The reference sample is the one used in the previous section but *without* the two Mexican bonds and the two Russian bonds, which remained in default during all of the 1924–1939. Hence the sample consists of 131 bonds. Tables 7.6–7.9 display average cumulative default rates for each of the four agencies.

Observe at the start that default rates for the lowest ratings (DDD and below for Fitch, Caa and below for Moody's, C* and below for Poor's, and C and below for Standard Statistics) are not computed. This is because such ratings concerned defaulting bonds exclusively, as stated by the four agencies in their rating definitions (see Sect. 3.2). That being said, comparing the quality of ratings issued by the four agencies still raises two difficulties.

First, how can one determine a fitted rating bracket suitable for comparing the default rates of the four agencies? There is no problem choosing the top rating of the

**Table 7.6** Fitch average cumulative default rates, 1924–1939

| In % | Year 1 | Year 2 | Year 3 | Year 4 | Year 5 | Year 6 | Year 7 | Year 8 | Year 9 | Year 10 |
|---|---|---|---|---|---|---|---|---|---|---|
| AAA | 0.00 | 0.00 | 0.00 | 0.00 | 1.04 | 1.04 | 1.04 | 1.04 | 1.04 | 1.04 |
| AA | 0.00 | 1.43 | 3.03 | 4.83 | 5.83 | 5.83 | 5.83 | 5.83 | 5.83 | 5.83 |
| A | 1.41 | 7.33 | 13.73 | 19.90 | 24.11 | 27.54 | 29.46 | 30.98 | 31.98 | 34.54 |
| BBB | 5.36 | 8.67 | 16.63 | 23.58 | 30.36 | 35.49 | 44.98 | 54.15 | 63.97 | 66.09 |
| BB | 5.88 | 14.00 | 20.47 | 29.07 | 39.58 | 46.90 | 54.49 | 66.90 | 71.63 | 76.36 |
| B | 21.21 | 30.67 | 34.13 | 34.13 | 34.13 | 47.31 | 64.87 | 64.87 | 64.87 | 64.87 |
| CCC | 61.11 | 77.78 | 83.33 | 88.89 | 94.44 | 100.00 | 100.00 | 100.00 | 100.00 | 100.00 |
| CC | 42.86 | 100.00 | 100.00 | 100.00 | 100.00 | 100.00 | 100.00 | 100.00 | 100.00 | 100.00 |
| C | 0.00 | 0.00 | 0.00 | 50.00 | 100.00 | 100.00 | 100.00 | 100.00 | 100.00 | 100.00 |
| DDD | N.A. | N.A. | N.A. | N.A. | N.A. | N.A. | N.A. | N.A. | N.A. | N.A. |
| DD | N.A. | N.A. | N.A. | N.A. | N.A. | N.A. | N.A. | N.A. | N.A. | N.A. |
| D | N.A. | N.A. | N.A. | N.A. | N.A. | N.A. | N.A. | N.A. | N.A. | N.A. |

*Note*: N.A. not applicable
*Sources*: Author's computations based on *Fitch Bond Books*

**Table 7.7** Moody's average cumulative default rates, 1924–1939

| In % | Year 1 | Year 2 | Year 3 | Year 4 | Year 5 | Year 6 | Year 7 | Year 8 | Year 9 | Year 10 |
|---|---|---|---|---|---|---|---|---|---|---|
| Aaa | 0.00 | 0.00 | 0.00 | 0.00 | 0.00 | 0.00 | 0.00 | 0.00 | 0.00 | 0.00 |
| Aa | 0.00 | 0.00 | 0.00 | 1.22 | 1.89 | 2.61 | 3.48 | 4.63 | 6.19 | 6.19 |
| A | 2.68 | 6.46 | 12.89 | 18.31 | 22.81 | 26.17 | 30.60 | 33.75 | 35.62 | 37.96 |
| Baa | 6.84 | 17.29 | 27.15 | 36.82 | 47.09 | 56.37 | 68.64 | 85.75 | 88.60 | 88.60 |
| Ba | 20.45 | 31.64 | 38.48 | 44.63 | 48.20 | 52.71 | 57.68 | 60.33 | 71.66 | 77.96 |
| B | 10.00 | 21.25 | 34.38 | 50.78 | 75.39 | 75.39 | 75.39 | 75.39 | 75.39 | 75.39 |
| Caa | N.A. | N.A. | N.A. | N.A. | N.A. | N.A. | N.A. | N.A. | N.A. | N.A. |
| Ca | N.A. | N.A. | N.A. | N.A. | N.A. | N.A. | N.A. | N.A. | N.A. | N.A. |
| C | N.A. | N.A. | N.A. | N.A. | N.A. | N.A. | N.A. | N.A. | N.A. | N.A. |

*Note*: N.A. not applicable
*Sources*: Author's computations based on *Moody's Manuals*

**Table 7.8** Poor's average cumulative default rates, 1924–1939

| In % | Year 1 | Year 2 | Year 3 | Year 4 | Year 5 | Year 6 | Year 7 | Year 8 | Year 9 | Year 10 |
|---|---|---|---|---|---|---|---|---|---|---|
| A**** | 0.00 | 0.00 | 0.00 | 0.00 | 0.00 | 0.00 | 0.00 | 0.00 | 0.00 | 0.00 |
| A*** | 0.00 | 0.00 | 0.00 | 0.00 | 0.00 | 0.00 | 0.00 | 0.00 | 0.00 | 0.00 |
| A** | 0.00 | 0.00 | 0.00 | 0.00 | 0.00 | 0.00 | 0.00 | 0.00 | 0.00 | 0.00 |
| A* | 0.00 | 0.00 | 1.02 | 3.35 | 4.69 | 6.31 | 6.31 | 6.31 | 6.31 | 6.31 |
| A | 3.25 | 7.69 | 11.62 | 16.56 | 19.03 | 20.99 | 23.11 | 25.67 | 26.83 | 26.83 |
| B** | 5.05 | 9.96 | 18.91 | 22.00 | 27.15 | 32.01 | 36.01 | 39.38 | 43.56 | 46.24 |
| B* | 5.33 | 14.28 | 22.85 | 34.25 | 45.52 | 56.42 | 69.03 | 77.11 | 82.83 | 85.95 |
| B | 32.08 | 50.60 | 61.34 | 66.17 | 71.81 | 75.33 | 78.86 | 82.38 | 85.90 | 89.43 |
| C** | 25.00 | 100.00 | 100.00 | 100.00 | 100.00 | 100.00 | 100.00 | 100.00 | 100.00 | 100.00 |
| C* | N.A. | N.A. | N.A. | N.A. | N.A. | N.A. | N.A. | N.A. | N.A. | N.A. |
| C | N.A. | N.A. | N.A. | N.A. | N.A. | N.A. | N.A. | N.A. | N.A. | N.A. |

*Note*: N.A. not applicable
*Sources*: Author's computations based on *Poor's Volumes*

## 7.3 Analysis of Average Cumulative Default Rates

**Table 7.9** Standard Statistics average cumulative default rates, 1924–1939

| In % | Year 1 | Year 2 | Year 3 | Year 4 | Year 5 | Year 6 | Year 7 | Year 8 | Year 9 | Year 10 |
|---|---|---|---|---|---|---|---|---|---|---|
| A1+ | 0.00 | 0.00 | 0.00 | 0.00 | 0.00 | 0.00 | 0.00 | 0.00 | 0.00 | 0.00 |
| A1 | 0.00 | 1.29 | 2.69 | 4.29 | 5.17 | 5.17 | 5.17 | 5.17 | 5.17 | 5.17 |
| A | 2.62 | 5.66 | 11.01 | 15.93 | 20.32 | 23.84 | 27.35 | 32.39 | 34.90 | 36.38 |
| B1+ | 3.97 | 10.88 | 14.83 | 20.38 | 22.37 | 26.01 | 30.28 | 33.95 | 36.23 | 36.23 |
| B1 | 7.74 | 16.69 | 25.62 | 31.34 | 39.66 | 50.63 | 65.26 | 75.19 | 83.46 | 90.07 |
| B | 14.29 | 31.09 | 51.04 | 66.71 | 73.84 | 77.11 | 80.38 | 83.65 | 86.92 | 90.19 |
| C1+ | 66.67 | 66.67 | 66.67 | 83.33 | 100.00 | 100.00 | 100.00 | 100.00 | 100.00 | 100.00 |
| C1 | 100.00 | 100.00 | 100.00 | 100.00 | 100.00 | 100.00 | 100.00 | 100.00 | 100.00 | 100.00 |
| C | N.A. | N.A. | N.A. | N.A. | N.A. | N.A. | N.A. | N.A. | N.A. | N.A. |
| D1+ | N.A. | N.A. | N.A. | N.A. | N.A. | N.A. | N.A. | N.A. | N.A. | N.A. |
| D1 | N.A. | N.A. | N.A. | N.A. | N.A. | N.A. | N.A. | N.A. | N.A. | N.A. |
| D | N.A. | N.A. | N.A. | N.A. | N.A. | N.A. | N.A. | N.A. | N.A. | N.A. |
| E | N.A. | N.A. | N.A. | N.A. | N.A. | N.A. | N.A. | N.A. | N.A. | N.A. |

*Note: N.A.* not applicable
*Sources:* Author's computations based on *Standard Bond Books*

**Table 7.10** Rating equivalence for the four CRAs

|  | Fitch | Moody's | Poor's | Standard Statistics |
|---|---|---|---|---|
| First category | AAA | Aaa | Hybrid A** | A1+ |
| Second category | AA | Aa | A* | A1 |
| Third category | A | A | A | A |

*Sources*: Author's classification

bracket: it is the maximum rating that each agency can assign (i.e., AAA for Fitch, Aaa for Moody's, A**** for Poor's, and A1+ for Standard Statistics), but establishing the minimum rating is not so straightforward. The absence in the 1920s of a cutoff between investment- and speculative-grade issues means that one cannot simply assess the minimum rating (see Moody's 2004; Flandreau et al. 2010). However the analysis of rating definitions presented in Chap. 3 indicates that bonds rated BBB by Fitch, Baa by Moody's, B** by Poor's, and B1+ by Standard Statistics were all characterized by a "speculative element". In contrast, bonds rated A (i.e., one notch higher) were systematically considered sound by the four agencies. It is therefore reasonable to consider the A rating category as a satisfactory minimum rating.[3]

The second difficulty is linked to the differing granularity of the agencies' rating scales. The Poor's rating scale had more notches than its competitors for high-end bonds (A****, A***, A** and A*). This problem can be overcome by translating the Poor's categories (A****, A***, A**, and A*) to those used by Fitch, Moody's, and Standard Statistics as follows. The A****, A***, and A** rating categories are aggregated to form a hybrid A** rating category as well as a unique hybrid default rate for the A****–A** bracket to facilitate comparisons with the default rates of bonds rated AAA by Fitch, Aaa by Moody's, and A1+ by Standard Statistics. Default rates associated with the hybrid A** rating category are equal to those of bonds originally rated A** (default rates for bonds originally rated A****, A***, and A** are equal to zero for all horizons). Thus, in the remaining of this chapter, the A** rating category corresponds to Poor's original A****–A** bracket. Table 7.10 shows how this procedure homogenizes and renders equivalent the first three rating categories across agencies.

Given the ratings equivalence summarized in Table 7.10, it is possible to assess rating accuracy by examining default rates of bonds rated in the first three categories. A first measure of this accuracy is to assess for a given time horizon, which agency has the lowest default rate for the first rating category and then (if rates are equal) to look at the second and third rating categories.

At the 1-year horizon, default rates for bonds rated in the first two categories are equal to zero for all four agencies. However there are differences in the default rates of A-rated bonds: Fitch has the most accurate ratings, followed by Standard Statistics, Moody's, and Poor's. In this comparison, Fitch takes advantage of its

---

[3] Any comparison of the default rates of bonds rated BBB/Baa/B**/B1+ would be irrelevant given their appreciable level of risk.

## 7.3 Analysis of Average Cumulative Default Rates

**Table 7.11** Average cumulative default rates for the first two rating categories, 1–10-year horizons

|  | Ratings considered | Y 1 | Y 2 | Y 3 | Y 4 | Y 5 | Y 6 | Y 7 | Y 8 | Y 9 | Y 10 |
|---|---|---|---|---|---|---|---|---|---|---|---|
| Fitch | AAA–AA | **0.00** | 0.72 | 1.53 | 2.43 | 3.45 | 3.45 | 3.45 | 3.45 | 3.45 | 3.45 |
| Moody's | Aaa–Aa | **0.00** | **0.00** | **0.00** | **0.68** | **1.06** | **1.48** | **1.96** | 2.56 | 3.34 | 3.34 |
| Poor's | A**–A* | **0.00** | **0.00** | 0.38 | 1.24 | 1.73 | 2.30 | 2.30 | **2.30** | **2.30** | **2.30** |
| Standard Statistics | A1+–A1 | **0.00** | 0.63 | 1.32 | 2.09 | 2.52 | 2.52 | 2.52 | 2.52 | 2.52 | 2.52 |

*Sources*: Author's computations

**Table 7.12** Average cumulative default rates for the first three rating categories, 1–10-year horizons

|  | Ratings considered | Y 1 | Y 2 | Y 3 | Y 4 | Y 5 | Y 6 | Y 7 | Y 8 | Y 9 | Y 10 |
|---|---|---|---|---|---|---|---|---|---|---|---|
| Fitch | AAA–A | **0.68** | 3.88 | 7.41 | 10.88 | 13.48 | 15.22 | 16.20 | 16.95 | 17.42 | 18.69 |
| Moody's | Aaa–A | 1.21 | 2.86 | 5.58 | 8.20 | 10.22 | 11.74 | 13.78 | 15.49 | 16.79 | 17.94 |
| Poor's | A**–A | 1.40 | 3.32 | **5.26** | 7.91 | **9.27** | **10.50** | **11.56** | **12.82** | **13.36** | **13.36** |
| Standard Statistics | A1+–A | 1.14 | **2.78** | 5.40 | **7.89** | 9.93 | 11.36 | 12.70 | 14.71 | 15.75 | 16.43 |

*Sources*: Author's computations

early downgrading of the Chilean bonds that defaulted between August 1931 and January 1932; the other three agencies had left their ratings unchanged.

At the 2-year horizon, Moody's has the most accurate ratings because two bonds rated AA by Fitch (two Dominican bonds) and two bonds rated A1 by Standard Statistics (one Dominican bond and one Panamanian bond) defaulted. Moody's and Poor's default rates are equal to zero for the first two rating categories, but Moody's ratings outperformed Poor's because of a lower default rate for the third rating category (A).

At the 3-year horizon, Moody's is still the top CRA. It holds this leadership until the 8-year horizon, aided by the increasing default rates of bonds rated A* by Poor's (default of the 1930 Cuban bond and a Panamanian bond), A1 by Standard Statistics (Dominican and Panamanian bonds), and AAA by Fitch (the 1924 German bond[4]). For the 9-and 10-year horizons, Moody's loses its leadership position to Standard Statistics.

The second way to measure rating accuracy is to aggregate the highest ratings, for a given time horizon, in order to assess which agency had the lowest default rates for the first two and the first three rating categories. This computation permits one to answer the following question: What percentage of bonds rated in the first two and first three rating categories defaulted at the time horizon *t*? These new average cumulative default rates are presented in Tables 7.11 and 7.12 (for each time horizon, the boldface entries indicate the best performances).

---

[4] The German Government External 7% Gold Loan of 1924 (Dawes Loan) was the sole bond to be given the highest rating by an agency and then subsequently default.

For the first two rating categories (Table 7.11), default rates are equal to zero for all four CRAs at the 1-year horizon. At the 2-year horizon, Moody's and Poor's share the leadership whereas, from the 3- to the 7-year horizons, Moody's has the most accurate ratings. Afterwards, this latter agency loses its leadership position to Poor's.

For the first three rating categories (Table 7.12), Fitch ratings perform the best at the 1-year horizon. In the medium-term (2- to 5-year horizons), Standard Statistics and Poor's ratings have the most accurate default rates. From the 5-year horizon onward, Poor's ratings are the best. It is also worth noting that Fitch default rates are systematically the highest in the 2- to 10-year horizons for the AAA–AA as well as the AAA–A brackets.

## 7.4 Concluding Remarks

Several conclusions may be drawn from this chapter.

First, the four agencies failed to anticipate the sovereign debt crisis that began in 1931, and they overreacted by making massive downgrades during 1931–1933. Nonetheless, the low default rates for bonds rated in the first two rating categories – together with the higher default rates for lower rating classes – show that Fitch, Moody's, Poor's, and Standard Statistics successfully discriminated among foreign government bonds.

Second, the rating performances (as measured by cumulative default rates) are not widely dispersed. If the highest rating category (AAA, Aaa, A**, and A1+) only is counted, reflecting the highest level of risk aversion, then default rates are equal to zero for all four agencies in both the short and medium term. In contrast, long-term Fitch ratings turn out to be slightly less accurate. For the intermediate level of risk aversion (i.e., the first two rating categories), rating performances of the four agencies are equal in the short term; however, Moody's and Poor's ratings are the leaders in the medium and long term, respectively. Note that, in the long run, the default rate gap between Poor's and Fitch (whose rates are the highest) is only 1.15 points. The gap increases significantly when the risk aversion level is lower (first three rating categories): Fitch has the lowest default rates in the short term but the highest rates in the medium/long term. Table 7.13 summarizes these accuracy measures by horizon and level of risk aversion. These results would have been particularly

**Table 7.13** Best-performing CRAs by risk aversion and time horizon

| | Short term | Medium term | Long term |
|---|---|---|---|
| Maximum risk aversion | All four agencies | All four agencies | Moody's, Poor's, and Standard Statistics |
| Intermediate risk aversion | All four agencies | Moody's | Poor's |
| Minimum risk aversion | Fitch | Poor's and Standard Statistics | Poor's |

*Sources*: Author's classification

useful for investors, who could have chosen securities based on ratings that reflected tolerance to risk and investment horizon.

Third, these results suggest that the most reactive and volatile ratings are the most accurate in the short run (Fitch). In contrast, the most stable ratings perform best in the medium/long run (Moody's and Poor's particularly). Standard Statistics turns out to have employed a hybrid rating policy. The findings reported here are in line with Flandreau et al. (2010) research work. They imply that two rating policies existed in the 1920–1930s: one, as used by Poor's and Moody's, that analyzed sovereign risk "through the cycle"; and one, as employed by Fitch, that was based on a short-term analysis.

# References

Eichengreen B. and Portes R. (1986), "Debt and Default in the 1930s", *European Economic Review*, Vol.30, No.3.

Eichengreen B. and Werley C. (1988), "How the Bondholders Fared: Realized Rates of Return on Foreign Dollar Bonds Floated in the 1920s", *University of California at Berkeley, Economic Working Paper 8869*.

Fitch (various years), *Fitch Bond Books*.

Flandreau M., Gaillard N. and Packer F. (2010), "To Err Is Human: Rating Agencies and the Interwar Foreign Government Debt Crisis", *BIS Working Paper No.335*, December.

Harold G. (1938), *Bond Ratings as an Investment Guide*, Ronald Press Company, New York.

Hickman W. B. (1958), *Corporate Bond Quality and Investor Experience*, Princeton University Press, Princeton.

Hickman W. B. (1960), *Statistical Measures of Corporate Bond Financing since 1900*, Princeton University Press, Princeton.

Mintz I. (1951), *Deterioration in the Quality of Foreign Bonds Issued in the United States 1920–30*, NBER, Cambridge.

Moody's Investors Service (various years), *Moody's Manuals*.

Moody's Investors Service (1995), "Corporate Bond Defaults and Default Rates 1970–1994", January.

Moody's Investors Service (2004), "Tracing the Origins of Investment Grade", January.

Palyi M. (1938), "Bank Portfolios and the Control of the Capital Market", *Journal of Business of the University of Chicago*, Vol.11, No.1.

Poor's (various years), *Poor's Volumes*.

Rippy J. F. (1950), "A Bond-Selling Extravaganza of the 1920's", *Journal of Business of the University of Chicago*, Vol.23, No.4.

Standard Statistics (various years), *Standard Bond Books*.

Winkler M. (1933), *Foreign Bonds – An Autopsy*, Roland Swain Company, Philadelphia.

# Chapter 8
# Consistency and Performance of Sovereign Ratings Since the 1980s

This chapter compares the consistency and accuracy of sovereign ratings issued by Fitch, Moody's, and S&P from January 1987 to January 2011. Sovereign rating policies have refined considerably – and information availability has been much enhanced – since 1918, so this chapter is more exhaustive than Chap. 7. Section 8.1 reviews the literature. Section 8.2 studies rating outlooks and reviews, which did not exist in the interwar years, and shows that the three CRAs are more prone to upgrade sovereigns with a positive outlook or a positive watch than to downgrade issuers with a negative outlook or a negative watch. Focusing on the stability of sovereign ratings, Sect. 8.3 finds that rating changes by Moody's are the least frequent, but have the greatest magnitude. Section 8.4 compares the accuracy of Fitch, Moody's, and S&P sovereign ratings. It turns out that S&P ratings are slightly more accurate in the short term, whereas Moody's ratings perform better in the medium term. Section 8.5 concludes.

## 8.1 Review of the Literature

This chapter refers to three strands of the literature.

The first group of papers consists of those that specifically analyze rating migration rates. Focusing on corporate ratings, Nickell et al. (2000) and Moody's (2003b) emphasize the stability and cyclicality of migration rates. Hu et al. (2002), noting that the lack of historical data for sovereigns precludes the computation of migration rates, use an ordered probit model to estimate these transition matrices. Moody's (2003a) computes the first sovereign migration rates for the period 1985–2002 and concludes that sovereign ratings are more stable than corporate ratings. Moody's also finds that upgrades and downgrades by more than one notch are more numerous in the corporate area. Similar studies conducted by Fitch and S&P yield comparable results. More interestingly, Altman and Rijken (2004) analyze the main factors underlying the stability of credit ratings and find that rating agencies have a "through the cycle" methodology. Confirming Altman and Rijken's work, Moody's (2006) explains that its current rating system embodies a trade-off between accuracy and stability.

The second category of papers deals with the different ways to estimate rating performances. Moody's (1995) studies its own corporate ratings for 1970–1994, computing marginal and cumulative default rates. Unsurprisingly, the agency demonstrates the accuracy of its investment-grade ratings. Moody's (1997) broadens the historical scope of its study by examining the years 1920–1996; since then, the agency has updated its reports annually. KMV (1998) warns against the excessive use of default rates to assess rating quality. They argue that since there is so little homogeneity of default rates within a rating category the outliers (which artificially increase average default rates) must be dropped. Moody's (2000) refines its assessment of the quality of corporate ratings by using cumulative accuracy profiles (CAPs) and accuracy ratios (ARs), which are designed to estimate the agency's ability to assign low ratings to issuers that will default and high ratings to those that will not.[1] These various measures of rating accuracy, extended to Moody's sovereign ratings in 2003 (Moody's 2003a), have been adopted by S&P, but not by Fitch; see S&P (2011) and Fitch (2011) for the latest reports.

The third kind of study emphasizes the importance of rating outlooks and reviews. Moody's (2004) documents corporate rating transition rates during the 1995–2003 period conditional on rating Watchlist, outlook, and rating history. Rating outlooks and reviews turn out to be powerful indicators of the likely direction and timing of future rating actions. Fitch (2005) and S&P (2010a) provide comparable studies for sovereign rating outlooks and reviews, finding that they have a significant impact on their respective rating changes.

## 8.2  Sovereign Rating Reviews and Outlooks

Rating reviews[2] are opinions regarding the likely direction of a rating over the short term (see Fitch 2009; Moody's 2010b; S&P 2010b). Rating outlooks assess the potential direction of a rating over the short-medium term. S&P (2010b) indicates that its rating outlooks typically extend from 6 months to 2 years. For Fitch rating outlooks, the time horizon is 1–2 years (Fitch 2009). Moody's is less precise: its rating outlooks are expected to apply over "the medium term" (Moody's 2010b).

Rating reviews and rating outlooks are two types of indicators that are intended to complement ratings and to help investors anticipate the likely change in issuer credit quality. These indicators are mutually exclusive; that is, an issuer cannot be assigned an outlook and be placed on CreditWatch at the same time.

---

[1] Rating a defaulter too high is a Type I error; rating a nondefaulter too low is a Type II error.
[2] The terms "rating review," "CreditWatch," "Rating Watch," and "Watchlist" are used interchangeably hereafter.

## 8.2 Sovereign Rating Reviews and Outlooks

Sections 8.2.1 and 8.2.2 investigate the frequency and duration of rating reviews and of rating outlooks and assess the likelihood that these indicators ultimately result in an upgrade or downgrade. Section 8.2.3 computes the probability that downgrades and upgrades are preceded by rating reviews or outlook assignments.

### 8.2.1 Sovereign Rating Reviews

A rating can be placed on review for possible upgrade (a.k.a. on positive watch), on review for possible downgrade (negative watch), or more rarely on review with direction uncertain.[3] The rating is removed from the Watchlist once it is upgraded, downgraded, or confirmed.

S&P, Moody's, and Fitch started placing sovereign ratings on Watchlist on 7 March 1991, 6 May 1992, and 13 November 1995, respectively. The three periods under study are 7 March 1991 to 1 January 2011, 6 May 1992 to 1 January 2011, and 19 May 2000 to 1 January 2011 for S&P, Moody's, and Fitch, respectively.[4] Tables 8.1–8.3 display summary statistics on the Fitch, Moody's, and S&P rating reviews.

First, the number of rating reviews varies across agencies: 171 ratings are placed on Watchlist by Moody's vs. 43 for Fitch and 78 for S&P. On average, a Moody's rating is put on Watchlist every 9.5 years. The frequency of S&P and Fitch rating reviews is much lower: 21 and 22.7 years, respectively.[5]

Second, in the sample periods, there is only one CreditWatch with direction uncertain, which was issued by S&P; all other rating watches are either positive watches or negative watches. The number of negative Watchlists exceeds the number of positive Watchlists in the case of Fitch and S&P. In contrast, Moody's reviews for possible upgrade are more numerous than its reviews for possible downgrade. S&P did not place any sovereign rating on CreditWatch with positive implications until July 2010, which confirms that S&P considers the Watchlist an indicator of likely downgrades. In this regard, S&P's policy differs from that of Fitch and Moody's.

A third observation is that the great majority of ratings under positive watch are eventually upgraded: from 95.1% for Moody's to 100% for Fitch. In contrast, the percentage of ratings under negative watch that are downgraded is significantly lower: 67.7, 69.7, and 72.5% for Fitch, S&P, and Moody's, respectively. Hence, one might conclude that CRAs are more reluctant to downgrade than to upgrade, or that governments under negative watch manage to reassure rating analysts about the creditworthiness of their country.

Fourth, examining the duration of CreditWatches shows that reviews for possible upgrade are resolved in a shorter period of time than are reviews for possible

---

[3] This is Moody's term. Fitch and S&P use the terms "evolving" and "developing" (respectively) in such cases.

[4] Fitch Rating Watches are examined only from 19 May 2000, after Fitch IBCA merged with Duff and Phelps.

[5] Author's computations.

**Table 8.1** Fitch rating reviews, 19 May 2000 to 1 January 2011

| Rating review direction | Rating review termination | Number | Average duration (days) | Minimum duration (days) | Maximum duration (days) | Standard deviation (days) | % of all respective reviews | % of all rating reviews |
|---|---|---|---|---|---|---|---|---|
| Review for possible upgrade | Upgrade | 12 | 52 | 13 | 111 | 28 | 100.00 | 27.91 |
|  | Downgrade | 0 | NA | NA | NA | NA | 0.00 | 0.00 |
|  | Rating confirmed | 0 | NA | NA | NA | NA | 0.00 | 0.00 |
| *All reviews for possible upgrade* |  | *12* | *52* | *13* | *111* | *28* | *100.00* | *27.91* |
| Review for possible downgrade | Upgrade | 1 | 263 | 263 | 263 | NA | 3.23 | 2.33 |
|  | Downgrade | 21 | 94 | 2 | 448 | 103 | 67.74 | 48.84 |
|  | Rating confirmed | 9 | 145 | 33 | 442 | 136 | 29.03 | 20.93 |
| *All reviews for possible downgrade* |  | *31* | *114* | *2* | *448* | *116* | *100.00* | *72.09* |
| Evolving rating watch | Upgrade | 0 | NA | NA | NA | NA | NA | 0.00 |
|  | Downgrade | 0 | NA | NA | NA | NA | NA | 0.00 |
|  | Rating confirmed | 0 | NA | NA | NA | NA | NA | 0.00 |
| *All evolving rating watches* |  | *0* | *NA* | *NA* | *NA* | *NA* | *NA* | *0.00* |
| **All rating reviews** |  | **43** | **97** | **2** | **448** | **103** | **100.00** | **100.00** |

*Sources*: Author's computations based on http://www.fitchratings.com
*Notes*: Percentages may not total 100% due to rounding. NA not applicable

8.2 Sovereign Rating Reviews and Outlooks

**Table 8.2** Moody's rating reviews, 6 May 1992 to 1 January 2011

| Rating review direction | Rating review termination | Number | Average duration (days) | Minimum duration (days) | Maximum duration (days) | Standard deviation (days) | % of all respective reviews | % of all rating reviews |
|---|---|---|---|---|---|---|---|---|
| Review for possible upgrade | Upgrade | 97 | 73 | 11 | 221 | 42 | 95.10 | 56.73 |
| | Downgrade | 0 | NA | NA | NA | NA | 0.00 | 0.00 |
| | Rating confirmed | 5 | 123 | 82 | 150 | 26 | 4.90 | 2.92 |
| *All reviews for possible upgrade* | | *102* | *76* | *11* | *221* | *43* | *100.00* | *59.65* |
| Review for possible downgrade | Upgrade | 0 | NA | NA | NA | NA | 0.00 | 0.00 |
| | Downgrade | 50 | 87 | 8 | 570 | 89 | 72.46 | 29.24 |
| | Rating confirmed | 19 | 93 | 22 | 160 | 37 | 27.54 | 11.11 |
| *All reviews for possible downgrade* | | *69* | *88* | *8* | *570* | *78* | *100.00* | *40.35* |
| Review with direction uncertain | Upgrade | 0 | NA | NA | NA | NA | NA | 0.00 |
| | Downgrade | 0 | NA | NA | NA | NA | NA | 0.00 |
| | Rating confirmed | 0 | NA | NA | NA | NA | NA | 0.00 |
| *All reviews with direction uncertain* | | *0* | *NA* | *NA* | *NA* | *NA* | *NA* | *0.00* |
| **All rating reviews** | | ***171*** | ***81*** | ***8*** | ***570*** | ***60*** | ***100.00*** | ***100.00*** |

*Sources*: Author's computations based on http://www.moodys.com
*Notes*: Percentages may not total 100% due to rounding. NA denotes not applicable

**Table 8.3** S&P rating reviews, 7 March 1991 to 1 January 2011

| Rating review direction | Rating review termination | Number | Average duration (days) | Minimum duration (days) | Maximum duration (days) | Standard deviation (days) | % of all respective reviews | % of all rating reviews |
|---|---|---|---|---|---|---|---|---|
| Review for possible upgrade | Upgrade | 1 | 7 | 7 | 7 | NA | 100.00 | 1.28 |
|  | Downgrade | 0 | NA | NA | NA | NA | 0.00 | 0.00 |
|  | Rating confirmed | 0 | NA | NA | NA | NA | 0.00 | 0.00 |
| *All reviews for possible upgrade* |  | *1* | *7* | *7* | *7* | *NA* | *100.00* | *1.28* |
| Review for possible downgrade | Upgrade | 0 | NA | NA | NA | NA | 0.00 | 0.00 |
|  | Downgrade | 53 | 47 | 2 | 218 | 45 | 69.74 | 67.95 |
|  | Rating confirmed | 23 | 97 | 7 | 345 | 93 | 30.26 | 29.49 |
| *All reviews for possible downgrade* |  | *76* | *62* | *2* | *345* | *67* | *100.00* | *97.44* |
| Developing Creditwatch | Upgrade | 1 | 33 | 33 | 33 | NA | 100.00 | 1.28 |
|  | Downgrade | 0 | NA | NA | NA | NA | 0.00 | 0.00 |
|  | Rating confirmed | 0 | NA | NA | NA | NA | 0.00 | 0.00 |
| *All developing Creditwatches* |  | *1* | *33* | *33* | *33* | *NA* | *100.00* | *1.28* |
| **All rating reviews** |  | **78** | **61** | **2** | **345** | **66** | **100.00** | **100.00** |

*Sources:* Author's computations based on http://www.standardandpoors.com
*Notes:* Percentages may not total 100% due to rounding. NA denotes not applicable

downgrade. Moreover, ratings under positive (negative) watch that are eventually upgraded (downgraded) are resolved in a shorter period of time than those that result in a rating confirmation. So the longer the Rating Watch, the higher the probability that the agency confirms the rating.

Finally, S&P's Rating Watches are resolved within shorter periods (61 days on average) than are those of Moody's and Fitch (81 and 97 days, respectively). This is consistent with the duration of S&P's Watchlists, which never exceeds 1 year – contrary to what is observed for Fitch and Moody's.

CreditWatches provide investors with relevant informational content. A high percentage of sovereign ratings placed on review for possible upgrade (downgrade) are eventually upgraded (downgraded) within 3 months on average, which is in line with the rating policies of all three CRAs.

## 8.2.2 Sovereign Rating Outlooks

There are four categories of rating outlooks. A "positive outlook" means that a rating may be raised, and a "negative outlook" means that a rating may be lowered. A "stable outlook" means that a rating is not likely to change, whereas a "developing outlook" (termed "evolving" by Fitch) means that a rating contingent may be raised or lowered upon some event.

S&P, Moody's, and Fitch began issuing sovereign rating outlooks on 26 June 1989, 7 March 1997, and 21 September 2000, respectively. The three periods under study are 26 June 1989 to 1 January 2011, 7 March 1997 to 1 January 2011, and 21 September 2000 to 1 January 2011 for S&P, Moody's, and Fitch, respectively. Tables 8.4–8.6 give summary statistics on the Fitch, Moody's, and S&P outlooks.

Observe first that the number of outlooks varies across CRAs: 874 outlooks are assigned by S&P vs. 509 for Moody's and 439 for Fitch. On average, S&P assigns a new outlook every 1.8 years. The frequency of Fitch and Moody's outlooks is lower: respectively 2.2 and 2.75 years.[6]

Second, the samples include only four developing outlooks (two assigned by Moody's and two assigned by S&P). All other outlooks are positive, stable, or negative. Stable outlooks account for 50% of all outlooks assigned. The number of positive outlooks exceeds the number of negative outlooks in the case of Fitch and Moody's, yet S&P negative outlooks are more numerous than its positive outlooks. However, the distribution of positive and negative outlooks is fairly well balanced in each agency: the largest gap is observed for Moody's, whose positive outlooks outnumber negative outlooks by roughly 20%.

Third, more than 70% of Fitch and S&P positive outlooks is eventually upgraded vs. less than 35% for Moody's. It is interesting that when all positive actions are considered (i.e., when upgrades and positive watches are combined), the Moody's percentage soars to 76% – exceeding slightly Fitch's and S&P's percentages. Other positive outlooks

---

[6] Author's computations.

Table 8.4 Fitch rating outlooks, 21 September 2000 to 1 January 2011

| Outlook direction | Outlook termination | Number | Average duration (days) | Minimum duration (days) | Maximum duration (days) | Standard deviation (days) | % of all respective outlooks | % of all outlooks |
|---|---|---|---|---|---|---|---|---|
| Positive outlook | Upgrade | 73 | 374 | 50 | 1,347 | 276 | 71.57 | 16.63 |
| | Downgrade | 1 | 509 | 509 | 509 | NA | 0.98 | 0.23 |
| | Positive watch | 2 | 246 | 203 | 289 | 61 | 1.96 | 0.46 |
| | Negative watch | 0 | NA | NA | NA | NA | 0.00 | 0.00 |
| | Positive outlook | NA | NA | NA | NA | NA | NA | NA |
| | Negative outlook | 0 | NA | NA | NA | NA | 0.00 | 0.00 |
| | Stable outlook | 26 | 413 | 8 | 785 | 206 | 25.49 | 5.92 |
| | Evol. outlook | 0 | NA | NA | NA | NA | 0.00 | 0.00 |
| | Rating withdrawn | 0 | NA | NA | NA | NA | 0.00 | 0.00 |
| *All positive outlooks* | | *102* | *383* | *8* | *1,347* | *256* | *100.00* | *23.23* |
| Negative outlook | Upgrade | 1 | 164 | 164 | 164 | NA | 1.01 | 0.23 |
| | Downgrade | 58 | 203 | 13 | 875 | 167 | 58.59 | 13.21 |
| | Positive watch | 0 | NA | NA | NA | NA | 0.00 | 0.00 |
| | Negative watch | 5 | 194 | 42 | 330 | 119 | 5.05 | 1.14 |
| | Positive outlook | 1 | 134 | 134 | 134 | NA | 1.01 | 0.23 |
| | Negative outlook | NA | NA | NA | NA | NA | NA | NA |
| | Stable outlook | 34 | 482 | 125 | 1,260 | 297 | 34.34 | 7.74 |
| | Evol. outlook | 0 | NA | NA | NA | NA | 0.00 | 0.00 |
| | Rating withdrawn | 0 | NA | NA | NA | NA | 0.00 | 0.00 |
| *All negative outlooks* | | *99* | *297* | *13* | *1,260* | *254* | *100.00* | *22.55* |

## 8.2 Sovereign Rating Reviews and Outlooks

| | | | | | | | | |
|---|---|---|---|---|---|---|---|---|
| Stable outlook | Upgrade | 58 | 653 | 56 | 2,278 | 460 | 24.37 | 13.21 |
| | Downgrade | 13 | 819 | 231 | 3,045 | 883 | 5.46 | 2.96 |
| | Positive watch | 8 | 487 | 53 | 1,180 | 386 | 3.36 | 1.82 |
| | Negative watch | 12 | 517 | 48 | 3,088 | 832 | 5.04 | 2.73 |
| | Positive outlook | 84 | 624 | 33 | 1,950 | 464 | 35.29 | 19.13 |
| | Negative outlook | 58 | 568 | 33 | 2,158 | 466 | 24.37 | 13.21 |
| | Stable outlook | NA | NA | NA | NA | NA | NA | NA |
| | Evol. outlook | 0 | NA | NA | NA | NA | 0.00 | 0.00 |
| | Rating withdrawn | 5 | 940 | 458 | 2,045 | 641 | 2.10 | 1.14 |
| *All stable outlooks* | | *238* | *625* | *33* | *3,088* | *517* | *100.00* | *54.21* |
| Evolving outlook | Upgrade | 0 | NA | NA | NA | NA | 0.00 | 0.00 |
| | Downgrade | 0 | NA | NA | NA | NA | 0.00 | 0.00 |
| | Positive watch | 0 | NA | NA | NA | NA | 0.00 | 0.00 |
| | Negative watch | 0 | NA | NA | NA | NA | 0.00 | 0.00 |
| | Positive outlook | 0 | NA | NA | NA | NA | 0.00 | 0.00 |
| | Negative outlook | 0 | NA | NA | NA | NA | 0.00 | 0.00 |
| | Stable outlook | 0 | NA | NA | NA | NA | 0.00 | 0.00 |
| | Evol. outlook | NA | NA | NA | NA | NA | NA | NA |
| | Rating withdrawn | 0 | NA | NA | NA | NA | 0.00 | 0.00 |
| *All evolving outlooks* | | *0* | *NA* | *NA* | *NA* | *NA* | *NA* | *0.00* |
| **All outlooks** | | **439** | **495** | **8** | **3,088** | **442** | **100.00** | **100.00** |

*Sources*: Author's computations based on http://www.fitchratings.com
*Notes*: Percentages may not total 100% due to rounding. NA denotes not applicable

Table 8.5 Moody's rating outlooks, 7 March 1997 to 1 January 2011

| Outlook direction | Outlook termination | Number | Average duration (days) | Minimum duration (days) | Maximum duration (days) | Standard deviation (days) | % of all respective outlooks | % of all outlooks |
|---|---|---|---|---|---|---|---|---|
| Positive outlook | Upgrade | 42 | 349 | 29 | 1,471 | 324 | 34.71 | 8.25 |
| | Downgrade | 0 | NA | NA | NA | NA | 0.00 | 0.00 |
| | Positive watch | 50 | 339 | 69 | 928 | 202 | 41.32 | 9.82 |
| | Negative watch | 0 | NA | NA | NA | NA | 0.00 | 0.00 |
| | Positive outlook | NA | NA | NA | NA | NA | NA | NA |
| | Negative outlook | 3 | 562 | 117 | 1,120 | 511 | 2.48 | 0.59 |
| | Stable outlook | 25 | 530 | 62 | 1,068 | 323 | 20.66 | 4.91 |
| | Dev. outlook | 1 | 84 | 84 | 84 | NA | 0.83 | 0.20 |
| | Rating withdrawn | 0 | NA | NA | NA | NA | 0.00 | 0.00 |
| All positive outlooks | | 121 | 385 | 29 | 1,471 | 292 | 100.00 | 23.77 |
| Negative outlook | Upgrade | 1 | 415 | 415 | 415 | NA | 0.98 | 0.20 |
| | Downgrade | 35 | 181 | 8 | 1,333 | 246 | 34.31 | 6.88 |
| | Positive watch | 0 | NA | NA | NA | NA | 0.00 | 0.00 |
| | Negative watch | 27 | 182 | 15 | 805 | 182 | 26.47 | 5.30 |
| | Positive outlook | 1 | 580 | 580 | 580 | NA | 0.98 | 0.20 |
| | Negative outlook | NA | NA | NA | NA | NA | NA | NA |
| | Stable outlook | 38 | 486 | 17 | 1,609 | 340 | 37.25 | 7.47 |
| | Dev. outlook | 0 | NA | NA | NA | NA | 0.00 | 0.00 |
| | Rating withdrawn | 0 | NA | NA | NA | NA | 0.00 | 0.00 |
| All negative outlooks | | 102 | 301 | 8 | 1,609 | 306 | 100.00 | 20.04 |

## 8.2 Sovereign Rating Reviews and Outlooks

| | | | | | | |
|---|---|---|---|---|---|---|
| Stable outlook | Upgrade | 52 | 1,002 | 16 | 3,031 | 739 | 18.31 | 10.22 |
| | Downgrade | 25 | 647 | 18 | 3,213 | 807 | 8.80 | 4.91 |
| | Positive watch | 37 | 783 | 127 | 4,769 | 808 | 13.03 | 7.27 |
| | Negative watch | 22 | 872 | 76 | 4,396 | 1,133 | 7.75 | 4.32 |
| | Positive outlook | 94 | 746 | 66 | 3,308 | 638 | 33.10 | 18.47 |
| | Negative outlook | 53 | 781 | 16 | 4,196 | 892 | 18.66 | 10.41 |
| | Stable outlook | NA | NA | NA | NA | NA | NA | NA |
| | Dev. outlook | 0 | NA | NA | NA | NA | 0.00 | 0.00 |
| | Rating withdrawn | 1 | 2,340 | 2,340 | 2,340 | NA | 0.35 | 0.20 |
| All stable outlooks | | 284 | 811 | 16 | 4,769 | 795 | 100.00 | 55.80 |
| Developing outlook | Upgrade | 1 | 282 | 282 | 282 | NA | 50.00 | 0.20 |
| | Downgrade | 0 | NA | NA | NA | NA | 0.00 | 0.00 |
| | Positive watch | 0 | NA | NA | NA | NA | 0.00 | 0.00 |
| | Negative watch | 0 | NA | NA | NA | NA | 0.00 | 0.00 |
| | Positive outlook | 0 | NA | NA | NA | NA | 0.00 | 0.00 |
| | Negative outlook | 0 | NA | NA | NA | NA | 0.00 | 0.00 |
| | Stable outlook | 1 | 78 | 78 | 78 | NA | 50.00 | 0.20 |
| | Dev. outlook | NA | NA | NA | NA | NA | NA | NA |
| | Rating withdrawn | 0 | NA | NA | NA | NA | 0.00 | 0.00 |
| All developing outlooks | | 2 | 180 | 78 | 282 | 144 | 100.00 | 0.39 |
| All outlooks | | 509 | 605 | 8 | 4,769 | 667 | 100.00 | 100.00 |

*Sources*: Author's computations based on http://www.moodys.com
*Note*: Percentages may not total 100% due to rounding. NA denotes not applicable

**Table 8.6** S&P rating outlooks, 26 June 1989 to 1 January 2011

| Outlook direction | Outlook termination | Number | Average duration (days) | Minimum duration (days) | Maximum duration (days) | Standard deviation (days) | % of all respective outlooks | % of all outlooks |
|---|---|---|---|---|---|---|---|---|
| Positive outlook | Upgrade | 146 | 406 | 21 | 1,395 | 258 | 70.53 | 16.70 |
|  | Downgrade | 0 | NA | NA | NA | NA | 0.00 | 0.00 |
|  | Positive watch | 0 | NA | NA | NA | NA | 0.00 | 0.00 |
|  | Negative watch | 1 | 400 | 400 | 400 | NA | 0.48 | 0.11 |
|  | Positive outlook | NA | NA | NA | NA | NA | NA | NA |
|  | Negative outlook | 1 | 1,809 | 1,809 | 1,809 | NA | 0.48 | 0.11 |
|  | Stable outlook | 59 | 425 | 86 | 2,416 | 367 | 28.50 | 6.75 |
|  | Dev. outlook | 0 | NA | NA | NA | NA | 0.00 | 0.00 |
|  | Rating withdrawn | 0 | NA | NA | NA | NA | 0.00 | 0.00 |
| All positive outlooks |  | 207 | 418 | 21 | 2,416 | 307 | 100.00 | 23.68 |
| Negative outlook | Upgrade | 1 | 305 | 305 | 305 | NA | 0.43 | 0.11 |
|  | Downgrade | 125 | 166 | 4 | 1,251 | 209 | 53.65 | 14.30 |
|  | Positive watch | 0 | NA | NA | NA | NA | 0.00 | 0.00 |
|  | Negative watch | 19 | 248 | 32 | 853 | 208 | 8.15 | 2.17 |
|  | Positive outlook | 5 | 432 | 153 | 836 | 287 | 2.15 | 0.57 |
|  | Negative outlook | NA | NA | NA | NA | NA | NA | NA |
|  | Stable outlook | 82 | 426 | 22 | 1,410 | 294 | 35.19 | 9.38 |
|  | Dev. outlook | 0 | NA | NA | NA | NA | 0.00 | 0.00 |
|  | Rating withdrawn | 1 | 54 | 54 | 54 | NA | 0.43 | 0.11 |
| All negative outlooks |  | 233 | 292 | 4 | 1,410 | 264 | 100.00 | 26.66 |

## 8.2 Sovereign Rating Reviews and Outlooks

| | | | | | | | |
|---|---|---|---|---|---|---|---|
| Stable outlook | Upgrade | 93 | 628 | 80 | 2,454 | 486 | 21.53 | 10.64 |
| | Downgrade | 26 | 659 | 61 | 4,259 | 846 | 6.02 | 2.97 |
| | Positive watch | 1 | 66 | 66 | 66 | NA | 0.23 | 0.11 |
| | Negative watch | 38 | 480 | 64 | 1,514 | 410 | 8.80 | 4.35 |
| | Positive outlook | 143 | 709 | 51 | 4,207 | 616 | 33.10 | 16.36 |
| | Negative outlook | 130 | 798 | 13 | 7,269 | 1,022 | 30.09 | 14.87 |
| | Stable outlook | NA | NA | NA | NA | NA | NA | NA |
| | Dev. outlook | 0 | NA | NA | NA | NA | 0.00 | 0.00 |
| | Rating withdrawn | 1 | 1,520 | 1,520 | 1,520 | NA | 0.23 | 0.11 |
| *All stable outlooks* | | *432* | *696* | *13* | *7,269* | *745* | *100.00* | *49.43* |
| Developing outlook | Upgrade | 2 | 142 | 35 | 248 | NA | 100.00 | 0.23 |
| | Downgrade | 0 | NA | NA | NA | NA | 0.00 | 0.00 |
| | Positive watch | 0 | NA | NA | NA | NA | 0.00 | 0.00 |
| | Negative watch | 0 | NA | NA | NA | NA | 0.00 | 0.00 |
| | Positive outlook | 0 | NA | NA | NA | NA | 0.00 | 0.00 |
| | Negative outlook | 0 | NA | NA | NA | NA | 0.00 | 0.00 |
| | Stable outlook | 0 | NA | NA | NA | NA | 0.00 | 0.00 |
| | Dev. outlook | NA | NA | NA | NA | NA | NA | NA |
| | Rating withdrawn | 0 | NA | NA | NA | NA | 0.00 | 0.00 |
| *All developing outlooks* | | *2* | *142* | *35* | *248* | *NA* | *100.00* | *0.23* |
| **All outlooks** | | **874** | **521** | **4** | **7,269** | **589** | **100.00** | **100.00** |

*Sources*: Author's computations based on http://www.standardandpoors.com
*Notes*: Percentages may not total 100% due to rounding. NA denotes not applicable

are generally changed to stable. Less than 0.5% of positive outlooks leads to a negative action (i.e., to a downgrade, a negative watch, or a negative outlook).

Fourth, the percentage of negative outlooks that are eventually downgraded (or lead to a negative action) is significantly lower: 34.3% (60.8%), 53.6% (61.8%), and 58.6% (63.6%) for Moody's, S&P, and Fitch, respectively. Other negative outlooks are generally changed to stable. The proportion of negative outlooks that result in a positive action is slightly above 2%. As before, one may well presume that CRAs are more reluctant to downgrade than to upgrade.

Fifth, stable outlooks that finish with a positive action outnumber those that finish with a negative action: 63 vs. 34.9% for Fitch, 64.4 vs. 35.2% for Moody's, and 54.9 vs. 44.9% for S&P. These findings could mean that there is an upward bias in the rating policies of Fitch and Moody's and, to a lesser extent, S&P.

Sixth, examining the duration of outlooks shows that negative outlooks are resolved in shorter periods of time than positive outlooks: 297 vs. 383 days for Fitch, 301 vs. 385 days for Moody's, and 292 vs. 418 days for S&P. Naturally enough, outlooks that move in the expected direction (i.e., positive outlooks that result in a positive action and negative outlooks that result in a negative action) are resolved more quickly than are outlooks that move in the unexpected direction. These gaps are even larger for (a) negative outlooks assigned by the three CRAs and (b) all of the Moody's outlooks.

Seventh, resolving stable outlooks takes much more time than resolving positive and negative outlooks: 625, 696, and 811 days for Fitch, S&P, and Moody's, respectively. These longer periods are not surprising given that negative and positive outlooks are intended to be temporary signals.

Positive and negative outlooks are, on average, resolved within 10–14 months; this is consistent with the agencies' rating policy. The proportion of positive (negative) outlooks that are eventually upgraded (downgraded) is much higher for Fitch and S&P than for Moody's, which is more prone to place on review for possible upgrade (downgrade) a rating that is assigned a positive (negative) outlook. These findings highlight the importance of Watchlist signals in Moody's rating policy.

### 8.2.3 Outlook/Watchlist Status Prior to Rating Change Announcements

This section answers the following question: What is the current status of sovereign ratings when they are upgraded or downgraded?

The three periods under study are 7 March 1991 to 1 January 2011, 7 March 1997 to 1 January 2011, and 21 September 2000 to 1 January 2011 for S&P, Moody's, and Fitch, respectively.[7] Tables 8.7–8.9 provide information about the current status of Fitch, Moody's, and S&P ratings at the time of their upgrade or downgrade.

---

[7] The starting date of each period corresponds to the first day on which the respective agencies assigned both rating watches and outlooks to sovereign issuers.

## 8.2 Sovereign Rating Reviews and Outlooks

**Table 8.7** Current rating status at the time of Fitch rating changes, 21 September 2000 to 1 January 2011

| Rating change | Current status at time of the rating change | Investment-grade ratings (%) | Speculative-grade ratings (%) | All ratings (%) |
|---|---|---|---|---|
| Downgrade | Positive watch | 0.00 | 0.00 | 0.00 |
| | Negative watch | 13.16 | 29.09 | 22.58 |
| | Evolving watch | 0.00 | 0.00 | 0.00 |
| | Positive outlook | 0.00 | 1.82 | 1.08 |
| | Negative outlook | 78.95 | 50.91 | 62.37 |
| | Stable outlook | 7.89 | 18.18 | 13.98 |
| | Evolving outlook | 0.00 | 0.00 | 0.00 |
| | *Total* | *100.00* | *100.00* | *100.00* |
| Upgrade | Positive watch | 10.00 | 5.41 | 7.64 |
| | Negative watch | 0.00 | 1.35 | 0.69 |
| | Evolving watch | 0.00 | 0.00 | 0.00 |
| | Positive outlook | 50.00 | 51.35 | 50.69 |
| | Negative outlook | 0.00 | 1.35 | 0.69 |
| | Stable outlook | 40.00 | 40.54 | 40.28 |
| | Evolving outlook | 0.00 | 0.00 | 0.00 |
| | *Total* | *100.00* | *100.00* | *100.00* |

*Sources*: Author's computations based on http://www.fitchratings.com
*Note*: Percentages may not total 100% due to rounding

**Table 8.8** Current rating status at the time of Moody's rating changes, 7 March 1997 to 1 January 2011

| Rating change | Current status at time of the rating change | Investment-grade ratings (%) | Speculative-grade ratings (%) | All ratings (%) |
|---|---|---|---|---|
| Downgrade | Positive watch | 0.00 | 0.00 | 0.00 |
| | Negative watch | 51.43 | 29.51 | 37.50 |
| | Uncertain watch | 0.00 | 0.00 | 0.00 |
| | Positive outlook | 0.00 | 0.00 | 0.00 |
| | Negative outlook | 34.29 | 37.70 | 36.46 |
| | Stable outlook | 14.29 | 32.79 | 26.04 |
| | Developing outlook | 0.00 | 0.00 | 0.00 |
| | *Total* | *100.00* | *100.00* | *100.00* |
| Upgrade | Positive watch | 49.47 | 38.46 | 44.51 |
| | Negative watch | 0.00 | 0.00 | 0.00 |
| | Uncertain watch | 0.00 | 0.00 | 0.00 |
| | Positive outlook | 23.16 | 25.64 | 24.28 |
| | Negative outlook | 0.00 | 1.28 | 0.58 |
| | Stable outlook | 27.37 | 33.33 | 30.06 |
| | Developing outlook | 0.00 | 1.28 | 0.58 |
| | *Total* | *100.00* | *100.00* | *100.00* |

*Sources*: Author's computations based on http://www.moodys.com
*Note*: Percentages may not total 100% due to rounding

**Table 8.9** Current rating status at the time of S&P rating changes, 7 March 1991 to 1 January 2011

| Rating change | Current status at time of the rating change | Investment-grade ratings (%) | Speculative-grade ratings (%) | All ratings (%) |
|---|---|---|---|---|
| Downgrade | Positive watch | 0.00 | 0.00 | 0.00 |
| | Negative watch | 24.05 | 28.10 | 26.50 |
| | Developing watch | 0.00 | 0.00 | 0.00 |
| | Positive outlook | 0.00 | 0.00 | 0.00 |
| | Negative outlook | 64.56 | 57.85 | 60.50 |
| | Stable outlook | 11.39 | 14.05 | 13.00 |
| | Developing outlook | 0.00 | 0.00 | 0.00 |
| | *Total* | *100.00* | *100.00* | *100.00* |
| Upgrade | Positive watch | 0.00 | 0.83 | 0.41 |
| | Negative watch | 0.00 | 0.00 | 0.00 |
| | Developing watch | 0.00 | 0.83 | 0.41 |
| | Positive outlook | 64.75 | 54.55 | 59.67 |
| | Negative outlook | 0.00 | 0.83 | 0.41 |
| | Stable outlook | 35.25 | 41.32 | 38.27 |
| | Developing outlook | 0.00 | 1.65 | 0.82 |
| | *Total* | *100.00* | *100.00* | *100.00* |

*Sources*: Author's computations based on http://www.standardandpoors.com
*Note*: Percentages may not total 100% due to rounding

First, the percentage of downgrades that are preceded by a negative watch or a negative outlook outnumbers that of upgrades that are preceded by a positive watch or a positive outlook: 84.9 vs. 58.3% for Fitch, 74 vs. 68.8% for Moody's, and 87 vs. 60.1% for S&P. This gap is the reason for the higher proportion of upgrades that are preceded by a stable outlook. These findings indicate that rating agencies are more reluctant to downgrade than to upgrade a country that has a stable outlook.

A second observation is that these results are even more striking when speculative-grade ratings are considered: 33.3, 40.5, and 41.3% of the speculative-grade ratings upgraded by Moody's, Fitch, and S&P (respectively) are preceded by a stable outlook. These percentages support the view that speculative-grade rating outlooks convey less relevant information than do investment-grade rating outlooks. This assumption is confirmed by the exclusive occurrence of speculative-grade ratings among those rating watches and outlooks that lead to an unexpected rating change (i.e., positive watches and positive outlooks that result in a downgrade and negative watches and negative outlooks that result in an upgrade).

Third, the most frequent status at the time of Moody's upgrades (downgrades) is being on the positive (negative) Watchlist. This contrasts with Fitch and S&P, where the most common rating status at time of upgrades (downgrades) is the positive (negative) outlook. As a result, Moody's outlooks provide less information about likely rating changes than do Fitch and S&P outlooks.

In conclusion, Watchlist signals are the most reliable indicators of rating changes; the positive and negative outlooks assigned by Fitch and S&P also have predictive power concerning likely rating changes. Next, there is an upward bias to the rating policies of all three CRAs, as indicated by the greater probability of positive outlooks and positive watches resulting in an upgrade than the probability of negative outlooks and negative watches resulting in a downgrade. Finally, it is worth considering a suggestion to improve the consistency of rating actions: all upgrades (downgrades) could be preceded by a positive (negative) outlook or a positive (negative) watch.[8] This procedure would reduce to zero the probability that a rating with a stable outlook is upgraded or downgraded, thereby enhancing the predictive power of outlooks and Watchlist signals.

## 8.3 Stability of Sovereign Ratings

Rating changes are decisive actions that reflect the strengthening or the worsening of the sovereign issuer's financial position. This section investigates the stability of sovereign ratings issued by the three main CRAs. Section 8.3.1 studies the frequency and magnitude of rating changes. Section 8.3.2 provides an exhaustive analysis of migration rates. Section 8.3.3 presents an original comparison of Fitch, Moody's, and S&P rating reversals.

### 8.3.1 Frequency and Magnitude of Rating Changes

Table 8.10 displays the distribution of Fitch, Moody's, and S&P upgrades and downgrades.

The S&P rating changes outnumber those of Fitch and Moody's: 471 vs. 242 and 347, respectively. On average, an S&P rating is modified every 3.7 vs. 3.8 years for a Fitch rating and 5.2 years for a Moody's rating.[9] The number of upgrade announcements far exceeds the number of downgrade announcements: 147 upgrades vs. 95 downgrades for Fitch, 211 vs. 136 for Moody's, and 260 vs. 211 for S&P. This finding is in line with the results in Sect. 8.1 showing that positive outlooks and watches outnumber negative outlooks and watches.

The most massive wave of upgrades is observed for Moody's in 2002. This record high, which is related to the agency's revised country ceiling policy (described in Chap. 3), paved the way for a series of upgrades by Fitch and S&P during 2003–2004. The number of downgrades peaks in 2008, when S&P negative rating changes greatly exceed those of its competitors.

---

[8] Obviously, this would *not* mean that all positive (negative) outlooks and watches would automatically result in an upgrade (a downgrade).
[9] Author's computations.

**Table 8.10** Distribution of Fitch, Moody's, and S&P rating changes, 1 January 1987 to 1 January 2011

| | Fitch UP | Moody's UP | S&P UP | Fitch DN | Moody's DN | S&P DN | Fitch UP-to-DN ratio | Moody's UP-to-DN ratio | S&P UP-to-DN ratio |
|---|---|---|---|---|---|---|---|---|---|
| 1987 | NA | 0 | 0 | NA | 4 | 0 | NA | 0.00 | NA |
| 1988 | NA | 0 | 0 | NA | 0 | 0 | NA | NA | NA |
| 1989 | NA | 0 | 1 | NA | 5 | 2 | NA | 0.00 | 0.50 |
| 1990 | NA | 3 | 0 | NA | 3 | 2 | NA | 1.00 | 0.00 |
| 1991 | NA | 1 | 6 | NA | 4 | 3 | NA | 0.25 | 2.00 |
| 1992 | NA | 1 | 0 | NA | 2 | 2 | NA | 0.50 | 0.00 |
| 1993 | NA | 2 | 4 | NA | 2 | 3 | NA | 1.00 | 1.33 |
| 1994 | NA | 6 | 4 | NA | 6 | 4 | NA | 1.00 | 1.00 |
| 1995 | NA | 6 | 11 | NA | 3 | 1 | NA | 2.00 | 11.00 |
| 1996 | NA | 9 | 8 | NA | 1 | 2 | NA | 9.00 | 4.00 |
| 1997 | NA | 13 | 7 | NA | 10 | 9 | NA | 1.30 | 0.78 |
| 1998 | NA | 6 | 5 | NA | 23 | 24 | NA | 0.26 | 0.21 |
| 1999 | NA | 8 | 12 | NA | 4 | 11 | NA | 2.00 | 1.09 |
| 2000 | NA | 11 | 13 | NA | 4 | 6 | NA | 2.75 | 2.17 |
| 2001 | 12 | 9 | 17 | 17 | 7 | 18 | 0.71 | 1.29 | 0.94 |
| 2002 | 16 | 27 | 16 | 10 | 6 | 14 | 1.60 | 4.50 | 1.14 |
| 2003 | 23 | 19 | 21 | 9 | 8 | 12 | 2.56 | 2.38 | 1.75 |
| 2004 | 24 | 7 | 29 | 2 | 3 | 10 | 12.00 | 2.33 | 2.90 |
| 2005 | 19 | 12 | 24 | 8 | 4 | 7 | 2.38 | 3.00 | 3.43 |
| 2006 | 13 | 20 | 21 | 2 | 1 | 7 | 6.50 | 20.00 | 3.00 |
| 2007 | 12 | 17 | 25 | 3 | 1 | 5 | 4.00 | 17.00 | 5.00 |
| 2008 | 10 | 8 | 11 | 17 | 9 | 29 | 0.59 | 0.89 | 0.38 |
| 2009 | 3 | 11 | 3 | 18 | 17 | 25 | 0.17 | 0.65 | 0.12 |
| 2010 | 15 | 15 | 22 | 9 | 9 | 15 | 1.67 | 1.67 | 1.47 |

*Sources*: Author's computations

*Notes*: "UP" and "DN" denote "upgrades" and "downgrades," respectively. NA denotes not applicable. The counting of Fitch rating changes starts on 1 January 2001, i.e., the first civil year after Fitch IBCA merged with Duff and Phelps

Not surprisingly, the upgrade-to-downgrade ratios are correlated to business cycles. In times of sovereign debt crisis, currency crisis, or economic recession (e.g., 1992, 1997–1998, 2001, and 2008–2009), these ratios are lower than unity; however, they soar during boom periods (e.g., 1995–1996, 2004–2007). These findings support the view that sovereign ratings have procyclical effects (see Ferri et al. 1999; Reisen and von Maltzan 1999).

Any examination of the *frequency* of rating changes must be complemented with one of the *magnitude* of rating changes – that is, taking into account the "upward notches" and "downward notches" in lieu of rating change events. Table 8.11 reveals that multi-notch upgrades and downgrades do exist, but account for a small portion of all rating changes.

The magnitude of rating changes is summarized in Table 8.12. One-notch rating changes account for the vast majority of all rating changes: 85.4, 83.1, and 72.6% for S&P, Fitch, and Moody's, respectively. The percentage of two-notch rating changes is quite low, except for Moody's: 7.9 and 9.5% for S&P and Fitch (respectively) vs. 21.6% for Moody's. Three-notch rating changes account for 2.3, 3.7, and 4.9% of all changes for S&P, Fitch, and Moody's, respectively. More-than-three-notch rating changes are less frequent at Moody's (0.9%) than at Fitch and S&P (3.7 and 4.5%). Overall, then, the average upgrades and downgrades for the three agencies turn out to be quite similar (see the last two lines of Table 8.12), as the numerous two-notch rating changes by Moody's are counterbalanced by the more-than-three-notch rating changes by Fitch and S&P.

These results must actually be interpreted in light of the occurrence of several multi-notch rating changes stemming from the downgrade to (and removal from) the default category. When defaulting sovereigns are dropped from the three samples,[10] the proportion of more-than-two-notch rating changes decreases dramatically for Fitch and S&P. The proportion of one-notch rating changes then reaches 91.4 and 93.5% for Fitch and S&P vs. 74.9% for Moody's. These results show that multi-notch upgrades and downgrades are much more common for Moody's than for Fitch and S&P. This discrepancy in rating practices is even more striking when migration rates are examined.

### 8.3.2 Rating Migration Matrices

Table 8.13 displays the annual frequency of rating changes. Note that the ratings assigned by Moody's are more stable than those assigned by Fitch and S&P. Also the proportion of one-notch rating changes reaches 17.9 and 17.8% for

---

[10]Defaulting countries are Argentina, the Dominican Republic, Ecuador, Indonesia, Jamaica, Russia, Ukraine, Uruguay, and Venezuela for the three agencies, plus: Moldova and the Seychelles for Fitch; Belize, Moldova, Pakistan, and Paraguay for Moody's; and Belize, Grenada, Pakistan, Paraguay, and the Seychelles for S&P.

**Table 8.11** Distribution of Fitch, Moody's, and S&P rating changes in notches, 1 January 1987 to 1 January 2011

| | Fitch UP | Moody's UP | S&P UP | Fitch DN | Moody's DN | S&P DN | Fitch UP-to-DN ratio | Moody's UP-to-DN ratio | S&P UP-to-DN ratio |
|---|---|---|---|---|---|---|---|---|---|
| 1987 | NA | 0 | 0 | NA | 7 | 0 | NA | 0.00 | NA |
| 1988 | NA | 0 | 0 | NA | 0 | 0 | NA | NA | NA |
| 1989 | NA | 0 | 1 | NA | 5 | 3 | NA | 0.00 | 0.33 |
| 1990 | NA | 3 | 0 | NA | 5 | 2 | NA | 0.60 | 0.00 |
| 1991 | NA | 2 | 7 | NA | 6 | 3 | NA | 0.33 | 2.33 |
| 1992 | NA | 2 | 0 | NA | 3 | 2 | NA | 0.67 | 0.00 |
| 1993 | NA | 2 | 4 | NA | 2 | 4 | NA | 1.00 | 1.00 |
| 1994 | NA | 7 | 4 | NA | 8 | 6 | NA | 0.88 | 0.67 |
| 1995 | NA | 6 | 13 | NA | 3 | 1 | NA | 2.00 | 13.00 |
| 1996 | NA | 11 | 9 | NA | 1 | 2 | NA | 11.00 | 4.50 |
| 1997 | NA | 14 | 7 | NA | 14 | 16 | NA | 1.00 | 0.44 |
| 1998 | NA | 7 | 7 | NA | 34 | 32 | NA | 0.21 | 0.22 |
| 1999 | NA | 10 | 20 | NA | 6 | 15 | NA | 1.67 | 1.33 |
| 2000 | NA | 12 | 25 | NA | 4 | 9 | NA | 3.00 | 2.78 |
| 2001 | 12 | 13 | 17 | 25 | 8 | 20 | 0.48 | 1.63 | 0.85 |
| 2002 | 17 | 49 | 19 | 14 | 11 | 18 | 1.21 | 4.45 | 1.06 |
| 2003 | 36 | 30 | 26 | 13 | 12 | 20 | 2.77 | 2.50 | 1.30 |
| 2004 | 26 | 8 | 33 | 3 | 4 | 18 | 8.67 | 2.00 | 1.83 |
| 2005 | 25 | 15 | 42 | 12 | 7 | 13 | 2.08 | 2.14 | 3.23 |
| 2006 | 13 | 23 | 22 | 2 | 1 | 7 | 6.50 | 23.00 | 3.14 |
| 2007 | 13 | 18 | 31 | 4 | 1 | 5 | 3.25 | 18.00 | 6.20 |
| 2008 | 10 | 9 | 11 | 24 | 15 | 38 | 0.42 | 0.60 | 0.29 |
| 2009 | 7 | 11 | 6 | 22 | 22 | 26 | 0.32 | 0.50 | 0.23 |
| 2010 | 27 | 17 | 26 | 15 | 18 | 21 | 1.80 | 0.94 | 1.24 |

*Sources*: Author's computations

*Notes*: UP and DN denote upgrades and downgrades, respectively. NA denotes not applicable. The counting of Fitch rating changes starts on 1 January 2001, i.e., the first civil year after Fitch IBCA merged with Duff and Phelps

8.3 Stability of Sovereign Ratings

**Table 8.12** Magnitude of Fitch, Moody's, and S&P rating changes, 1 January 1987 to 1 January 2011

| | All ratings | | | Nondefaulting ratings only | | |
|---|---|---|---|---|---|---|
| | Fitch | Moody's | S&P | Fitch | Moody's | S&P |
| UP by more than three notches (%) | 2.48 | 0.00 | 3.18 | 0.00 | 0.00 | 0.00 |
| UP by three notches (%) | 0.00 | 2.31 | 0.21 | 0.00 | 2.35 | 0.31 |
| UP by two notches (%) | 4.55 | 12.10 | 1.91 | 3.45 | 11.76 | 1.86 |
| UP by one notch (%) | 53.72 | 46.40 | 49.89 | 62.07 | 53.73 | 59.13 |
| DN by more than three notches (%) | 1.24 | 0.86 | 1.27 | 0.00 | 0.78 | 0.31 |
| DN by three notches (%) | 3.72 | 2.59 | 2.12 | 1.72 | 1.96 | 0.93 |
| DN by two notches (%) | 4.96 | 9.51 | 5.94 | 3.45 | 8.24 | 3.10 |
| DN by one notch (%) | 29.34 | 26.22 | 35.46 | 29.31 | 21.18 | 34.37 |
| *All rating changes (%)* | *100.00* | *100.00* | *100.00* | *100.00* | *100.00* | *100.00* |
| Average UP (notches) | 1.27 | 1.27 | 1.27 | 1.05 | 1.24 | 1.04 |
| Average DN (notches) | 1.41 | 1.45 | 1.33 | 1.20 | 1.46 | 1.15 |

*Sources*: Author's computations
*Notes*: UP and DN denote upgrades and downgrades, respectively. The period under consideration for Fitch rating changes is 1 January 2001 to 1 January 2011

**Table 8.13** Average annual frequency of Fitch, Moody's, and S&P rating changes, 1 January 1987 to 1 January 2011

| | Fitch | Moody's | S&P |
|---|---|---|---|
| No rating change (%) | 77.58 | 82.34 | 77.69 |
| UP by more than three notches (%) | 0.33 | 0.00 | 0.48 |
| UP by three notches (%) | 0.00 | 0.58 | 0.12 |
| UP by two notches (%) | 1.55 | 2.25 | 1.19 |
| UP by one notch (%) | 13.54 | 9.06 | 12.55 |
| DN by more than three notches (%) | 0.67 | 0.69 | 0.83 |
| DN by three notches (%) | 0.55 | 0.52 | 0.48 |
| DN by two notches (%) | 1.55 | 1.38 | 1.31 |
| DN by one notch (%) | 4.22 | 3.17 | 5.35 |
| *Total (%)* | *100.00* | *100.00* | *100.00* |

*Sources*: Author's computations
*Notes*: UP and DN denote upgrades and downgrades, respectively. The period under consideration for Fitch rating changes is 1 January 2001 to 1 January 2011

S&P and Fitch (respectively) vs. 12.2% for Moody's. These two findings confirm that Moody's rating changes are less frequent, but are of greater magnitude. This idiosyncratic rating policy can be checked through analysis of rating migration matrices.

Rating migration matrices provide a picture of changes in credit quality over time for the different rating categories. Tables 8.14–8.16 show average annual rating migration rates for Fitch, Moody's, and S&P, respectively.

Not surprisingly, the entire AAA and AA rating categories are much more stable than lower categories for the three CRAs. The stability of the AAA-rated sovereigns is impressive. Iceland was the only AAA-rated country to be massively downgraded

**Table 8.14** Average 1-year rating migration rates for Fitch, 1 January 2001 to 1 January 2011

|      | AAA  | AA+  | AA   | AA−  | A+   | A    | A−   | BBB+ | BBB  | BBB− | BB+  | BB   | BB−  | B+   | B    | B−   | CCC+ | CCC  | CCC− | CC   | C    | D     | WR   |
|------|------|------|------|------|------|------|------|------|------|------|------|------|------|------|------|------|------|------|------|------|------|-------|------|
| AAA  | **98.6** | 0.7  | 0.0  | 0.7  | 0.0  | 0.0  | 0.0  | 0.0  | 0.0  | 0.0  | 0.0  | 0.0  | 0.0  | 0.0  | 0.0  | 0.0  | 0.0  | 0.0  | 0.0  | 0.0  | 0.0  | 0.0   | 0.0  |
| AA+  | 13.5 | **83.8** | 2.7  | 0.0  | 0.0  | 0.0  | 0.0  | 0.0  | 0.0  | 0.0  | 0.0  | 0.0  | 0.0  | 0.0  | 0.0  | 0.0  | 0.0  | 0.0  | 0.0  | 0.0  | 0.0  | 0.0   | 0.0  |
| AA   | 0.0  | 11.7 | **83.3** | 1.7  | 1.7  | 1.7  | 0.0  | 0.0  | 0.0  | 0.0  | 0.0  | 0.0  | 0.0  | 0.0  | 0.0  | 0.0  | 0.0  | 0.0  | 0.0  | 0.0  | 0.0  | 0.0   | 0.0  |
| AA−  | 0.0  | 0.0  | 14.3 | **80.0** | 2.9  | 0.0  | 0.0  | 2.9  | 0.0  | 0.0  | 0.0  | 0.0  | 0.0  | 0.0  | 0.0  | 0.0  | 0.0  | 0.0  | 0.0  | 0.0  | 0.0  | 0.0   | 0.0  |
| A+   | 0.0  | 0.0  | 0.0  | 13.9 | **80.6** | 2.8  | 0.0  | 0.0  | 0.0  | 2.8  | 0.0  | 0.0  | 0.0  | 0.0  | 0.0  | 0.0  | 0.0  | 0.0  | 0.0  | 0.0  | 0.0  | 0.0   | 0.0  |
| A    | 0.0  | 0.0  | 0.0  | 0.0  | 18.0 | **76.0** | 2.0  | 4.0  | 0.0  | 0.0  | 0.0  | 0.0  | 0.0  | 0.0  | 0.0  | 0.0  | 0.0  | 0.0  | 0.0  | 0.0  | 0.0  | 0.0   | 0.0  |
| A−   | 0.0  | 0.0  | 0.0  | 0.0  | 0.0  | 18.4 | **75.5** | 6.1  | 0.0  | 0.0  | 0.0  | 0.0  | 0.0  | 0.0  | 0.0  | 0.0  | 0.0  | 0.0  | 0.0  | 0.0  | 0.0  | 0.0   | 0.0  |
| BBB+ | 0.0  | 0.0  | 0.0  | 0.0  | 0.0  | 5.3  | 13.2 | **63.2** | 13.2 | 5.3  | 0.0  | 0.0  | 0.0  | 0.0  | 0.0  | 0.0  | 0.0  | 0.0  | 0.0  | 0.0  | 0.0  | 0.0   | 0.0  |
| BBB  | 0.0  | 0.0  | 0.0  | 0.0  | 0.0  | 0.0  | 6.3  | 12.5 | **75.0** | 4.2  | 2.1  | 0.0  | 0.0  | 0.0  | 0.0  | 0.0  | 0.0  | 0.0  | 0.0  | 0.0  | 0.0  | 0.0   | 0.0  |
| BBB− | 0.0  | 0.0  | 0.0  | 0.0  | 0.0  | 0.0  | 0.0  | 0.0  | 20.4 | **72.2** | 5.6  | 0.0  | 0.0  | 0.0  | 1.9  | 0.0  | 0.0  | 0.0  | 0.0  | 0.0  | 0.0  | 0.0   | 0.0  |
| BB+  | 0.0  | 0.0  | 0.0  | 0.0  | 0.0  | 0.0  | 0.0  | 0.0  | 0.0  | 18.2 | **75.8** | 6.1  | 0.0  | 0.0  | 0.0  | 0.0  | 0.0  | 0.0  | 0.0  | 0.0  | 0.0  | 0.0   | 0.0  |
| BB   | 0.0  | 0.0  | 0.0  | 0.0  | 0.0  | 0.0  | 0.0  | 0.0  | 0.0  | 2.4  | 22.0 | **68.3** | 4.9  | 0.0  | 0.0  | 0.0  | 0.0  | 0.0  | 0.0  | 0.0  | 0.0  | 2.4   | 0.0  |
| BB−  | 0.0  | 0.0  | 0.0  | 0.0  | 0.0  | 0.0  | 0.0  | 0.0  | 0.0  | 0.0  | 2.9  | 11.8 | **70.6** | 8.8  | 4.4  | 1.5  | 0.0  | 0.0  | 0.0  | 0.0  | 0.0  | 0.0   | 0.0  |
| B+   | 0.0  | 0.0  | 0.0  | 0.0  | 0.0  | 0.0  | 0.0  | 0.0  | 0.0  | 0.0  | 0.0  | 1.9  | 19.2 | **67.3** | 5.8  | 1.9  | 0.0  | 0.0  | 0.0  | 0.0  | 0.0  | 0.0   | 3.8  |
| B    | 0.0  | 0.0  | 0.0  | 0.0  | 0.0  | 0.0  | 0.0  | 0.0  | 0.0  | 0.0  | 0.0  | 0.0  | 1.8  | 17.5 | **71.9** | 5.3  | 1.8  | 1.8  | 0.0  | 0.0  | 0.0  | 0.0   | 0.0  |
| B−   | 0.0  | 0.0  | 0.0  | 0.0  | 0.0  | 0.0  | 0.0  | 0.0  | 0.0  | 0.0  | 0.0  | 0.0  | 0.0  | 2.1  | 19.1 | **63.8** | 0.0  | 4.3  | 2.1  | 2.1  | 0.0  | 0.0   | 6.4  |
| CCC+ | 0.0  | 0.0  | 0.0  | 0.0  | 0.0  | 0.0  | 0.0  | 0.0  | 0.0  | 0.0  | 0.0  | 0.0  | 0.0  | 0.0  | 0.0  | 40.0 | **40.0** | 20.0 | 0.0  | 0.0  | 0.0  | 0.0   | 0.0  |
| CCC  | 0.0  | 0.0  | 0.0  | 0.0  | 0.0  | 0.0  | 0.0  | 0.0  | 0.0  | 0.0  | 0.0  | 0.0  | 0.0  | 0.0  | 0.0  | 42.9 | 0.0  | **28.6** | 0.0  | 0.0  | 0.0  | 14.3  | 14.3 |
| CCC− | 0.0  | 0.0  | 0.0  | 0.0  | 0.0  | 0.0  | 0.0  | 0.0  | 0.0  | 0.0  | 0.0  | 0.0  | 0.0  | 0.0  | 0.0  | 0.0  | 0.0  | 0.0  | **75.0** | 0.0  | 0.0  | 0.0   | 25.0 |
| CC   | 0.0  | 0.0  | 0.0  | 0.0  | 0.0  | 0.0  | 0.0  | 0.0  | 0.0  | 0.0  | 0.0  | 0.0  | 0.0  | 0.0  | 0.0  | 0.0  | 0.0  | 0.0  | 0.0  | **0.0** | 0.0  | 0.0   | 0.0  |
| C    | 0.0  | 0.0  | 0.0  | 0.0  | 0.0  | 0.0  | 0.0  | 0.0  | 0.0  | 0.0  | 0.0  | 0.0  | 0.0  | 0.0  | 0.0  | 0.0  | 0.0  | 0.0  | 0.0  | 0.0  | **0.0** | 100.0 | 0.0  |
| D    | 0.0  | 0.0  | 0.0  | 0.0  | 0.0  | 0.0  | 0.0  | 0.0  | 0.0  | 0.0  | 0.0  | 0.0  | 0.0  | 0.0  | 9.1  | 9.1  | 0.0  | 9.1  | 0.0  | 0.0  | 0.0  | **72.7** | 0.0  |

*Sources*: Author's computations based on http://www.fitchratings.com

*Note*: WR denotes Withdrawn Rating

8.3 Stability of Sovereign Ratings

**Table 8.15** Average 1-year rating migration rates for Moody's, 1 January 1987 to 1 January 2011

|      | Aaa  | Aa1  | Aa2  | Aa3  | A1   | A2   | A3   | Baa1 | Baa2 | Baa3 | Ba1  | Ba2  | Ba3  | B1   | B2   | B3   | Caa1 | Caa2 | Caa3 | Ca   | C    | WR  |
|------|------|------|------|------|------|------|------|------|------|------|------|------|------|------|------|------|------|------|------|------|------|-----|
| Aaa  | 97.1 | 2.3  | 0.3  | 0.0  | 0.0  | 0.0  | 0.0  | 0.3  | 0.0  | 0.0  | 0.0  | 0.0  | 0.0  | 0.0  | 0.0  | 0.0  | 0.0  | 0.0  | 0.0  | 0.0  | 0.0  | 0.0 |
| Aa1  | 7.8  | 83.3 | 5.9  | 1.0  | 0.0  | 0.0  | 0.0  | 1.0  | 0.0  | 0.0  | 0.0  | 0.0  | 0.0  | 0.0  | 0.0  | 0.0  | 0.0  | 0.0  | 0.0  | 0.0  | 0.0  | 1.0 |
| Aa2  | 3.4  | 8.0  | 86.4 | 1.1  | 1.1  | 0.0  | 0.0  | 0.0  | 0.0  | 0.0  | 0.0  | 0.0  | 0.0  | 0.0  | 0.0  | 0.0  | 0.0  | 0.0  | 0.0  | 0.0  | 0.0  | 0.0 |
| Aa3  | 1.3  | 0.0  | 14.1 | 83.3 | 1.3  | 0.0  | 0.0  | 0.0  | 0.0  | 0.0  | 0.0  | 0.0  | 0.0  | 0.0  | 0.0  | 0.0  | 0.0  | 0.0  | 0.0  | 0.0  | 0.0  | 0.0 |
| A1   | 0.0  | 0.0  | 0.0  | 14.3 | 80.5 | 3.9  | 0.0  | 0.0  | 0.0  | 0.0  | 1.3  | 0.0  | 0.0  | 0.0  | 0.0  | 0.0  | 0.0  | 0.0  | 0.0  | 0.0  | 0.0  | 0.0 |
| A2   | 0.0  | 0.0  | 0.0  | 1.8  | 12.5 | 76.8 | 4.5  | 1.8  | 0.0  | 0.9  | 1.8  | 0.0  | 0.0  | 0.0  | 0.0  | 0.0  | 0.0  | 0.0  | 0.0  | 0.0  | 0.0  | 0.0 |
| A3   | 0.0  | 0.0  | 0.0  | 0.0  | 3.4  | 12.6 | 80.5 | 2.3  | 0.0  | 1.1  | 0.0  | 0.0  | 0.0  | 0.0  | 0.0  | 0.0  | 0.0  | 0.0  | 0.0  | 0.0  | 0.0  | 0.0 |
| Baa1 | 0.0  | 0.0  | 0.0  | 0.0  | 3.4  | 5.7  | 9.1  | 77.3 | 0.0  | 3.4  | 0.0  | 1.1  | 0.0  | 0.0  | 0.0  | 0.0  | 0.0  | 0.0  | 0.0  | 0.0  | 0.0  | 0.0 |
| Baa2 | 0.0  | 0.0  | 0.0  | 0.0  | 0.0  | 1.3  | 3.9  | 11.8 | 80.3 | 1.3  | 1.3  | 0.0  | 0.0  | 0.0  | 0.0  | 0.0  | 0.0  | 0.0  | 0.0  | 0.0  | 0.0  | 0.0 |
| Baa3 | 0.0  | 0.0  | 0.0  | 0.0  | 0.0  | 0.0  | 0.9  | 3.4  | 8.6  | 81.0 | 1.7  | 1.7  | 0.9  | 0.0  | 0.0  | 0.0  | 0.0  | 0.0  | 0.0  | 0.0  | 0.0  | 0.0 |
| Ba1  | 0.0  | 0.0  | 0.0  | 0.0  | 0.0  | 0.0  | 0.0  | 0.9  | 1.7  | 12.8 | 81.2 | 1.7  | 0.9  | 0.9  | 0.0  | 0.9  | 0.0  | 0.0  | 0.0  | 0.0  | 0.0  | 0.0 |
| Ba2  | 0.0  | 0.0  | 0.0  | 0.0  | 0.0  | 0.0  | 0.0  | 0.0  | 0.0  | 3.7  | 14.8 | 71.6 | 2.5  | 2.5  | 3.7  | 1.2  | 0.0  | 0.0  | 0.0  | 0.0  | 0.0  | 0.0 |
| Ba3  | 0.0  | 0.0  | 0.0  | 0.0  | 0.0  | 0.0  | 0.0  | 0.0  | 0.0  | 0.0  | 4.4  | 13.2 | 69.1 | 8.8  | 2.9  | 1.5  | 0.0  | 0.0  | 0.0  | 0.0  | 0.0  | 0.0 |
| B1   | 0.0  | 0.0  | 0.0  | 0.0  | 0.0  | 0.0  | 0.0  | 0.0  | 0.0  | 0.0  | 0.0  | 3.1  | 6.1  | 79.6 | 6.1  | 3.1  | 1.0  | 0.0  | 0.0  | 1.0  | 0.0  | 0.0 |
| B2   | 0.0  | 0.0  | 0.0  | 0.0  | 0.0  | 0.0  | 0.0  | 0.0  | 0.0  | 2.0  | 0.0  | 0.0  | 2.0  | 10.2 | 75.5 | 6.1  | 3.1  | 0.0  | 1.0  | 0.0  | 0.0  | 2.0 |
| B3   | 0.0  | 0.0  | 0.0  | 0.0  | 0.0  | 0.0  | 0.0  | 0.0  | 0.0  | 2.0  | 0.0  | 0.0  | 6.0  | 16.0 | 68.0 | 6.0  | 2.0  | 0.0  | 0.0  | 0.0  | 0.0 |
| Caa1 | 0.0  | 0.0  | 0.0  | 0.0  | 0.0  | 0.0  | 0.0  | 0.0  | 0.0  | 0.0  | 0.0  | 0.0  | 0.0  | 0.0  | 4.4  | 13.3 | 75.6 | 2.2  | 0.0  | 2.2  | 0.0  | 2.2 |
| Caa2 | 0.0  | 0.0  | 0.0  | 0.0  | 0.0  | 0.0  | 0.0  | 0.0  | 0.0  | 0.0  | 0.0  | 0.0  | 0.0  | 0.0  | 0.0  | 0.0  | 16.7 | 66.7 | 0.0  | 16.7 | 0.0  | 0.0 |
| Caa3 | 0.0  | 0.0  | 0.0  | 0.0  | 0.0  | 0.0  | 0.0  | 0.0  | 0.0  | 0.0  | 0.0  | 0.0  | 0.0  | 0.0  | 0.0  | 0.0  | 33.3 | 0.0  | 66.7 | 0.0  | 0.0  | 0.0 |
| Ca   | 0.0  | 0.0  | 0.0  | 0.0  | 0.0  | 0.0  | 0.0  | 0.0  | 0.0  | 0.0  | 0.0  | 0.0  | 0.0  | 0.0  | 0.0  | 0.0  | 50.0 | 0.0  | 25.0 | 25.0 | 0.0  | 0.0 |
| C    | 0.0  | 0.0  | 0.0  | 0.0  | 0.0  | 0.0  | 0.0  | 0.0  | 0.0  | 0.0  | 0.0  | 0.0  | 0.0  | 0.0  | 0.0  | 0.0  | 0.0  | 0.0  | 0.0  | 0.0  | **0.0**  | 0.0 |

*Sources*: Author's computations based on http://www.moodys.com
*Note*: WR denotes Withdrawn Rating

**Table 8.16** Average 1-year rating migration rates for S&P, 1 January 1987 to 1 January 2011

|  | AAA | AA+ | AA | AA- | A+ | A | A- | BBB+ | BBB | BBB- | BB+ | BB | BB- | B+ | B | B- | CCC+ | CCC | CCC- | CC | D | WR |
|---|---|---|---|---|---|---|---|---|---|---|---|---|---|---|---|---|---|---|---|---|---|---|
| AAA | **98.5** | 1.2 | 0.3 | 0.0 | 0.0 | 0.0 | 0.0 | 0.0 | 0.0 | 0.0 | 0.0 | 0.0 | 0.0 | 0.0 | 0.0 | 0.0 | 0.0 | 0.0 | 0.0 | 0.0 | 0.0 | 0.0 |
| AA+ | 8.3 | **87.0** | 3.7 | 0.9 | 0.0 | 0.0 | 0.0 | 0.0 | 0.0 | 0.0 | 0.0 | 0.0 | 0.0 | 0.0 | 0.0 | 0.0 | 0.0 | 0.0 | 0.0 | 0.0 | 0.0 | 0.0 |
| AA | 0.0 | 9.5 | **83.2** | 6.3 | 0.0 | 1.1 | 0.0 | 0.0 | 0.0 | 0.0 | 0.0 | 0.0 | 0.0 | 0.0 | 0.0 | 0.0 | 0.0 | 0.0 | 0.0 | 0.0 | 0.0 | 0.0 |
| AA- | 0.0 | 0.0 | 15.8 | **73.7** | 8.8 | 0.0 | 0.0 | 0.0 | 0.0 | 0.0 | 1.8 | 0.0 | 0.0 | 0.0 | 0.0 | 0.0 | 0.0 | 0.0 | 0.0 | 0.0 | 0.0 | 0.0 |
| A+ | 0.0 | 0.0 | 0.0 | 16.1 | **67.7** | 12.9 | 1.6 | 0.0 | 0.0 | 1.6 | 0.0 | 0.0 | 0.0 | 0.0 | 0.0 | 0.0 | 0.0 | 0.0 | 0.0 | 0.0 | 0.0 | 0.0 |
| A | 0.0 | 0.0 | 0.0 | 0.8 | 11.7 | **82.5** | 1.7 | 1.7 | 0.8 | 0.8 | 0.0 | 0.0 | 0.0 | 0.0 | 0.0 | 0.0 | 0.0 | 0.0 | 0.0 | 0.0 | 0.0 | 0.0 |
| A- | 0.0 | 0.0 | 0.0 | 0.0 | 1.1 | 16.3 | **78.3** | 4.3 | 0.0 | 0.0 | 0.0 | 0.0 | 0.0 | 0.0 | 0.0 | 0.0 | 0.0 | 0.0 | 0.0 | 0.0 | 0.0 | 0.0 |
| BBB+ | 0.0 | 0.0 | 0.0 | 0.0 | 0.0 | 1.8 | 21.4 | **60.7** | 12.5 | 1.8 | 1.8 | 0.0 | 0.0 | 0.0 | 0.0 | 0.0 | 0.0 | 0.0 | 0.0 | 0.0 | 0.0 | 0.0 |
| BBB | 0.0 | 0.0 | 0.0 | 0.0 | 0.0 | 0.0 | 3.8 | 21.8 | **62.8** | 7.7 | 2.6 | 0.0 | 0.0 | 1.3 | 0.0 | 0.0 | 0.0 | 0.0 | 0.0 | 0.0 | 0.0 | 0.0 |
| BBB- | 0.0 | 0.0 | 0.0 | 0.0 | 0.0 | 0.0 | 0.0 | 1.0 | 16.7 | **76.5** | 3.9 | 1.0 | 0.0 | 0.0 | 0.0 | 1.0 | 0.0 | 0.0 | 0.0 | 0.0 | 0.0 | 0.0 |
| BB+ | 0.0 | 0.0 | 0.0 | 0.0 | 0.0 | 0.0 | 0.0 | 0.0 | 2.2 | 16.5 | **71.4** | 8.8 | 0.0 | 0.0 | 0.0 | 0.0 | 1.1 | 0.0 | 0.0 | 0.0 | 0.0 | 0.0 |
| BB | 0.0 | 0.0 | 0.0 | 0.0 | 0.0 | 0.0 | 0.0 | 0.0 | 0.0 | 1.0 | 16.2 | **74.3** | 6.7 | 1.9 | 0.0 | 0.0 | 0.0 | 0.0 | 0.0 | 0.0 | 0.0 | 0.0 |
| BB- | 0.0 | 0.0 | 0.0 | 0.0 | 0.0 | 0.0 | 0.0 | 0.0 | 0.0 | 0.0 | 1.1 | 14.9 | **69.1** | 7.4 | 2.1 | 1.1 | 1.1 | 1.1 | 1.1 | 0.0 | 2.1 | 0.0 |
| B+ | 0.0 | 0.0 | 0.0 | 0.0 | 0.0 | 0.0 | 0.0 | 0.0 | 0.0 | 0.0 | 0.9 | 2.8 | 13.8 | **65.1** | 12.8 | 2.8 | 0.0 | 0.0 | 0.0 | 0.9 | 0.0 | 0.0 |
| B | 0.0 | 0.0 | 0.0 | 0.0 | 0.0 | 0.0 | 0.0 | 0.0 | 0.0 | 0.0 | 0.0 | 0.0 | 0.0 | 21.2 | **68.7** | 3.0 | 2.0 | 2.0 | 0.0 | 0.0 | 1.0 | 2.0 |
| B- | 0.0 | 0.0 | 0.0 | 0.0 | 0.0 | 0.0 | 0.0 | 0.0 | 0.0 | 0.0 | 0.0 | 5.6 | 20.4 | 5.6 | **64.8** | 1.9 | 1.9 | 0.0 | 1.9 | 0.0 | 3.7 | 0.0 |
| CCC+ | 0.0 | 0.0 | 0.0 | 0.0 | 0.0 | 0.0 | 0.0 | 0.0 | 0.0 | 0.0 | 0.0 | 0.0 | 7.7 | 7.7 | 7.7 | 38.5 | **46.2** | 0.0 | 0.0 | 0.0 | 0.0 | 0.0 |
| CCC | 0.0 | 0.0 | 0.0 | 0.0 | 0.0 | 0.0 | 0.0 | 0.0 | 0.0 | 0.0 | 0.0 | 0.0 | 0.0 | 0.0 | 0.0 | 40.0 | 20.0 | **20.0** | 0.0 | 20.0 | 0.0 | 0.0 |
| CCC- | 0.0 | 0.0 | 0.0 | 0.0 | 0.0 | 0.0 | 0.0 | 0.0 | 0.0 | 0.0 | 0.0 | 0.0 | 0.0 | 0.0 | 0.0 | 0.0 | 0.0 | 0.0 | **0.0** | 0.0 | 100.0 | 0.0 |
| CC | 0.0 | 0.0 | 0.0 | 0.0 | 0.0 | 0.0 | 0.0 | 0.0 | 0.0 | 0.0 | 0.0 | 0.0 | 50.0 | 0.0 | 50.0 | 50.0 | 0.0 | 0.0 | 0.0 | **0.0** | 0.0 | 0.0 |
| SD | 0.0 | 0.0 | 0.0 | 0.0 | 0.0 | 0.0 | 0.0 | 0.0 | 0.0 | 0.0 | 0.0 | 0.0 | 0.0 | 0.0 | 10.0 | 40.0 | 10.0 | 0.0 | 0.0 | 0.0 | **30.0** | 10.0 |

*Sources*: Author's computations based on http://www.standardandpoors.com

*Note*: WR denotes Withdrawn Rating

within a single year (one one-notch downgrade and two three-notch downgrades by Moody's in 2008). During the sample period, Iceland was never so highly rated by Fitch and S&P, as it was previously downgraded by both CRAs. Few AA-rated countries experience a more-than-three-notch worsening of their credit rating: only South Korea in 1998 (S&P) and Ireland in 2010 (Fitch and Moody's). Other investment-grade rating categories are less stable in part because they gather sovereign issuers with various economic profiles. Emerging countries in Eastern Europe, Asia, and the Middle East were upgraded from the BBB–A categories to the A–AA categories in the 2000s, whereas Eastern Asian countries in 1997–1998 as well as peripheral European countries (e.g., Baltic countries, Greece, Iceland, Ireland, and Portugal) in 2007–2010 followed the opposite course.

The higher proportion of rating changes among speculative-grade countries reflects the greater sensitivity of low-rated than investment-grade countries to business cycles. It is also consistent with Sect. 8.1, which shows that speculative-grade issuers with a stable outlook are more likely to be upgraded or downgraded than are investment-grade issuers with a stable outlook.

It is worth remarking that all defaulting issuers were rated in the speculative-grade category as of 1 January of the default year, which explains the higher proportion of multi-notch rating changes in the bottom part of Tables 8.14–8.16. Multi-notch downgrades hit countries that subsequently defaulted, whereas multi-notch upgrades involved sovereign issuers that recovered from default.

Migration rates covering more than 1 year are regularly published by rating agencies, but they can be deceptive because some ratings are upgraded and then downgraded (or vice versa) within 2–3 years, thereby biasing the percentages of rating changes downward. Actually, using migration rates underscore the relevance of examining rating reversals to measure rating consistency and stability over time.

### 8.3.3 Rating Reversals

Rating reversals are defined as the cases of CRAs assigning both upward and downward rating changes within a 12-month period. Tables 8.17–8.19 exhibit the list of rating reversals for Fitch, Moody's, and S&P, respectively.

The number of rating reversals varies across CRAs: it ranges from five for Moody's to nine for Fitch and 24 for S&P. This suggests that the frequency of rating reversals is positively correlated with the frequency of rating changes, as Moody's ratings are more stable and less likely to be reversed than Fitch and S&P ratings.

Twenty of the 38 rating reversals stem from the downgrade to (and then removal from) the default category; these reversals are italicized in the three tables. If these specific rating reversals are dropped, then all the remaining observations (except Kazakhstan and Estonia) concern speculative-grade issuers. This fact is consistent with previous results showing that speculative-grade ratings are more volatile than investment-grade ones. Of more relevance is that issuers whose ratings were reversed are countries that defaulted shortly before or after the reversal.

**Table 8.17** Fitch rating reversals, 1 January 2001 to 1 January 2011

| Country | Date | Rating action |
|---|---|---|
| *Argentina* | 14 January 2005 | Downgrade to D from DDD |
| | 3 June 2005 | Upgrade to DDD from D |
| *Dominican Republic* | 5 May 2005 | Downgrade to DDD from C |
| | 19 July 2005 | Upgrade to B– from DDD |
| *Ecuador* | 15 December 2008 | Downgrade to RD from CCC |
| | 4 September 2009 | Upgrade to CCC from RD |
| *Jamaica* | 3 February 2010 | Downgrade to RD from CCC |
| | 3 February 2010 | Upgrade to CCC from RD |
| *Moldova* | 28 June 2002 | Downgrade to DD from CC |
| | 4 February 2003 | Upgrade to B– from DD |
| Turkey | 25 March 2003 | Downgrade to B– from B |
| | 25 September 2003 | Upgrade to B from B– |
| Ukraine | 12 November 2009 | Downgrade to B– from B |
| | 6 July 2010 | Upgrade to B from B– |
| *Uruguay* | 16 May 2003 | Downgrade to DDD from C |
| | 17 June 2003 | Upgrade to B– from DDD |
| Venezuela | 10 January 2003 | Downgrade to CCC+ from B |
| | 23 June 2003 | Upgrade to B– from CCC+ |

*Sources*: Author's classification based on http://www.fitchratings.com

**Table 8.18** Moody's rating reversals, 1 January 1987 to 1 January 2011

| Country | Date | Rating action |
|---|---|---|
| Ecuador | 20 March 2008 | Upgrade to B3 from Caa2 |
| | 14 November 2008 | Downgrade to Caa1 from B3 |
| *Ecuador* | 16 December 2008 | Downgrade to Ca from Caa1 |
| | 24 September 2009 | Upgrade to Caa3 from Ca |
| Jamaica | 18 November 2009 | Downgrade to Caa1 from B2 |
| | 2 March 2010 | Upgrade to B3 from Caa1 |
| Moldova | 11 July 2002 | Downgrade to Ca from Caa1 |
| | 6 May 2003 | Upgrade to Caa1 from Ca |
| Peru | 19 September 2000 | Downgrade to B1 from Ba3 |
| | 5 October 2000 | Upgrade to Ba3 from B1 |

*Sources*: Author's classification based on http://www.moodys.com

The frequency of rating reversals would be even lower if agencies assigned more conservative and stable ratings to serial defaulters. For instance, it would have been more prudent to maintain Ecuador's rating in the CCC category than to change it eight times, as S&P did between 2000 (the year of Ecuador's recovery from its 1999 default) and 2008 (the year of its subsequent default).

This section has established that about 80% of sovereign ratings remain unchanged within the 1-year horizon. The stability is even greater for investment-grade issuers. Moody's ratings turn out to be more stable than Fitch and S&P ratings, but its rating changes have a larger magnitude. This fact is evidenced by the higher proportion of two-notch upgrades and downgrades by Moody's. More-than-three-notch rating

**Table 8.19** S&P rating reversals, 1 January 1987 to 1 January 2011

| Country | Date | Rating action |
|---|---|---|
| *Belize* | 7 December 2006 | *Downgrade to SD from CC* |
|  | 20 February 2007 | *Upgrade to B from SD* |
| *Dominican Republic* | 1 February 2005 | *Downgrade to SD from CC* |
|  | 29 June 2005 | *Upgrade to B from SD* |
| Ecuador | 28 August 2000 | Upgrade to B– from SD |
|  | 2 April 2001 | Downgrade to CCC+ from B– |
| Ecuador | 24 January 2005 | Upgrade to B– from CCC+ |
|  | 20 June 2005 | Downgrade to CCC+ from B– |
| Ecuador | 19 January 2007 | Downgrade to CCC from CCC+ |
|  | 20 November 2007 | Upgrade to B– from CCC |
| Ecuador | 20 November 2007 | Upgrade to B– from CCC |
|  | 14 November 2008 | Downgrade to CCC– from B– |
| *Ecuador* | 15 December 2008 | *Downgrade to SD from CCC–* |
|  | 15 June 2009 | *Upgrade to CCC+ from SD* |
| Estonia | 10 August 2009 | Downgrade to A– from A |
|  | 10 June 2010 | Upgrade to A from A– |
| *Grenada* | 30 December 2004 | *Downgrade to SD from B–* |
|  | 18 November 2005 | *Upgrade to B– from SD* |
| Grenada | 2 April 2007 | Downgrade to CCC+ from B– |
|  | 1 August 2007 | Upgrade to B– from CCC+ |
| *Indonesia* | 30 March 1999 | *Downgrade to SD from CCC+* |
|  | 31 March 1999 | *Upgrade to CCC+ from SD* |
| *Indonesia* | 17 April 2000 | *Downgrade to SD from CCC+* |
|  | 2 October 2000 | *Upgrade to B– from SD* |
| *Indonesia* | 23 April 2002 | *Downgrade to SD from CCC* |
|  | 5 September 2002 | *Upgrade to CCC+ from SD* |
| *Jamaica* | 14 January 2010 | *Downgrade to SD from CCC* |
|  | 24 February 2010 | *Upgrade to B– from SD* |
| Kazakhstan | 2 November 2006 | Upgrade to BBB from BBB– |
|  | 8 October 2007 | Downgrade to BBB– from BBB |
| Lebanon | 31 January 2008 | Downgrade to CCC+ from B– |
|  | 5 August 2008 | Upgrade to B– from CCC+ |
| *Pakistan* | 29 January 1999 | *Downgrade to SD from CC* |
|  | 21 December 1999 | *Upgrade to B– from SD* |
| Pakistan | 14 November 2008 | Downgrade to CCC from CCC+ |
|  | 19 December 2008 | Upgrade to CCC+ from CCC |
| South Korea | 22 December 1997 | Downgrade to B+ from BBB– |
|  | 18 February 1998 | Upgrade to BB+ from B+ |
| Turkey | 25 April 2000 | Upgrade to B+ from B |
|  | 23 February 2001 | Downgrade to B from B+ |
| *Uruguay* | 16 May 2003 | *Downgrade to SD from CC* |
|  | 2 June 2003 | *Upgrade to B– from SD* |
| Venezuela | 13 December 2002 | Downgrade to CCC+ from B– |
|  | 30 July 2003 | Upgrade to B– from CCC+ |
| Venezuela | 25 August 2004 | Upgrade to B from B– |
|  | 18 January 2005 | Downgrade to SD from B |
| *Venezuela* | 18 January 2005 | *Downgrade to SD from B* |
|  | 3 March 2005 | *Upgrade to B from SD* |

*Sources*: Author's classification based on http://www.standardandpoors.com

change announcements, which involve countries that are about to default or have recovered from default, cast doubt on consistency of the ratings. First, such announcements reflect an inability of CRAs to anticipate currency and debt crises (from the Asian crisis in 1997–1998 to the Greek debt crisis in 2010), which have resulted in multi-notch downgrades. Second, they reveal the inadequacy of rating scales at the bottom of the speculative grade category. Are the CCC+, CCC, CCC−, CC, and C rating categories used by Fitch and S&P actually relevant?[11] They contribute to inflating artificially the magnitude of rating changes for defaulting issuers. From this standpoint, the rating scale implemented by Moody's has led to the appreciable greater stability of its ratings.

## 8.4 Accuracy of Sovereign Ratings

Although consistency and stability are valuable measures of ratings performance, they must be complemented by assessment of the *accuracy* of ratings. This objective may be pursued in three ways: examination of ratings prior to default (Sect. 8.4.1); computation of cumulative default rates (Sect. 8.4.2); and computation of ARs (Sect. 8.4.3).

As in Chap. 7, these measurements aim to compare the accuracy of ratings assigned by the different credit raters. Hence, this section examines a unique sample composed of 747 annual observations for 84 sovereign issuers rated simultaneously by Fitch, Moody's, and S&P from 1 January 2001 to 1 January 2011. An unexpected difficulty arises because rating agencies do not entirely agree on which countries defaulted during this period. For example, S&P considers Venezuela to be a country that defaulted in 2005, but Fitch and Moody's do not. This problem is overcome by selecting all default events listed in the sovereign transition and default studies released by the three agencies (Fitch 2011; Moody's 2010a; S&P 2011). This results in seven sovereign defaults between 1 January 2001 and 1 January 2011: Argentina (2001), Indonesia (2002), Uruguay (2003), the Dominican Republic (2005), Venezuela (2005), Ecuador (2008), and Jamaica (2010).[12]

### *8.4.1 Ratings Prior to Default*

Table 8.20 reports the ratings assigned by Fitch, Moody's, and S&P to these seven countries at various times prior to their default date.[13]

---

[11] The C rating category is not used by S&P.

[12] Five other countries that defaulted during this period are dropped from the sample because they were not assigned a rating by all three agencies: Moldova (2002), Paraguay (2003), Grenada (2004), Belize (2006), and Seychelles (2008).

[13] The ratings at time of default are not provided because the dates of defaults differ across agencies.

## 8.4 Accuracy of Sovereign Ratings

**Table 8.20** Fitch, Moody's, and S&P ratings at various times prior to default

| | Date of default | Fitch | | | | Moody's | | | | S&P | | | |
|---|---|---|---|---|---|---|---|---|---|---|---|---|---|
| | | M | M–3 | M–6 | M–12 | M | M–3 | M–6 | M–12 | M | M–3 | M–6 | M–12 |
| ARG | Nov 2001 | CCC– | B– | B+ | BB | Caa3 | Caa1 | B2 | B1 | CC | B– | B+ | BB |
| IDN | Apr 2002 | B– | B– | B– | B– | B3 | B3 | B3 | B3 | CCC | CCC | CCC+ | B– |
| URY | May 2003 | C | B– | B | BB+ | B3 | B3 | B3 | Baa3 | CC | B– | B | BB+ |
| VEN | Jan 2005 | B+ | B+ | B– | B– | B2 | B2 | Caa1 | Caa1 | B | B | CCC+ | CCC+ |
| DOM | Apr 2005 | CCC+ | CCC+ | CCC+ | CCC+ | B3 | B3 | B3 | B3 | SD | CC | CC | CC |
| ECU | Dec 2008 | CCC | CCC | CCC | CCC | Caa1 | B3 | B3 | Caa2 | CCC– | B– | B– | B– |
| JAM | Jan 2010 | CCC | B | B | B | Caa1 | B2 | B2 | B1 | CCC | CCC+ | B– | B |

*Notes*: M, M–3, M–6, and M–12 refer to the ratings at the beginning of the month of the default, and of the third, the sixth, and the twelfth month preceding the default, respectively. S&P downgraded the Dominican Republic to SD as early as February 2005. ARG, IDN, URY, VEN, DOM, ECU, JAM refer to Argentina, Indonesia, Uruguay, Venezuela, Dominican Republic, Ecuador, and Jamaica, respectively

*Sources*: http://www.fitchratings.com, http://www.moodys.com, and http://www.standardandpoors.com

S&P ratings are systematically the lowest at the beginning of the month M of the default, which supports the view that their ratings are adjusted more severely in the event of a default. At the other moments in time (M–3, M–6, and M–12), a default-by-default analysis is required. S&P issued the lowest ratings to Indonesia, Jamaica, and the Dominican Republic during the 12 months preceding their respective defaults. Fitch had the most conservative approach regarding Ecuador. Although the case of Venezuela is specific because Fitch and Moody's did not view this country as defaulting, it is worth noting that all three CRAs upgraded the country prior to the default event. This suggests how untimely positive rating actions may be for countries rated at the bottom of the speculative-grade category. Moody's assigned the most accurate ratings to Argentina, downgrading the country (to B1 from Ba3) on 6 October 1999 – far in advance of its competitors. S&P and Fitch did not downgrade Argentina until 14 November 2000 and 20 March 2001, respectively. Even after this first downgrade, S&P and Fitch ratings were higher than Moody's (BB– and BB– vs. B1). The story is quite the opposite for Uruguay, as Moody's was the last agency to downgrade the country to the speculative-grade category (on 3 May 2002 vs. 14 February 2002 and 13 March 2002 for S&P and Fitch, respectively). Moody's poor performance with regard to Uruguay's rating results from overoptimism about the country's economic resilience at a time when Argentina's economy was collapsing (Moody's 2001).

If all defaulting countries and times are considered, then S&P ratings turn out to be slightly more accurate. That being said, this result may be skewed because Fitch, Moody's, and S&P rating scales are only roughly equivalent. Moreover, Moody's ratings reflect both a probability of default and an expected recovery in the event of default, which contributes to enhancing the rating of several countries (e.g., the Dominican Republic, Indonesia, Uruguay), thus penalizing Moody's performance. Hence, other measures are needed to assess ratings accuracy; these include both average cumulative default rates and ARs.

## 8.4.2 Average Cumulative Default Rates

Tables 8.21–8.23 present the average cumulative default rates of cohorts of Fitch-, Moody's-, and S&P-rated countries formed at the beginning of each year from 1 January 2001 to 1 January 2011. The tables show 1- to 5-year average cumulative default rates, from which many relevant conclusions can be drawn.

First, for the sample under examination, no country rated in the BBB/Baa2 category or above by Fitch, Moody's, and S&P defaulted between 1 January 2001 and 1 January 2011. The highest rating assigned to a sovereign issuer that subsequently defaulted (i.e., Uruguay) is the same for the three agencies: BBB–/Baa3. This default affects the 2-year default rates and beyond. That the highest default rates are observed for S&P is a consequence of this agency having the smallest number of countries rated BBB–. For the opposite reason, the lowest default rates are observed for Moody's.

8.4 Accuracy of Sovereign Ratings

**Table 8.21** Fitch average cumulative default rates, 1 January 2001 to 1 January 2011

| In % | Year 1 | Year 2 | Year 3 | Year 4 | Year 5 |
| --- | --- | --- | --- | --- | --- |
| AAA | 0.00 | 0.00 | 0.00 | 0.00 | 0.00 |
| AA+ | 0.00 | 0.00 | 0.00 | 0.00 | 0.00 |
| AA | 0.00 | 0.00 | 0.00 | 0.00 | 0.00 |
| AA− | 0.00 | 0.00 | 0.00 | 0.00 | 0.00 |
| A+ | 0.00 | 0.00 | 0.00 | 0.00 | 0.00 |
| A | 0.00 | 0.00 | 0.00 | 0.00 | 0.00 |
| A− | 0.00 | 0.00 | 0.00 | 0.00 | 0.00 |
| BBB+ | 0.00 | 0.00 | 0.00 | 0.00 | 0.00 |
| BBB | 0.00 | 0.00 | 0.00 | 0.00 | 0.00 |
| BBB− | 0.00 | 2.50 | 5.65 | 5.65 | 5.65 |
| BB+ | 0.00 | 0.00 | 0.00 | 0.00 | 0.00 |
| BB | 2.78 | 2.78 | 2.78 | 2.78 | 2.78 |
| BB− | 0.00 | 0.00 | 0.00 | 4.17 | 9.21 |
| B+ | 4.00 | 4.00 | 8.80 | 13.87 | 13.87 |
| B | 3.23 | 10.39 | 14.29 | 14.29 | 14.29 |
| B− | 4.17 | 17.23 | 21.37 | 25.74 | 25.74 |
| CCC+ | 33.33 | 33.33 | 33.33 | 33.33 | 55.56 |
| CCC | 66.67 | 66.67 | 66.67 | 66.67 | 66.67 |
| CCC− | NR | NR | NR | NR | NR |
| CC | NR | NR | NR | NR | NR |
| C | NR | NR | NR | NR | NR |

*Sources*: Author's computations based on http://www.fitchratings.com
*Note*: NR denotes that no issuer was assigned the corresponding rating at the beginning of a year

**Table 8.22** Moody's average cumulative default rates, 1 January 2001 to 1 January 2011

| In % | Year 1 | Year 2 | Year 3 | Year 4 | Year 5 |
| --- | --- | --- | --- | --- | --- |
| Aaa | 0.00 | 0.00 | 0.00 | 0.00 | 0.00 |
| Aa1 | 0.00 | 0.00 | 0.00 | 0.00 | 0.00 |
| Aa2 | 0.00 | 0.00 | 0.00 | 0.00 | 0.00 |
| Aa3 | 0.00 | 0.00 | 0.00 | 0.00 | 0.00 |
| A1 | 0.00 | 0.00 | 0.00 | 0.00 | 0.00 |
| A2 | 0.00 | 0.00 | 0.00 | 0.00 | 0.00 |
| A3 | 0.00 | 0.00 | 0.00 | 0.00 | 0.00 |
| Baa1 | 0.00 | 0.00 | 0.00 | 0.00 | 0.00 |
| Baa2 | 0.00 | 0.00 | 0.00 | 0.00 | 0.00 |
| Baa3 | 0.00 | 2.08 | 4.36 | 4.36 | 4.36 |
| Ba1 | 0.00 | 0.00 | 0.00 | 0.00 | 0.00 |
| Ba2 | 0.00 | 0.00 | 0.00 | 0.00 | 0.00 |
| Ba3 | 0.00 | 0.00 | 0.00 | 0.00 | 0.00 |
| B1 | 2.00 | 4.08 | 6.48 | 9.32 | 9.32 |
| B2 | 3.57 | 7.76 | 7.76 | 12.62 | 17.47 |
| B3 | 11.11 | 14.53 | 18.25 | 18.25 | 18.25 |
| Caa1 | 12.50 | 37.50 | 46.43 | 54.08 | 54.08 |
| Caa2 | 33.33 | 33.33 | 33.33 | 33.33 | 66.67 |
| Caa3 | 0.00 | 0.00 | 0.00 | 0.00 | 0.00 |

*Sources*: Author's computations based on http://www.moodys.com
*Note*: NR denotes that no issuer was assigned the corresponding rating at the beginning of a year

**Table 8.23** S&P average cumulative default rates, 1 January 2001 to 1 January 2011

| In % | Year 1 | Year 2 | Year 3 | Year 4 | Year 5 |
|---|---|---|---|---|---|
| AAA | 0.00 | 0.00 | 0.00 | 0.00 | 0.00 |
| AA+ | 0.00 | 0.00 | 0.00 | 0.00 | 0.00 |
| AA | 0.00 | 0.00 | 0.00 | 0.00 | 0.00 |
| AA− | 0.00 | 0.00 | 0.00 | 0.00 | 0.00 |
| A+ | 0.00 | 0.00 | 0.00 | 0.00 | 0.00 |
| A | 0.00 | 0.00 | 0.00 | 0.00 | 0.00 |
| A− | 0.00 | 0.00 | 0.00 | 0.00 | 0.00 |
| BBB+ | 0.00 | 0.00 | 0.00 | 0.00 | 0.00 |
| BBB | 0.00 | 0.00 | 0.00 | 0.00 | 0.00 |
| BBB− | 0.00 | 2.94 | 6.41 | 6.41 | 6.41 |
| BB+ | 0.00 | 0.00 | 0.00 | 0.00 | 0.00 |
| BB | 0.00 | 0.00 | 0.00 | 0.00 | 0.00 |
| BB− | 2.63 | 2.63 | 2.63 | 2.63 | 2.63 |
| B+ | 0.00 | 0.00 | 0.00 | 0.00 | 0.00 |
| B | 3.57 | 7.28 | 11.31 | 19.76 | 24.48 |
| B− | 7.41 | 14.81 | 14.81 | 14.81 | 14.81 |
| CCC+ | 0.00 | 14.29 | 38.78 | 47.52 | 56.27 |
| CCC | 66.67 | 83.33 | 83.33 | 83.33 | 83.33 |
| CCC− | NR | NR | NR | NR | NR |
| CC | 100.00 | 100.00 | 100.00 | 100.00 | 100.00 |

*Sources*: Author's computations based on http://www.standardandpoors.com

*Note*: NR denotes that no issuer was assigned the corresponding rating at the beginning of a year

Second, there were no defaults within the entire Moody's Ba rating category. The same cannot be said for Fitch and S&P, whose BB and BB− categories (respectively) include default events. As a result, Moody's outperforms its competitors with respect to the top speculative-grade rating categories.

Third, the default rates for the B+/B1 category are not homogeneous across rating agencies: they range from 0% for S&P over all time horizons to 13.87% for Fitch over the 4- and 5-year horizons. The S&P B+ default rates are troublesome in that they ought to be higher than its BB− default rates. In fact, examining the B−B−/B2−B3 categories reveals that Fitch and Moody's default rates do increase as the credit quality declines. However, this path is observed for S&P only over the 1-, 2-, and 3-year horizons.

Fourth, all the CCC/Caa rating categories (and below) exhibit the highest default rates. Yet some categories contain no issuer (e.g., the S&P CCC− and the Fitch CCC−, CC, and C categories) or, more embarrassingly, a single issuer that did not default (e.g., the Moody's Caa3 category). These results highlight the need for all three CRAs to reduce the number of low speculative-grade rating categories.

This analysis of average cumulative default rates shows the performance of Fitch, Moody's, and S&P to be similar in that their investment-grade rating categories are safe (except for BBB−/Baa3). However, the absence of defaults in the entire Ba rating category gives Moody's the most accurate ratings.

### 8.4.3 Cumulative Accuracy Profiles and Accuracy Ratios

The last measurement of rating accuracy consists of tracing CAP curves and computing ARs. Both CAPs and ARs are designed to establish whether CRAs manage to assign low ratings to issuers that default and high ratings to issuers that do not.

A CAP curve is used to facilitate a visual and qualitative assessment of ratings performance. It is constructed by sorting the sovereign issuers from lowest to highest rating and then plotting, for each rating category, the percentage of defaults accounted for by sovereigns with the same or a lower rating against the percentage of all sovereigns with the same or a lower rating. The further the CAP curve bows toward the upper left corner, the greater the fraction of all defaults that are accounted for by the lowest rating categories (see Moody's 2000 for an exhaustive explanation).

Figures 8.1–8.3 depict the 1-, 3-, and 5-year CAP curves for the sample covering all the countries rated simultaneously by Fitch, Moody's, and S&P from 1 January 2001 through 1 January 2011. For the three time horizons, examining CAP curves does not reveal which agency's ratings are the most powerful predictor of default because the curves cross one another. For this reason, computing ARs is necessary in order to compare the ratings performance of Fitch, Moody's, and S&P.

The AR compresses the information depicted in the CAP curve into a single summary statistic: it is the ratio of the area between the CAP curve and the 45° line to the total area above the 45° line. ARs range between −1 and 1, where 1 represents

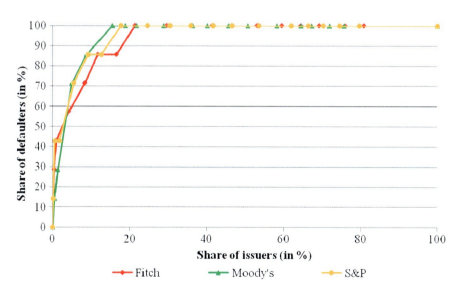

**Fig. 8.1** One-year cumulative accuracy profiles (CAPs), 1 January 2001 to 1 January 2011. *Sources*: Author's computations

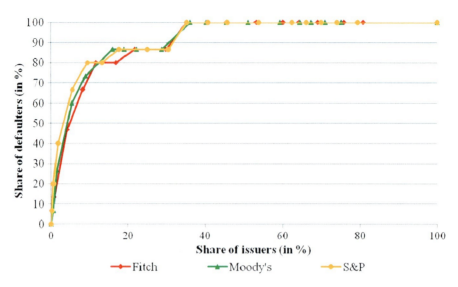

**Fig. 8.2** Three-year CAPs, 1 January 2001 to 1 January 2011. *Sources*: Author's computations

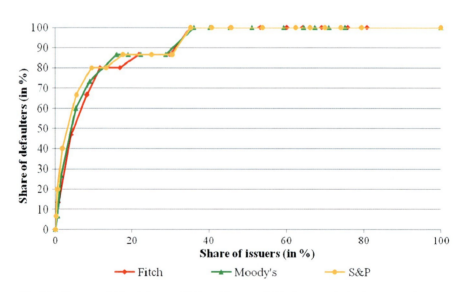

**Fig. 8.3** Five-year CAPs, 1 January 2001 to 1 January 2011. *Sources*: Author's computations

## 8.4 Accuracy of Sovereign Ratings

**Table 8.24** Accuracy ratios, 1 January 2001 to 1 January 2011

|  | One-year accuracy ratio | Three-year accuracy ratio | Five-year accuracy ratio |
|---|---|---|---|
| Fitch | 0.890 | 0.819 | 0.817 |
| Moody's | 0.915 | 0.835 | 0.852 |
| S&P | 0.914 | 0.847 | 0.852 |

*Sources*: Author's computations

maximum accuracy (i.e., all defaulters are assigned the lowest rating) and −1 represents worst performance (i.e., all defaulters are assigned the highest rating). The formula is as follows:

$$\text{AR} = 2\left[\left[\sum_{R_i = R_1, \ldots, R_{\max}} \frac{(D_{R_i} + D_{R_{i-1}})(N_{R_i} - N_{R_{i-1}})}{2DN}\right] - 0.5\right],$$

where
$D$ = total number of defaults;
$N$ = total number of issuers;
$R_i$ = rating of a given agency;
$D_{R_i}$ = total number of defaults rated $R_i$ and less;
$N_{R_i}$ = total number of issuers rated $R_i$ and less;
$D_0 = 0$; and
$N_0 = 0$.

Table 8.24 presents the 1-, 3-, and 5-year ARs for the three agencies. ARs during the period of study are much higher than those observed for the interwar years (see Flandreau et al. 2010). This gap is likely due not only to the greater efficiency of modern credit ratings but also, and even more probably, to the massive and unprecedented wave of sovereign defaults during the 1930s.

Three-year ARs are lower than 1-year ARs, but surprisingly they turn out to be lower than 5-year ARs, too. These unexpected results reflect two circumstances: (a) the investment-grade ratings assigned to Uruguay 4 and 5 years (i.e., in 2000 and 1999) prior to its default in May 2003 are not included in the sample; and (b) the low ratings assigned to defaulting countries 4 and 5 years prior to their bankruptcy enhance the 5-year ARs of Moody's and S&P.

Fitch ARs are the lowest for the three time horizons. At the 1-year horizon, Fitch is in third position mainly because it assigned, at the beginning of a year, the highest rating (of all three CRAs) to a country that defaulted later that year. On 1 January 2001, Argentina – which became insolvent in November 2001 – was rated BB by Fitch vs. BB− and B1 by S&P and Moody's, respectively. At each time horizon, Fitch is penalized because it has the highest proportion of defaulting countries among the whole BB rating category.

The ARs for Moody's and S&P are very close, except at the 3-year horizon. An in-depth analysis of Moody's and S&P ARs and CAPs is needed to compare the performance of these two agencies. As shown in Figs. 8.1–8.3, S&P ratings provide a better rank ordering of sovereign risk among the higher-risk portion of the rating scale (i.e., the whole B rating category and below). In contrast, Moody's ratings are more accurate when ranking countries within the whole Ba rating category. In other words, S&P ratings are more subject to Type I errors (rating a defaulter too high), whereas Moody's ratings are more subject to Type II errors (rating a nondefaulter too low). At the 1- and 5-year horizons, effects of the Type I errors by S&P nearly balance those of the Type II errors by Moody's. Yet at the 3-year horizon, effects of Moody's Type II errors are greater than those of S&P Type I errors, which propels S&P to the top position.

A different sample can be used to compare directly the performance of Moody's and S&P. This sample includes all countries rated simultaneously by the two agencies between 1 January 1987 and 1 January 2011, and it yields 1,492 annual observations for 98 countries. The defaulting countries account for all default events listed in the sovereign transition and default studies released by the two agencies (Moody's 2010a; S&P 2011): Pakistan (1999), Russia (1999), Indonesia (1999, 2000, and 2002), Argentina (2001), Paraguay (2003), Uruguay (2003), the Dominican Republic (2005), Venezuela (2005), Belize (2006), Ecuador (2008), and Jamaica (2010).[14]

Figures 8.4–8.6 depict the 1-, 3-, and 5-year CAP curves. At the three time horizons, S&P ratings are more accurate across the B rating category and below, whereas Moody's ratings provide the better rank ordering across the Ba rating

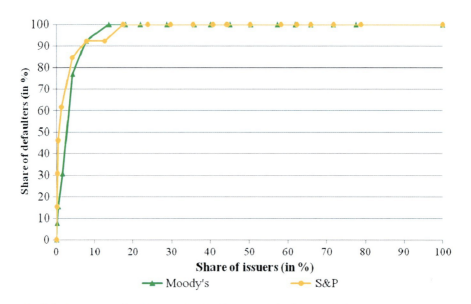

**Fig. 8.4** One-year CAPs, 1 January 1987 to 1 January 2011. *Sources*: Author's computations

---

[14] Three other countries that defaulted during this period are dropped from the sample because they were not assigned a rating by both agencies: Moldova (2002), Grenada (2004), and Seychelles (2008).

8.4 Accuracy of Sovereign Ratings

**Fig. 8.5** Three-year CAPs, 1 January 1987 to 1 January 2011. *Sources*: Author's computations

**Fig. 8.6** Five-year CAPs, 1 January 1987 to 1 January 2011. *Sources*: Author's computations

**Table 8.25** Accuracy ratios, 1 January 1987 to 1 January 2011

|         | One-year accuracy ratio | Three-year accuracy ratio | Five-year accuracy ratio |
|---------|-------------------------|---------------------------|--------------------------|
| Moody's | 0.935                   | 0.840                     | 0.787                    |
| S&P     | 0.950                   | 0.823                     | 0.761                    |

*Sources*: Author's computations

category and above. But such comparison of CAP curves does not establish which agency's ratings are the best predictor of default because, as mentioned previously, the curves cross each other. Therefore, computing ARs is the best way to measure the ratings performance of Moody's and S&P.

Table 8.25 summarizes the ARs for these two agencies. The S&P ARs are better at the 1-year horizon, but the Moody's ratings outperform in the longer term. There are two reasons why S&P exhibits lower performance than Moody's at the 3- and 5-year horizons. First, S&P assigned the higher rating to a country that subsequently defaulted: Indonesia was rated BBB by S&P (vs. Baa3 by Moody's) from 3 to 5 years prior to its 1999 and 2000 defaults. Second, defaulting sovereign issuers that were rated within the BB category by S&P prior to their bankruptcy outnumber those rated within the Ba rating category by Moody's. Symmetrically, the lower performance of Moody's at the 1-year horizon originates in the higher proportion of nondefaulting countries among the higher-risk portion of the rating scale (i.e., the B3, Caa1, Caa2, and Caa3 categories).

These findings are particularly relevant to guiding investment decisions. The S&P ratings are more suitable for short-term strategies, whereas the Moody's ratings provide the most valuable information in the medium term. For investment-grade bondholders, the ratings of the two agencies are roughly equivalent. For speculative-grade bondholders, the analysis must be qualified. S&P ratings are less reliable for upper speculative-grade bond investors (Type I errors), whereas Moody's ratings are less accurate for lower speculative-grade bond investors (Type II errors).

## 8.5 Conclusions

This chapter sheds new light on the consistency and accuracy of sovereign ratings assigned by Fitch, Moody's, and S&P ratings since 1987.

First of all, Moody's ratings are generally more stable than Fitch and S&P ratings. However, Moody's adjusts its ratings more severely through multi-notch upgrades and downgrades. The three CRAs make consistent use of rating outlooks and reviews, and most of their upgrades (downgrades) are preceded by a positive (negative) outlook or review.

Second, the expected hierarchy of cumulative default rates (i.e., higher default rates observed for lower rating categories) as well as high ARs support the view that Fitch, Moody's, and S&P manage to discriminate between defaulters and nondefaulters. The examination of ARs at different time horizons reveals that S&P is the most accurate agency in the short term and that Moody's is the most accurate in the medium term. Fitch's comparatively poor performance is linked to its delay in downgrading some sovereign issuers that experienced severe financial difficulties (e.g., Argentina in 2001). It is reasonable to assume that as relatively new player in the sovereign rating business Fitch lagged behind its competitors when it came to adjusting ratings.

Finally, upgrades tend to soar in times of low risk aversion (e.g., 1995–1996 and 2004–2007), whereas downgrades are more numerous in times of high risk aversion (e.g., 1992, 1997–1998, 2001, 2008–2009). These findings suggest that sovereign ratings have procyclical effects on sovereign bond markets, a hypothesis that is tested in Chap. 8.

# References

Altman E. I. and Rijken H. A. (2004), "How Rating Agencies Achieve Rating Stability", *Journal of Banking & Finance*, Vol. 28, No. 11.
Ferri G., Liu L.-G. and Stiglitz J. (1999), "The Procyclical Role of Rating Agencies: Evidence from the East Asian Crisis", *Economic Notes, Banca Monte dei Paschi di Siena SpA*, No.3.
Fitch Ratings (2005), "Fitch Sovereign Rating Outlook and Watch Study", 25 November.
Fitch Ratings (2009), "Definitions of Ratings and Other Scales", March.
Fitch Ratings (2011), "Sovereign 2010 Transition and Default Study", 23 March.
Flandreau M., Gaillard N. and Packer F. (2010), "To Err Is Human: Rating Agencies and the Interwar Foreign Government Debt Crisis", *BIS Working Papers No. 335*, December.
Hu Y-T., Kiesel R. and Perraudin W. (2002), "The Estimation of Transition Matrices for Sovereign Credit Ratings", *Journal of Banking and Finance*, Vol.26.
KMV Corporation (1998), *Uses and Abuses of Bond Default Rates*, 3 March.
Moody's Investors Service (1995), "Corporate Bond Defaults and Default Rates 1970–1994", January.
Moody's Investors Service (1997), "Historical Default Rates of Corporate Bond Issuers 1920–1996", January.
Moody's Investors Service (2000), "Benchmarking Quantitative Default Risk Models: A Validation Methodology", March.
Moody's Investors Service (2001), "Uruguay: A Stable Credit in a Volatile Region", December.
Moody's Investors Service (2003a), "Sovereign Bond Defaults, Rating Transitions, and Recoveries (1985–2002)", February.
Moody's Investors Service (2003b), "Measuring the Performance of Corporate Bond Ratings", April.
Moody's Investors Service (2004), "Rating Transitions and Defaults Conditional on Watchlist, Outlook and Rating History", February.
Moody's Investors Service (2006), "Analyzing the Tradeoff between Ratings Accuracy and Stability", September.
Moody's Investors Service (2010a), "Sovereign Default and Recovery Rates, 1983–2009", April.
Moody's Investors Service (2010b), "Rating Symbols and Definitions", May.
Nickell P., Perraudin W. and Varotto S. (2000), "Stability of Rating Transitions", *Journal of Banking and Finance*, Vol. 24.
Reisen H. and von Maltzan J. (1999), "Boom and Bust and Sovereign Ratings", *OECD Development Centre, Working Papers No.148*.
Standard & Poor's (2010a), "Outlooks: The Sovereign Credit Weathervane, 2009/2010 Update", 20 April.
Standard & Poor's (2010b), "Standard & Poor's Ratings Definitions", 3 May.
Standard & Poor's (2011), "Default, Transition, and Recovery: Sovereign Defaults and Rating Transition Data, 2010 Update", 23 February.

# Chapter 9
# Fitch, Moody's, and S&P Sovereign Ratings and EMBI Global Spreads: Lessons from 1993–2007

The past two decades have seen a remarkable growth in sovereign bond debt issued by emerging countries. This evolution was accompanied by the extensive use of the JP Morgan Emerging Markets Bond Index (EMBI) among investors. The EMBI, a total-return index that tracks the traded market for U.S. dollar-denominated Brady and other similar sovereign restructured bonds, was successively transformed into the EMBI+ and the EMBI Global (EMBIG) so as to include US dollar local markets instruments, performing loans, Eurobonds, and investment-grade issuers (JP Morgan 1995, 1999). These indices provide investors with a well-defined performance benchmark and a vehicle for analyzing sovereign risk and returns. It is therefore relevant to compare them with FC ratings assigned by Fitch, Moody's, and S&P.

The purpose of this chapter is to examine the correlation between JP Morgan EMBIG spreads and Fitch, Moody's, and S&P sovereign ratings for the period December 1993 to February 2007 and also to assess the impact of spreads on ratings and vice versa. Analyzing the perception of sovereign risk by the market, on the one hand, and by CRAs, on the other hand, should be all the more instructive because the period under study covers subperiods of extremely high risk aversion (the Tequila crisis of December 1994 to March 1995, the Russian crisis of July to September 1998, the Argentina's default in November 2001, and Brazil's default risk of June 2002 to March 2003) and also years of very low risk aversion in 2005–2007 (driven by high levels of liquidity, increasing commodity prices, the rapid pace of economic growth, and continued improvement in the credit quality of emerging economies).

In Sect. 9.1, I review the literature on sovereign market spreads. The correlation between EMBIG spreads and Fitch, Moody's, and S&P ratings is studied in Sect. 9.2. Section 9.3 focuses on how ratings adjust to market spreads. Section 9.4 analyzes the reaction of market spreads to upgrades and downgrades. Section 9.5 concludes.

## 9.1 Review of the Literature

The first relevant piece of the literature concerns analysis of the determinants of sovereign spreads. Using primary yields as a measure of credit risk, Eichengreen and Mody (1998) find that changes in macroeconomic fundamentals explain only a fraction of the spread compression observed between 1991 and 1996. Ferrucci (2003) and Rowland and Torres (2004) investigate the determinants of EMBIG secondary market spreads. Ferrucci (2003) states that markets take into account macroeconomic fundamentals when pricing sovereign risk, but also insists on the role for such external factors as global liquidity conditions and U.S. equity prices. Rowland and Torres (2004) list six key variables: GDP growth rate and the ratios of total external debt to GDP, total external debt to exports, foreign reserves to GDP, exports to GDP, and debt service to GDP. Baldacci et al. (2008) find that both fiscal and political factors are determinants of country risk premiums as measured by sovereign bond spreads.

The literature dealing with sovereign ratings can be divided into three main categories. The first group of papers investigates the determinants of sovereign ratings (see Chaps. 5 and 6). The second line of research examines the alleged procyclicality of sovereign ratings during financial crises. For Ferri et al. (1999), Moody's and S&P failed to predict the Asian crisis and even exacerbated it by downgrading Asian countries more than was justified by the fundamentals. Kräussl (2000) disagrees, arguing that massive downgrades do not necessarily intensify a crisis (e.g., South Korea in 1997). Mora (2006) investigates the role of CRAs in the Asian crisis and shows that ratings are sticky rather than procyclical. The third type of papers, much more in line with this chapter, studies the relationships between spreads and sovereign ratings. Cantor and Packer (1996) look at the period 1987–1994 and conclude that the impact of a rating change on spreads is greater if it is made by Moody's or if it is related to speculative-grade countries. Larraín et al. (1997) find a significant impact for negative rating actions published by Moody's and S&P during 1987–1996. They conclude that CRAs have the potential to attenuate boom-bust spread cycles. Analyzing Fitch, Moody's, and S&P rating and outlook changes that occurred between 1989 and 1997, Reisen and von Maltzan (1999) show that downgrades have a significant impact on spreads, unlike upgrades, which are anticipated by the market. Sy (2001) emphasizes that the strong negative relationship between ratings and EMBI+ spreads declines during periods of market turbulence (e.g., 1997–1998). Moreover, he finds evidence of asymmetric adjustments of spreads and ratings following disagreements between the market and rating agencies.

## 9.2 Correlations Between EMBIG Spreads and Fitch, Moody's, and S&P Ratings

### 9.2.1 Data Description

Sovereigns must be assigned a FC rating by at least one of the three CRAs (Fitch, Moody's, and S&P) and also be included in the EMBIG benchmark as of 28 February 2006 in order to be included in the database. This criterion results in

## 9.2 Correlations Between EMBIG Spreads and Fitch, Moody's, and S&P Ratings

**Table 9.1** Linear transformation of ratings

| Fitch | | Moody's | | S&P | |
| --- | --- | --- | --- | --- | --- |
| Rating | Numerical transformation | Rating | Numerical transformation | Rating | Numerical transformation |
| AAA | 23 | Aaa | 20 | AAA | 22 |
| AA+ | 22 | Aa1 | 19 | AA+ | 21 |
| AA | 21 | Aa2 | 18 | AA | 20 |
| AA– | 20 | Aa3 | 17 | AA– | 19 |
| A+ | 19 | A1 | 16 | A+ | 18 |
| A | 18 | A2 | 15 | A | 17 |
| A– | 17 | A3 | 14 | A– | 16 |
| BBB+ | 16 | Baa1 | 13 | BBB+ | 15 |
| BBB | 15 | Baa2 | 12 | BBB | 14 |
| BBB– | 14 | Baa3 | 11 | BBB– | 13 |
| BB+ | 13 | Ba1 | 10 | BB+ | 12 |
| BB | 12 | Ba2 | 9 | BB | 11 |
| BB– | 11 | Ba3 | 8 | BB– | 10 |
| B+ | 10 | B1 | 7 | B+ | 9 |
| B | 9 | B2 | 6 | B | 8 |
| B– | 8 | B3 | 5 | B– | 7 |
| CCC+ | 7 | Caa1 | 4 | CCC+ | 6 |
| CCC | 6 | Caa2 | 3 | CCC | 5 |
| CCC– | 5 | Caa3 | 2 | CCC– | 4 |
| CC | 4 | Ca | 1 | CC | 3 |
| C | 3 | C | 0 | C | 2 |
| DDD | 2 | | | SD | 1 |
| DD | 1 | | | D | 0 |
| D | 0 | | | | |

selecting 32 sovereigns: Argentina, Brazil, Bulgaria, Chile, China, Colombia, Dominican Republic, Ecuador, Egypt, El Salvador, Hungary, Indonesia, Lebanon, Malaysia, Mexico, Morocco, Nigeria, Pakistan, Panama, Peru, the Philippines, Poland, Russia, Serbia, South Africa, Thailand, Tunisia, Turkey, Ukraine, Uruguay, Venezuela, and Vietnam.

I use EMBIG monthly stripped spreads from December 1993 to February 2007 (i.e., 159 months) for each country in the sample. Fitch, Moody's, and S&P FC ratings are those ratings at the end of each month from December 1993 to February 2007.[1] They are transformed into numerical values using a linear scale (Table 9.1).

Each agency has its own numerical scale; higher ratings correspond to higher values. Starting points of the series differ across countries, indices, and rating agencies. As a result, I have three samples of unbalanced panel data for Fitch, Moody's, and S&P, respectively (Table 9.2).

---

[1] In this chapter, Fitch sovereign ratings include the credit ratings assigned by IBCA and Duff & Phelps prior to their merger with Fitch in 1997 and 2000, respectively.

**Table 9.2** Description of the three samples

| Countries | Periods under consideration | | |
| --- | --- | --- | --- |
| | Fitch ratings | Moody's ratings | S&P ratings |
| Argentina | 1997:05–2007:02 | 1993:12–2007:02 | 1993:12–2007:02 |
| Brazil | 1994:12–2007:02 | 1994:04–2007:02 | 1994:12–2007:02 |
| Bulgaria | 1998:04–2007:02 | 1996:09–2007:02 | 1998:11–2007:02 |
| Chile | 1999:05–2007:02 | 1999:05–2007:02 | 1999:05–2007:02 |
| China | 1997:12–2007:02 | 1994:03–2007:02 | 1994:03–2007:02 |
| Colombia | 1994:12–2007:02 | 1997:02–2007:02 | 1997:02–2007:02 |
| Dominican Republic | 2000:08–2007:02 | 2001:11–2007:02 | 2001:11–2007:02 |
| Ecuador | 2002:11–2007:02 | 1997:07–2007:02 | 2000:07–2007:02 |
| Egypt | 2001:07–2007:02 | 2001:07–2007:02 | 2001:07–2007:02 |
| El Salvador | 2002:04–2007:02 | 2002:04–2007:02 | 2002:04–2007:02 |
| Hungary | 1999:01–2007:02 | 1999:02–2007:02 | 1999:01–2007:02 |
| Indonesia | 2004:05–2007:02 | 2004:05–2007:02 | 2004:05–2007:02 |
| Lebanon | 1998:04–2007:02 | 1998:04–2007:02 | 1998:04–2007:02 |
| Malaysia | 1998:08–2007:02 | 1996:10–2007:02 | 1996:10–2007:02 |
| Mexico | 1996:12–2007:02 | 1993:12–2007:02 | 1993:12–2007:02 |
| Morocco | NA | 1999:07–2006:11 | 1998:03–2006:11 |
| Nigeria | 2006:01–2007:02 | NA | 2006:02–2007:02 |
| Pakistan | NA | 2001:06–2007:02 | 2001:06–2007:02 |
| Panama | 1998:09–2007:02 | 1997:01–2007:02 | 1997:01–2007:02 |
| Peru | 1999:10–2007:02 | 1999:07–2007:02 | 1997:12–2007:02 |
| Philippines | 1999:07–2007:02 | 1997:12–2007:02 | 1997:12–2007:02 |
| Poland | 1996:12–2007:02 | 1995:06–2007:02 | 1995:06–2007:02 |
| Russia | 1997:12–2007:02 | 1997:12–2007:02 | 1997:12–2007:02 |
| Serbia | 2005:07–2007:02 | NA | 2005:07–2007:02 |
| South Africa | 1994:12–2007:02 | 1994:12–2007:02 | 1994:12–2007:02 |
| Thailand | 1998:05–2006:03 | 1997:05–2006:03 | 1997:05–2006:03 |
| Tunisia | 2002:05–2007:02 | 2002:05–2007:02 | 2002:05–2007:02 |
| Turkey | 1996:12–2007:02 | 1996:06–2007:02 | 1996:06–2007:02 |
| Ukraine | 2001:06–2007:02 | 2001:12–2007:02 | 2001:12–2007:02 |
| Uruguay | 2001:05–2007:02 | 2001:05–2007:02 | 2001:05–2007:02 |
| Venezuela | 1997:09–2007:02 | 1993:12–2007:02 | 1993:12–2007:02 |
| Vietnam | 2005:11–2007:02 | 2005:11–2007:02 | 2005:11–2007:02 |

*Sources*: Datastream, http://www.fitchratings.com, http://www.moodys.com, and http://www.standardandpoors.com

*Notes*: Morocco and Pakistan were not rated by Fitch as of 28 February 2006. Nigeria and Serbia were not rated by Moody's as of 28 February 2006. NA denotes not applicable

### *9.2.2 A Univariate Model of Spreads*

A univariate model of EMBIG spreads is developed here to determine differences in sovereign risk assessment between the market and the three CRAs. I use an unbalanced panel data estimation of log spreads on Fitch, Moody's, and S&P ratings. The relationship between spreads and ratings can be expressed as follows:

$$\text{Log}(\text{EMBIG})_{it} = \alpha_i + \beta\,\text{RAT}_{it} + \varepsilon_{it},$$

## 9.3 Adjustments of Ratings to Market Spreads

**Table 9.3** Unbalanced panel estimation results, pooling

|  | Dependent variable: Log(EMBIG spreads) | | |
| --- | --- | --- | --- |
|  | [1] | [2] | [3] |
| Fitch ratings | −0.229 (61.778) | | |
| Moody's ratings | | −0.231 (65.910) | |
| S&P ratings | | | −0.233 (68.424) |
| Constant | 8.471 (179.755) | 7.867 (229.476) | 8.297 (210.685) |
| Adjusted $R^2$ | 0.596 | 0.582 | 0.600 |
| Number of observations | 2,585 | 3,124 | 3,123 |

*Notes*: Absolute *t* statistics are in *parentheses*. All results are significant at the 5% level

for countries $i = 1, 2, 3, \ldots, 32$ and periods $t = 1, 2, 3 \ldots, 159$. The dependent variable Log(EMBIG) is the log of EMBIG spreads, and the independent variable RAT is the rating issued by each agency.

Two series of regressions are run: the first with a common intercept ($\alpha_i = \alpha$) and the second with fixed effects (the model specification $\alpha_i$). Results with a common intercept are presented in Table 9.3. Not surprisingly, there is a robust negative correlation between sovereign spreads and Fitch, Moody's, and S&P ratings. It is worth noting that Moody's ratings are slightly less correlated to spreads than are the other two agencies'.

Results with fixed effects (Table 9.4) show a stronger negative correlation between spreads and ratings. Constant terms must be interpreted carefully. Sovereigns with the highest intercepts are either countries that remained in default for a long time (Argentina and Russia) or countries with high risk premia (Brazil, Colombia, and the Philippines). Indonesia, Serbia, Vietnam, and Nigeria, lately integrated in the samples (May 2004, July 2005, November 2005, and January 2006, respectively), took advantage of the prevailing low risk aversion and thus have the lowest intercepts.

## 9.3 Adjustments of Ratings to Market Spreads

### 9.3.1 Adjustments of Ratings to Excessively High/Low Spreads

Spreads are considered excessively high (low), i.e., are outliers, when they are higher (lower) than rating-based spreads, or fitted spreads, by more than one standard deviation. Fitted spreads are obtained from the unbalanced panel data estimation with fixed effects (Sect. 9.2). The percentage of outliers (4.6, 5.5, and 7.5% for Fitch, S&P, and Moody's, respectively) shows that Moody's disagrees with the market more often than do other two agencies. In contrast, Fitch ratings tend to stick the market.

For the three agencies, I assess whether there was an upgrade, a downgrade, or no rating change within the month and the 3 months following excessively low and high spreads. Tables 9.5–9.7 present these rating adjustments for the three agencies.

**Table 9.4** Unbalanced panel estimation results, fixed effects

|  | Dependent variable: Log(EMBIG spreads) | | |
|---|---|---|---|
|  | [1] | [2] | [3] |
| Fitch ratings | −0.228 (34.943) | | |
| Moody's ratings | | −0.268 (38.173) | |
| S&P ratings | | | −0.236 (44.693) |
| Fixed effects | | | |
| Argentina | 8.571 | 8.500 | 8.758 |
| Brazil | 8.825 | 8.325 | 8.736 |
| Bulgaria | 8.395 | 7.813 | 8.201 |
| Chile | 8.737 | 8.335 | 8.683 |
| China | 8.449 | 8.373 | 7.998 |
| Colombia | 8.813 | 8.570 | 8.762 |
| Dominican Republic | 8.010 | 7.972 | 7.921 |
| Ecuador | 8.380 | 8.074 | 8.312 |
| Egypt | 7.978 | 7.652 | 7.843 |
| El Salvador | 8.529 | 8.515 | 8.404 |
| Hungary | 7.841 | 8.028 | 7.748 |
| Indonesia | 7.967 | 7.201 | 7.648 |
| Lebanon | 7.945 | 7.516 | 7.786 |
| Malaysia | 8.636 | 8.538 | 8.645 |
| Mexico | 8.709 | 8.687 | 8.751 |
| Morocco | | 8.233 | 8.337 |
| Nigeria | 7.612 | | 7.411 |
| Pakistan | | 7.284 | 7.725 |
| Panama | 8.812 | 8.512 | 8.545 |
| Peru | 8.602 | 8.117 | 8.552 |
| Philippines | 8.872 | 8.506 | 8.720 |
| Poland | 8.501 | 8.495 | 8.340 |
| Russia | 8.820 | 8.519 | 8.358 |
| Serbia | 7.889 | | 7.746 |
| South Africa | 8.367 | 8.391 | 8.339 |
| Thailand | 8.022 | 7.888 | 8.059 |
| Tunisia | 8.265 | 8.012 | 8.156 |
| Turkey | 8.363 | 7.979 | 8.056 |
| Ukraine | 8.117 | 7.498 | 7.822 |
| Uruguay | 8.395 | 7.831 | 8.165 |
| Venezuela | 8.808 | 8.451 | 8.600 |
| Vietnam | 7.492 | 7.129 | 7.438 |
| Adjusted $R^2$ | 0.704 | 0.707 | 0.733 |
| Number of observations | 2,585 | 3,124 | 3,123 |

*Notes*: Absolute $t$ statistics are in *parentheses*. All results are significant at the 5% level

Like Sy (2001), I consider that ratings are expected to be upgraded (respectively downgraded) when spreads turn out to be excessively low (respectively high).

The results merit several comments. First, the overall stability of ratings is striking: 87 and 77% of ratings (average of the three agencies) remain unchanged 1 and 3 months, respectively, after excessively high and low spreads.

9.3 Adjustments of Ratings to Market Spreads

**Table 9.5** Fitch rating adjustments to excessively low/high spreads

Excessively low spreads

| Ratings | Expected upgrade (%) | Unexpected downgrade (%) | No change (%) |
|---|---|---|---|
| 1 month later | 4.5 | 0.0 | 95.5 |
| 3 months later | 6.2 | 0.0 | 93.8 |

Excessively high spreads

| Ratings | Expected downgrade (%) | Unexpected upgrade (%) | No change (%) |
|---|---|---|---|
| 1 month later | 16.7 | 0.0 | 83.3 |
| 3 months later | 28.9 | 0.0 | 71.1 |

*Sources*: Author's computations

**Table 9.6** Moody's rating adjustments to excessively low/high spreads

Excessively low spreads

| Ratings | Expected upgrade (%) | Unexpected downgrade (%) | No change (%) |
|---|---|---|---|
| 1 month later | 2.6 | 0.0 | 97.4 |
| 3 months later | 6.1 | 0.0 | 93.9 |

Excessively high spreads

| Ratings | Expected downgrade (%) | Unexpected upgrade (%) | No change (%) |
|---|---|---|---|
| 1 month later | 9.9 | 0.8 | 89.3 |
| 3 months later | 17.4 | 1.6 | 81.0 |

*Sources*: Author's computations

**Table 9.7** S&P rating adjustments to excessively low/high spreads

Excessively low spreads

| Ratings | Expected upgrade (%) | Unexpected downgrade (%) | No change (%) |
|---|---|---|---|
| 1 month later | 9.6 | 0.0 | 90.4 |
| 3 months later | 21.3 | 0.0 | 78.7 |

Excessively high spreads

| Ratings | Expected downgrade (%) | Unexpected upgrade (%) | No change (%) |
|---|---|---|---|
| 1 month later | 15.4 | 0.0 | 84.6 |
| 3 months later | 26.9 | 0.0 | 73.1 |

*Sources*: Author's computations

Second, Moody's ratings are the most stable: 85 and 95.5% of unchanged ratings following excessively high and low spreads, respectively (average of 1- and 3-month terms for the two percentages) vs. 77 and 94.5% for Fitch vs. 79 and 84.5% for S&P.

Third, rating changes are asymmetric. The three agencies are more reluctant to upgrade when spreads are excessively low than to downgrade when spreads are excessively high. This trend is particularly strong for Fitch and Moody's: the percentage of downgrades following excessively high spreads is on average three times the percentage of upgrades following excessively low spreads. This asymmetric adjustment is weaker for S&P, essentially because this agency is much more prompt to upgrade following excessively low spreads (Table 9.7) than is Fitch or Moody's.

Fourth, Fitch and S&P do not adjust their ratings against the market's view: they do not downgrade (upgrade) countries with excessively low (high) spreads. Moody's has done so twice.[2]

Fifth, the percentage of outliers by year and rating agency (Figs. 9.1–9.3) reveals that major disagreements between CRAs and the market occur in 1994–1995, 1998 and 2006, i.e., during periods of historically high and low spreads. For instance, risk aversion is much higher among investors than among agencies' analysts at the peak of the Russian crisis in August 1998.[3] In contrast, spreads are excessively low in 2005–2006 when compared to rating-based spreads.

Sixth, the divergence in assessing sovereign creditworthiness is significant when Moody's rating-based spreads are taken into account for the historically low spreads

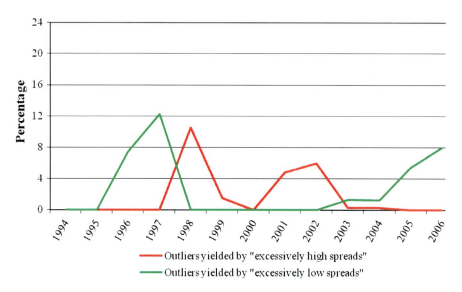

**Fig. 9.1** Outliers yielded by excessively high/low actual spreads when actual spreads are compared to Fitch rating-based spreads. *Note*: None of the 32 countries in the sample was rated by Fitch as of 31 December 1993. *Sources*: Author's computations

---

[2] Moody's upgraded Pakistan in February 2002 and Argentina in June 2005 at a time when the spreads of the two countries were excessively high.

[3] August 1998 was the month with the highest spreads for the period under study.

9.3 Adjustments of Ratings to Market Spreads 157

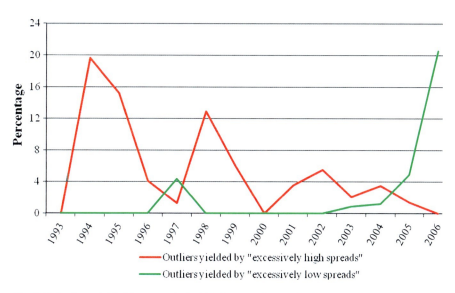

**Fig. 9.2** Outliers yielded by excessively high/low actual spreads when actual spreads are compared to Moody's rating-based spreads. *Sources*: Author's computations

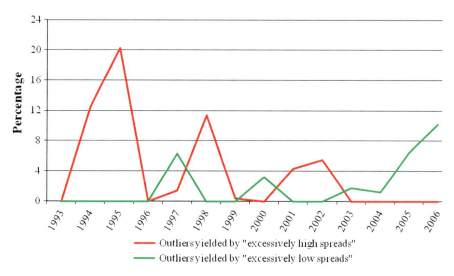

**Fig. 9.3** Outliers yielded by excessively high/low actual spreads when actual spreads are compared to S&P rating-based spreads. *Sources*: Author's computations

of 2006 (more than 20% of outliers, Fig. 9.2) and early 2007. This may lead one to view Moody's rating policy as being more conservative than Fitch and S&P.

These findings are consistent with Sy's results for January 1994 to April 2001, which indicate that the relationship between ratings and market spreads is weaker in times of financial turmoil. They also show that sovereign ratings are not as procyclical as the literature claims (Ferri et al. 1999; Reisen and von Maltzan 1999). For instance, the three agencies downgraded only 26% of the countries in my sample between July 1997 (the beginning of the Asian crisis) and December 1998. In the same way, CRAs tended to moderate the market euphoria in 2005–2007: 38% of all countries in the sample were upgraded between June 2005 (the month when the EMBIG Composite fell below the psychological threshold of 300 basis points for the first time) and April 2007.[4] Not surprisingly, S&P was more prone to upgrade (47%) than Fitch (37%) and Moody's (30%).

### 9.3.2 Adjustments of Ratings to Strong Increase/Decrease in Spreads

Increases (respectively decreases) in spreads are considered strong when they rise (respectively fall) by at least 25% within a month.[5] For each strong increase or decrease in spreads that occurs during month M, I assess whether there is an upgrade, a downgrade, or no rating change during the month M − 1, the month M, the month

**Table 9.8** Fitch rating changes to strong decrease/increase in spreads

| Strong decrease in spreads | | | |
|---|---|---|---|
| Ratings | Expected upgrade (%) | Unexpected downgrade (%) | No change (%) |
| 1 month before | 0.0 | 0.0 | 100.0 |
| Same month | 1.6 | 1.6 | 96.8 |
| 1 month later | 3.2 | 0.0 | 96.8 |
| 3 months later | 8.3 | 1.6 | 90.1 |
| Strong increase in spreads | | | |
| Ratings | Expected downgrade (%) | Unexpected upgrade (%) | No change (%) |
| 1 month before | 4.1 | 0.0 | 95.9 |
| Same month | 8.1 | 2.4 | 89.5 |
| 1 month later | 8.1 | 0.8 | 91.1 |
| 3 months later | 12.2 | 2.4 | 85.4 |

*Sources*: Author's computations

---

[4] The two percentages are weighted averages based on Fitch, Moody's, and S&P downgrades for July 1997–December 1998 and Fitch, Moody's, and S&P upgrades for June 2005–April 2007 (author's calculations).

[5] Here I continue using monthly stripped spreads.

## 9.3 Adjustments of Ratings to Market Spreads

**Table 9.9** Moody's rating changes to strong decrease/increase in spreads

Strong decrease in spreads

| Ratings | Expected upgrade (%) | Unexpected downgrade (%) | No change (%) |
|---|---|---|---|
| 1 month before | 0.0 | 1.4 | 98.6 |
| Same month | 4.3 | 4.3 | 91.4 |
| 1 month later | 2.9 | 1.4 | 95.7 |
| 3 months later | 7.2 | 1.4 | 91.4 |

Strong increase in spreads

| Ratings | Expected downgrade (%) | Unexpected upgrade (%) | No change (%) |
|---|---|---|---|
| 1 month before | 2.9 | 0.0 | 97.1 |
| Same month | 4.7 | 1.7 | 93.6 |
| 1 month later | 8.1 | 0.6 | 91.3 |
| 3 months later | 16.3 | 1.7 | 82.0 |

*Sources*: Author's computations

**Table 9.10** S&P rating changes to strong decrease/increase in spreads

Strong decrease in spreads

| Ratings | Expected upgrade (%) | Unexpected downgrade (%) | No change (%) |
|---|---|---|---|
| 1 month before | 1.4 | 1.4 | 97.2 |
| Same month | 5.6 | 0.0 | 94.4 |
| 1 month later | 1.4 | 0.0 | 98.6 |
| 3 months later | 6.9 | 1.4 | 91.7 |

Strong increase in spreads

| Ratings | Expected downgrade (%) | Unexpected upgrade (%) | No change (%) |
|---|---|---|---|
| 1 month before | 1.7 | 0.0 | 98.3 |
| Same month | 8.7 | 0.0 | 91.3 |
| 1 month later | 9.8 | 0.6 | 89.6 |
| 3 months later | 17.9 | 2.9 | 79.2 |

*Sources*: Author's computations

M+1, and the period M+1–M+3. The results (see Tables 9.8–9.10)[6] confirm previous conclusions: there is an overall stability of ratings as well as an asymmetry of rating changes (more downgrades than upgrades).

More than 12% of strong increases in spreads is preceded or accompanied by a Fitch downgrade the previous month or the same month; the percentage reaches 10.4% for S&P, but only 7.6% for Moody's. This may prove that Fitch partly anticipates spread increases by downgrading early, whereas S&P and Moody's adjust their ratings later (12% of downgrades for Fitch between months M+1 and M+3 vs. 16 and 18% for Moody's and S&P, respectively).

---

[6] I consider that ratings are expected to be upgraded (respectively downgraded) when there is a strong decrease (respectively increase) in spreads.

The study of the upgrades preceding and following strong declines in spreads discloses that S&P is slightly quicker to anticipate the decrease in risk aversion by upgrading in the month M − 1 or the month M. Moody's ratings are much less sensitive to strong spread decreases in that the total number of upgrades is equal to the total number of downgrades for the period from M − 1 to M + 1 (Table 9.9). Once again, these findings corroborate that Moody's ratings are less correlated to the market.

## 9.4 Reaction of Market Spreads to Rating Changes

This section aims to measure the impact of sovereign rating changes on EMBIG spreads. I list all upgrades and downgrades for the same sample of 32 emerging countries between 31 December 1993 and 28 February 2007 (Table 9.11).

The day of each rating change is day 0, and all spreads take the value 100 for the day prior to the rating change (day −1).[7] Then I compute the average evolution of spreads for the 30 trading days before and after upgrade and downgrade announcements by Fitch, Moody's, and S&P (Figs. 9.4–9.9).[8]

Not surprisingly, Fitch, Moody's, and S&P downgrades (respectively upgrades) are, on average, preceded and followed by an increase (respectively decrease) in spreads. More precisely, the curve associated with Moody's upgrades (Fig. 9.5) is of a spread overshooting immediately after the upgrade, but beyond day +10 the curve unexpectedly rises. This move in the "wrong" direction may disclose a very short-term, but real impact of Moody's upgrades. Figure 9.8 shows that Moody's downgrades occurred in times of extreme financial stress: spreads increased by 60% between day −30 and day +30 (the percentage reaches only 47% for Fitch downgrades and 31% for S&P downgrades).

Table 9.11 Rating changes by agency, 31 December 1993 to 28 February 2007

| CRA | Number of upgrades | Number of downgrades | Total number of rating changes |
| --- | --- | --- | --- |
| Fitch | 58 | 43 | 101 |
| Moody's | 49 | 41 | 90 |
| S&P | 73 | 60 | 133 |
| Total | 180 | 144 | 324 |

*Note*: Author's computations
*Sources*: http://www.fitchratings.com, http://www.moodys.com, and http://www.standardandpoors.com

---

[7] I assume that all rating changes (day 0) occurred before the end of the trading day.
[8] Daily spreads are here used for the period 31 December 1993 to 28 February 2007.

9.4 Reaction of Market Spreads to Rating Changes

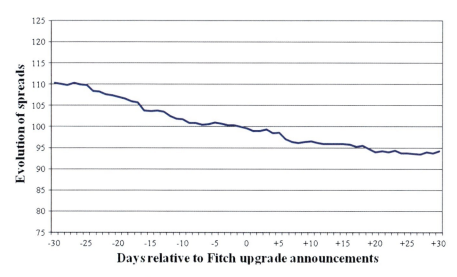

**Fig. 9.4** Evolution of EMBIG spreads before and after Fitch upgrade announcements. *Sources*: Author's computations

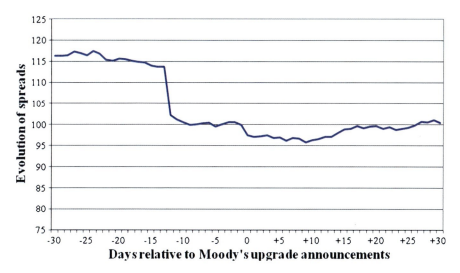

**Fig. 9.5** Evolution of EMBIG spreads before and after Moody's upgrade announcements. *Sources*: Author's computations

It is also important to highlight the regularity in the fall of the curve for Fitch upgrades and the rise of the curve for Fitch downgrades (Figs. 9.4 and 9.7, respectively). This supports the claim, mentioned previously, that Fitch ratings are more in line with the market. This hypothesis is also checked against the spread curve before

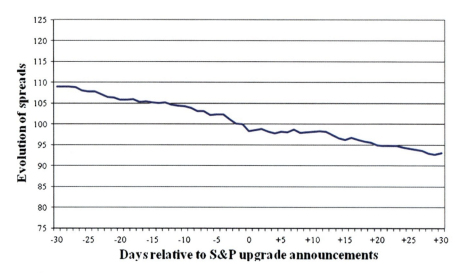

**Fig. 9.6** Evolution of EMBIG spreads before and after S&P upgrade announcements. *Sources*: Author's computations

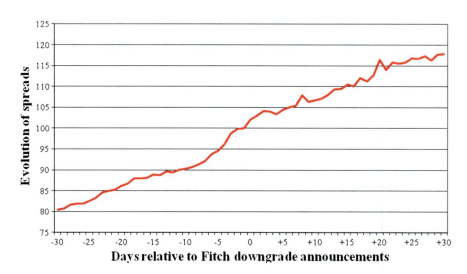

**Fig. 9.7** Evolution of EMBIG spreads before and after Fitch downgrade announcements. *Sources*: Author's computations

## 9.4 Reaction of Market Spreads to Rating Changes

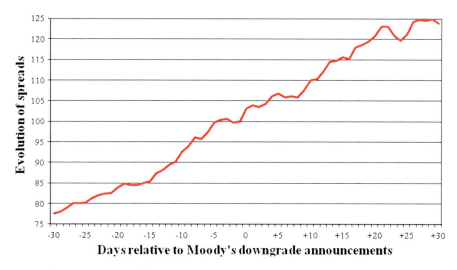

**Fig. 9.8** Evolution of EMBIG spreads before and after Moody's downgrade announcements. *Sources*: Author's computations

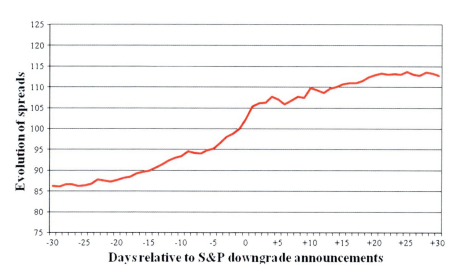

**Fig. 9.9** Evolution of EMBIG spreads before and after S&P downgrade announcements. *Sources*: Author's computations

and after S&P upgrades (Fig. 9.6). The slope of the spread curve for S&P downgrades (Fig. 9.9) is particularly sharp for the 2-day period following the downgrade (i.e., day 0 and day +1), which contrasts with the flat curve from day −30 to day −15 and from day +15 to day +30. This suggests an immediate impact of S&P downgrades on spreads.

In order to assess empirically the immediate impact of upgrades and downgrades on spreads, I run a series of regressions of the change in spreads (in percentage) between the end of the day −1 and the end of the day +1 [i.e., the evolution of spreads for (day 0; day +1)] against a set of explanatory variables that includes all rating changes, rating changes by each agency, the evolution of spreads (in percentage) during the 60 and 30 days preceding all rating changes, and preceding rating changes by each agency (i.e., from days −60 and −30 to day −1), as well as several dummies taking into account the investment-/speculative-grade cutoff (Table 9.12).

Regression results (Table 9.13) show that when all rating changes are tested they are significant and have the expected sign (regressions [1] and [2]). This immediate and expected impact on spreads is stronger than the change in spreads from days −60 and −30 to day −1. It is worth noting that neither the investment-grade status (regressions [3] and [4]) nor the upgrade from speculative grade to investment grade (regressions [5] and [6]) have any effect. However, the downgrade from investment grade to speculative grade (regressions [7] and [8]) is significant. This result can be partly explained by the fact that three of the eight downgrades from investment grade to speculative grade involved Uruguay and occurred in the aftermath of the Argentine default, in times of market stress.[9]

When rating changes are tested for each agency (Table 9.14), they are all significant, except for Fitch rating changes when tested with the evolution of spreads from day −60 to day −1. The variable capturing the evolution of spreads during the 30/60 days prior to the rating change is significant only once (regression [6]). These findings are particularly relevant because they prove that the increase/decrease in spreads within the 2 days (day 0 and day +1) following a Fitch, Moody's, or S&P downgrade/upgrade is more affected by the rating change itself than by the evolution of spreads between day −60/−30 and day −1.

The next step is to assess which agency's upgrades and downgrades have the most impact by taking into account the number of rating changes for each agency.[10] Thus, I run regressions of all spread changes for (day 0; day +1) (i.e., spread changes following all rating changes: downgrades and upgrades by Fitch, Moody's, and S&P) against Fitch upgrades, then against Fitch downgrades, Moody's upgrades, Moody's downgrades, S&P upgrades, and S&P downgrades, separately. I use a dummy variable taking the value 1 for the group tested and 0 otherwise. For instance,

---

[9] Uruguay was downgraded from investment grade to speculative grade on 14 February, 13 March, and 3 May 2002 by S&P, Fitch, and Moody's, respectively (see Chap. 8).

[10] This choice is implied by the fact that the number of rating changes differs across agencies (Table 9.11), and one could raise doubts about the influence of an agency whose upgrades and downgrades have an impact on spreads, but are very few.

## 9.4 Reaction of Market Spreads to Rating Changes

**Table 9.12** List of explanatory variables

| |
|---|
| ALLRAT is the number of upward/downward notches resulting from all rating changes (i.e., Fitch upgrades, Fitch downgrades, Moody's upgrades, Moody's downgrades, S&P upgrades, and S&P downgrades). For example: −2 for a two-notch downgrade and +1 for a one-notch upgrade |
| ASPR60 is the evolution of spreads (in percentage) during the 60 days preceding all rating changes (from day −60 to day −1) |
| ASPR30 is the evolution of spreads (in percentage) during the 30 days preceding all rating changes (from day −30 to day −1) |
| INV is a dummy taking the value 1 if the initial rating is in investment grade and 0 otherwise |
| GOINV is a dummy taking the value 1 if the initial rating is upgraded from speculative grade to investment grade and 0 otherwise |
| GOSPEC is a dummy taking the value 1 if the initial rating is downgraded from investment grade to speculative grade and 0 otherwise |
| ALLFI is the number of upward/downward notches resulting from all Fitch rating changes (i.e., Fitch upgrades and Fitch downgrades) |
| FISPR60 is the evolution of spreads (in percentage) during the 60 days preceding all Fitch rating changes (from day −60 to day −1) |
| FISPR30 is the evolution of spreads (in percentage) during the 30 days preceding all Fitch rating changes (from day −30 to day −1) |
| ALLMO is the number of upward/downward notches resulting from all Moody's rating changes (i.e., Moody's upgrades and Moody's downgrades) |
| MOSPR60 is the evolution of spreads (in percentage) during the 60 days preceding all Moody's rating changes (from day −60 to day −1) |
| MOSPR30 is the evolution of spreads (in percentage) during the 30 days preceding all Moody's rating changes (from day −30 to day −1) |
| ALLSP is the number of upward/downward notches resulting from all S&P rating changes (i.e., S&P upgrades and S&P downgrades) |
| SPSPR60 is the evolution of spreads (in percentage) during the 60 days preceding all S&P rating changes (from day −60 to day −1) |
| SPSPR30 is the evolution of spreads (in percentage) during the 30 days preceding all S&P rating changes (from day −30 to day −1) |
| FIUP is a dummy taking the value 1 for Fitch upgrades and 0 for all other rating changes (i.e., Fitch downgrades, Moody's upgrades, Moody's downgrades, S&P upgrades, and S&P downgrades) |
| FIDO is a dummy taking the value 1 for Fitch downgrades and 0 for all other rating changes |
| MOUP is a dummy taking the value 1 for Moody's upgrades and 0 for all other rating changes |
| MODO is a dummy taking the value 1 for Moody's downgrades and 0 for all other rating changes |
| SPUP is a dummy taking the value 1 for S&P upgrades and 0 for all other rating changes |
| SPDO is a dummy taking the value 1 for S&P downgrades and 0 for all other rating changes |

*Notes*: Fitch and S&P investment-grade ratings are BBB− and above. Moody's investment-grade ratings are Baa3 and above. Fitch and S&P speculative-grade ratings are BB+ and below. Moody's speculative-grade ratings are Ba1 and below

when Fitch upgrades are tested, the value for Fitch upgrades is 1, while Fitch downgrades and all Moody's and S&P rating changes take the value 0. Results are presented in Table 9.15.

First, both Fitch upgrades and downgrades do not seem to have a clear immediate impact on spreads (regressions [1] to [4]). This strengthens my previous results

**Table 9.13** Immediate impact of rating changes on EMBIG spreads

| | Dependent variable: evolution of EMBIG spreads for (day 0; day +1) | | | | | | | |
|---|---|---|---|---|---|---|---|---|
| | [1] | [2] | [3] | [4] | [5] | [6] | [7] | [8] |
| ALLRAT | **−1.227 (3.684)** | **−1.281 (3.882)** | **−1.266 (3.796)** | **−1.314 (3.986)** | **−1.170 (3.508)** | **−1.218 (3.684)** | **−1.135 (3.398)** | **1.167 (3.520)** |
| ASPR60 | **0.023 (2.558)** | | **0.023 (2.531)** | | **0.022 (2.446)** | | **0.023 (2.622)** | |
| ASPR30 | | **0.027 (2.166)** | | **0.028 (2.214)** | | **0.026 (2.077)** | | **0.029 (2.350)** |
| INV | | | 1.738 (1.480) | 1.925 (1.637) | | | | |
| GOINV | | | | | −4.372 (1.752) | −4.474 (1.791) | | |
| GOSPEC | | | | | | | **6.999 (2.153)** | **7.465 (2.288)** |
| Constant | 0.763 (1.418) | 0.793 (1.480) | 0.344 (0.566) | 0.318 (0.523) | 0.965 (1.760) | 0.995 (1.823) | 0.568 (1.047) | 0.566 (1.046) |
| Adjusted $R^2$ | 0.093 | 0.086 | 0.096 | 0.090 | 0.099 | 0.092 | 0.103 | 0.098 |
| Number of observations | 320 | 322 | 320 | 322 | 320 | 322 | 320 | 322 |

*Notes*: Absolute $t$ statistics are in *parentheses*. Coefficients with the expected sign and significant $t$ statistics (at the 5% level) are in **bold**. Because of missing EMBIG spread data for several countries 60 and 30 days before a rating change, the number of observations varies across regressions

## 9.4 Reaction of Market Spreads to Rating Changes

**Table 9.14** Immediate impact of rating changes on EMBIG spreads by agency

| | Dependent variable: evolution of EMBIG spreads for (day 0; day +1) | | | | | |
|---|---|---|---|---|---|---|
| | [1] | [2] | [3] | [4] | [5] | [6] |
| ALLFI | −0.922 (1.654) | | | | | |
| FISPR60 | 0.023 (1.523) | | | | | |
| FISPR30 | | 0.011 (0.507) | | | | |
| ALLMO | | **−1.197 (2.133)** | **−1.688 (2.029)** | **−1.807 (2.304)** | | |
| MOSPR60 | | | 0.016 (0.923) | | | |
| MOSPR30 | | | | 0.017 (0.710) | | |
| ALLSP | | | | | **−1.248 (2.567)** | **−1.185 (2.449)** |
| SPSPR60 | | | | | 0.028 (1.876) | |
| SPSPR30 | | | | | | **0.043 (2.134)** |
| Constant | 0.529 (0.646) | 0.748 (0.892) | 0.006 (0.005) | 0.075 (0.071) | 1.501 (1.647) | 1.407 (1.567) |
| Adjusted $R^2$ | 0.073 | 0.053 | 0.088 | 0.081 | 0.091 | 0.096 |
| Number of observations | 100 | 100 | 89 | 90 | 131 | 132 |

*Notes*: Absolute *t* statistics are in *parentheses*. Coefficients with the expected sign and significant *t* statistics (at the 5% level) are in **bold**. Because of missing EMBIG spread data for several countries 60 and 30 days before a rating change, the number of observations varies across regressions

**Table 9.15** Immediate impact of rating changes on EMBIG spreads by agency and type of rating change

Dependent variable: evolution of EMBIG spreads for (day 0; day +1)

| | [1] | [2] | [3] | [4] | [5] | [6] | [7] | [8] | [9] | [10] | [11] | [12] |
|---|---|---|---|---|---|---|---|---|---|---|---|---|
| ASPR60 | **0.036** | | **0.036** | | **0.033** | | **0.035** | | **0.034** | | **0.031** | |
| | **(4.200)** | | **(4.277)** | | **(3.978)** | | **(3.973)** | | **(4.007)** | | **(3.733)** | |
| ASPR30 | | **0.045** | | **0.045** | | **0.042** | | **0.043** | | **0.042** | | **0.039** |
| | | **(3.750)** | | **(3.787)** | | **(3.580)** | | **(3.579)** | | **(3.564)** | | **(3.372)** |
| FIUP | −1.158 | −1.320 | | | | | | | | | | |
| | (0.843) | (0.961) | | | | | | | | | | |
| FIDO | | | 1.174 | 1.237 | | | | | | | | |
| | | | (0.755) | (0.790) | | | | | | | | |
| MOUP | | | | | **−3.430** | **−3.630** | | | | | | |
| | | | | | **(2.365)** | **(2.509)** | | | | | | |
| MODO | | | | | | | 1.395 | 1.766 | | | | |
| | | | | | | | (0.845) | (1.097) | | | | |
| SPUP | | | | | | | | | −2.032 | −2.165 | | |
| | | | | | | | | | (1.603) | (1.708) | | |
| SPDO | | | | | | | | | | | **4.602** | **4.667** |
| | | | | | | | | | | | **(3.436)** | **(3.517)** |
| Constant | 0.590 | 0.654 | 0.219 | 0.250 | 0.947 | 1.003 | 0.221 | 0.208 | 0.866 | 0.928 | −0.387 | −0.386 |
| | (0.973) | (1.082) | (0.388) | (0.442) | (1.607) | (1.710) | (0.395) | (0.371) | (1.389) | (1.493) | (0.680) | (0.675) |
| Adjusted $R^2$ | 0.056 | 0.045 | 0.056 | 0.044 | 0.070 | 0.061 | 0.056 | 0.046 | 0.062 | 0.051 | 0.088 | 0.078 |
| Number of observations | 320 | 322 | 320 | 322 | 320 | 322 | 320 | 322 | 320 | 322 | 320 | 322 |

*Notes*: Absolute *t* statistics are in *parentheses*. Coefficients with the expected sign and significant *t* statistics (at the 5% level) are in **bold**. Because of missing EMBIG spread data for several countries 60 and 30 days before a rating change, the number of observations varies across regressions from testing simultaneously all rating changes and evolutions of spreads between days −60/−30 and day −1. Second, I find that Moody's upgrades and S&P downgrades have the greatest effect on spreads (regressions [5], [6], [11], and [12]). Observe that S&P downgrades have the most impact overall. Third, the effect that ratings have is not a function of the number of rating changes: Moody's upgrades have the biggest impact, yet are fewer than Fitch and S&P upgrades (Table 9.11). This point underscores the importance of the timing of rating changes. Fourth, the very low $R^2$ values in all regressions mean that investors' decisions are driven by issues other than rating changes. Fifth, my findings diverge from both Cantor and Packer's (1996) and Reisen and von Maltzan's (1999) in demonstrating that both Moody's upgrades and S&P downgrades have a significant impact on spreads. This is not surprising when one considers that the earlier papers focused on different periods (1987–1994 and 1989–1997, respectively) and included both emerging and advanced economies.

## 9.5 Conclusions

This chapter measures the interactions between JP Morgan EMBIG spreads and Fitch, Moody's, and S&P sovereign ratings for the period December 1993 to February 2007. The statistical analysis and empirical tests support several conclusions.

For the entire period overall, the market and the CRAs seem to have a common perception of sovereign risk. However, their perceptions tend to differ in times of extremely high risk aversion (1998) and low risk aversion (2005–2007). Therefore, the overreaction of CRAs during the Asian and the Russian crises in 1997 and 1998 is deceptive. The procyclicality of ratings holds partially for 1997–1998, but cannot be demonstrated either for 1994–1995 (the Tequila crisis) or for 2002, when investors feared that Brazil might default. Moreover, ratings moderated the market euphoria in 2005–2007: the majority of emerging countries' ratings remained unchanged during these 2 years. These findings remind that sovereign ratings reflect a "through the cycle" analysis, which explains the relatively small number of downgrades and upgrades for 1993–2007 (see Moody's ratings in particular). My last prominent conclusion concerns the impact of ratings on spreads. Moody's upgrades and S&P downgrades have the strongest impact, but rating changes are usually preceded by an evolution of spreads in the expected direction. These results show that ratings and spreads are interdependent even though their movements are far from synchronized.

## References

Baldacci E., Gupta S. and Mati A. (2008), "Is it (Still) Mostly Fiscal? Determinants of Sovereign Spreads in Emerging Markets", *IMF Working Paper, WP/08/259.*
Cantor R. and Packer F. (1996), "Determinants and Impacts of Sovereign Credit Ratings", *Economic Policy Review, Federal Reserve Bank of New York, October.*

Eichengreen B. and Mody A. (1998), "What Explains Changing Spreads on Emerging-Market Debt: Fundamentals or Market Sentiment?", *National Bureau of Economic Research, Working Paper No.6408*.

Ferri G., Liu L.-G. and Stiglitz J. (1999), "The Procyclical Role of Rating Agencies: Evidence from the East Asian Crisis", *Economic Notes, Banca Monte dei Paschi di Siena SpA*, No.3.

Ferrucci G. (2003), "Empirical determinants of emerging market economies' sovereign bond spreads", *Bank of England, Working Paper No.205*.

JP Morgan (1995), "Introducing the Emerging Markets Bond Index Plus (EMBI⁺)", *Methodology Brief*, 12 July.

JP Morgan (1999), "Introducing the JP Morgan Emerging Markets Bond Index Global (EMBI Global)", *Methodology Brief*, 3 August.

Kräussl R. (2000), "Sovereign Ratings and Their Impact on Recent Financial Crises", *Center for Financial Studies, Working Paper 2000, Frankfurt/Main*.

Larraín G., Reisen H. and von Maltzan J. (1997), "Emerging Market Risk and Sovereign Credit Ratings", *OECD Development Centre, Technical Paper No.124*.

Mora N. (2006), "Sovereign credit ratings: beyond reasonable doubt?", *Journal of Banking and Finance*, Vol.30, No.7.

Reisen H. and von Maltzan J. (1999), "Boom and Sovereign Ratings", *OECD Development Centre, Working Paper No.148*.

Rowland P. and Torres J. L. (2004), "Determinants of Spread and Creditworthiness for Emerging Market Sovereign Debt: A Panel Data Study", *Banco de la República, Colombia, Borrador de Economía 295*.

Sy A. (2001), "Emerging Market Bond Spreads and Sovereign Credit Ratings: Reconciling Market Views with Economic Fundamentals", *IMF Working Paper, WP/01/165*.

# Chapter 10
# The Limits of Sovereign Ratings in Light of the Greek Debt Crisis of 2009–2010

This chapter explains why the CRAs failed to anticipate the Greek debt crisis of 2009–2010 and maintained views that diverged from the market's during the crisis. Section 10.1 presents a review of the literature. Section 10.2 compares Fitch, Moody's, and S&P sovereign ratings with credit default swap-implied ratings (CDS-IRs) prior to and during the Greek debt crisis of November 2009 to May 2010. The main finding is that the risk of default reflected in the agencies' ratings at the end of the financial turmoil (i.e., in mid-May 2010, after the creation of the European stabilization mechanism was announced) was still lower than the risk reflected in the CDS-IRs at the beginning of the crisis (i.e., on 1 January 2010). Section 10.3 offers arguments to explain why CRAs "missed" the crisis. Two types of explanation emerge: first, the belief that an advanced country would not default; second, the use of ratings in regulatory capital standards, which served to inflate investment-grade sovereign ratings. Section 10.4 concludes.

## 10.1 Review of the Literature

This chapter incorporates themes from four categories of the literature.

The first group of papers studies market-implied ratings. Breger et al. (2003) derive equivalent ratings based on bond prices to reassess default risk. They demonstrate that classifying bonds using market data provides a more reliable basis for modeling return relationships and improving spread risk forecasts than does a classification driven by agencies' ratings. Comparing the accuracy and stability of its ratings with ratings inferred from bond spreads, Moody's (2003) finds that market-implied ratings are more accurate than Moody's ratings at the 1-year horizon; however, the two turn out to be equivalent at the 3-year horizon. Kou and Varotto (2008) refine Breger et al.'s (2003) approach by taking into account term structure effects and estimating separate boundaries for different maturities. They conclude that spread-implied ratings are powerful tools for predicting agencies' ratings.

The CRAs began to use market signals intensively in 2002, when Moody's launched its Market Implied Ratings services (for a description, see Moody's 2007b). Fitch (2007b) followed along these lines by developing a CDS-implied model that uses daily CDS market quotes to derive implied ratings.

A second area of research to which this chapter is related explores the sustainability of public debt. Reinhart et al. (2003) introduce the concept of "debt intolerance," which refers to the inability of some emerging economies to sustain a debt level that is manageable by the standards of more advanced countries. Their key finding is that a country's external debt intolerance can be explained by a small number of variables: default history, debt level, and macroeconomic stability. After examining several centuries of financial crises, Reinhart and Rogoff (2009) and Qian et al. (2011) assert that countries may "graduate" from serial default on sovereign debt. They consider a 20-year span without a debt crisis to be a significant milestone toward durable creditworthiness. Eichengreen and Hausmann (1999) offer a different approach by developing the concept of "original sin": the impossibility of a country to borrow abroad in its own currency or to borrow long-term even domestically. Eichengreen et al. (2005a, b) show that "original sin" is a widespread and persistent phenomenon that precludes borrowing in foreign currency debt and hinders economic development [for a recent update of their previous work, see Hausmann and Panizza 2010].

The third set of relevant papers focuses on the Greek debt crisis of 2009–2010 and can be summarized as the opposition of two views. Cottarelli et al. (2010) consider the default of an advanced country to be "unnecessary, undesirable, and unlikely." In particular, they argue that the cost of default would be considerable and would not solve the advanced countries' fundamental problem (i.e., primary deficits). They also emphasize that though painful the needed fiscal adjustments are feasible and would pave the way to a more stringent fiscal policy. However, Buiter and Rahbari (2010) question this opinion by recalling that the credit position of most advanced economies weakened in the 2000s. They cite three reasons for this evolution: strong demand for public spending, declining capacity to tax, and delay in fiscal adjustment for political reasons. They conclude that Greece is likely to restructure its debt in the short–medium term.

Finally, this chapter draws also from the literature dealing with the use of credit ratings in regulatory rules. Flandreau et al. (2010) study the context in which CRAs became the gatekeepers of the sovereign bond markets beginning in 1931. Cantor and Packer (1994) address the increasing role played by credit ratings in U.S. regulations since the 1980s. The Bank for International Settlements (2009) provides an updated compilation of the use of ratings in advanced countries' legislations, regulations, and supervisory policies. The Financial Stability Board (2010) argues that all references to credit ratings in standards, laws, and regulations should be removed or replaced; it suggests that market participants and institutional investors should make their own credit assessments and not rely mechanically on ratings. These recommendations echo Partnoy's (2002, 2009) views on the negative effects of using credit ratings for regulatory purpose.

## 10.2 Perception of Sovereign Risk During the Greek Debt Crisis: Ratings vs. CDS-IRs

This section provides a short chronology of the sovereign debt crisis that erupted in November 2009. It then presents the data employed and the method used to compare sovereign ratings and CDS-IRs. Finally, it analyzes the results obtained.

### 10.2.1 Chronicle of a Debt Crisis Foretold

In the wake of the mid-September 2008 collapse of Lehman Brothers, financial markets plunged into turmoil. Interbank rates and credit spreads soared to record levels, and fears of massive defaults surged. This extreme financial market stress forced several governments (in advanced and emerging countries both) to bail out banks, thus increasing public debt burdens. Uncertainty about the fiscal position of several eurozone members, combined with gloomy economic outlooks and weak banking systems, undermined the creditworthiness of four countries: Greece, Ireland, Portugal, and Spain. Figure 10.1 shows that Greece's and Ireland's 10-year CDSs began to widen from 65 and 45 basis points (bps) (respectively) the last week of September 2008 and reached 262 and 236 bps the first week of December 2008. Financial stress declined slightly until S&P downgraded Greece, Spain, and Portugal in January 2009 (see Table 10.1). Greece's and Ireland's 10-year CDSs fell again from March to October 2009. By the end of October 2009, the Greek government

**Fig. 10.1** 10-Year CDS in bps, 15 June 2008 to 15 June 2010. *Sources*: Datastream

**Table 10.1** Downgrades affecting eurozone members, 15 June 2008 to 15 June 2010

| Country | Fitch | Moody's | S&P |
|---|---|---|---|
| Greece | 22 October 2009: A → A− | 22 December 2009: A1 → A2 | 14 January 2009: A → A− |
|  | 8 December 2009: A− → BBB+ | 22 April 2010: A2 → A3 | 16 December 2009: A− → BBB+ |
|  | 9 April 2010: BBB+ → BBB− | 14 June 2010: A3 → Ba1 | 27 April 2010: BBB+ → BB+ |
| Ireland | 9 March 2009: AAA → AA+ | 6 July 2009: Aaa → Aa1 | 30 March 2009: AAA → AA+ |
|  | 4 November 2009: AA → AA− |  | 8 June 2009: AA+ → AA |
| Portugal | 24 March 2010: AA → AA− | No downgrade | 21 January 2009: AA− → A+ |
|  |  |  | 27 April 2010: A+ → A− |
| Spain | 28 May 2010: AAA → AA+ | No downgrade | 19 January 2009: AAA → AA+ |
|  |  |  | 28 April 2010: AA+ → AA |

*Sources*: http://www.fitchratings.com, http://www.moodys.com, and http://www.standardandpoors.com

revised its forecasted budget deficit upward to 12.5%, more than double the previous forecast. This announcement triggered another series of rating downgrades by the three principal CRAs in December. From then, CDS increases and rating cuts fed each other, which made it increasingly expensive for the Greek government to borrow. The end of the story is well known: after several months of negotiation, the European Union agreed to create new lending facilities for eurozone member states in financial distress. The 110 € billion support package for Greece was approved the first week of May; it consisted of an 80 € billion facility from the eurozone countries and a 30 € billion stand-by arrangement with the IMF.

The controversial role played by the rating agencies (particularly by S&P) during the Greek debt crisis made headlines. As during the Asian crisis, CRAs were held responsible for escalating financial stress by downgrading massively in April 2010. In fact, such assertions must be tested by comparing sovereign ratings and CDSs, which can be done by converting CDSs into CDS-IRs.

## *10.2.2 Data Description and Methods*

The database used in this chapter is described as follows. The countries under study are the sovereigns (both advanced and emerging countries in all regions) that are assigned an investment-grade or a BB+/Ba1 rating by at least one of the three main CRAs (Fitch, Moody's, and S&P), and for which a 10-year CDS is available during the period 1 January 2009 to 17 May 2010. Because there are not enough sovereign CDSs available for the countries rated in the speculative-grade category, the minimum rating considered here is BB+/Ba1.

Because of this data limitation, the BB+/Ba1 rating category was relabeled "SG" (i.e., speculative grade). The objective is to assign the SG classification to those countries whose CDS-IRs are BB+/Ba1, but could be even lower. The comparison of Fitch, Moody's, and S&P ratings with their respective CDS-IRs is made for six dates: 1 January 2009, 1 December 2009, 1 January 2010, 1 March 2010, 30 April 2010, and 17 May 2010. As a result, there are 18 samples. There is little variation across samples in the number of sovereigns under examination; this number ranges only from 50 to 53.

Estimates of the CDS-IRs were derived using the method developed by Breger et al. (2003) and refined by Kou and Varotto (2008). For each rating category, a penalty function $P(b)$ is computed that depends on the value of CDS boundaries. The penalty value increases when the CDS is outside the upper or lower boundaries that correspond to its rating. The penalty function is defined as follows:

$$P(b) = \frac{1}{m}\sum_{i=1}^{m}\max(c_{i,R_{a+1}} - b, 0) + \frac{1}{n}\sum_{j=1}^{n}\max(b - c_{j,R_a}, 0),$$

where
$R_a$ and $R_{a+1}$ are two adjacent rating categories with $R_{a+1}$ one notch higher than $R_a$;
$c_{i,R_{a+1}}$ is the CDS of country $i$ with the rating $R_{a+1}$;
$c_{j,R_a}$ is the CDS of country $j$ with the rating $R_a$;
$m$ is the total number of countries rated $R_{a+1}$;
$n$ is the total number of countries rated $R_a$; and
$b$ is CDS boundary between $R_a$ and $R_{a+1}$.

The optimum boundaries are those that minimize the penalty function for each pair of adjacent ratings. Once the optimum boundaries are obtained, it is possible to derive CDS-IRs.

### 10.2.3 "Sticky" Ratings vs. Volatile CDS-IRs

Tables 10.2–10.7 present the Fitch, Moody's, and S&P ratings and the CDS-IRs derived for all the eurozone members for the six dates.[1] As in Chap. 6, a significant disagreement between an agency and the market is considered significant when there is a more-than-two-notch gap between the actual rating and the CDS-IR.

On 1 January 2009 (i.e., 2 weeks before the first wave of S&P rating cuts that hit Greece, Spain, and Portugal), actual ratings and CDS-IRs are fairly close (with the exceptions of Ireland and Austria; see Table 10.2). One may suppose that market

---

[1] The results are reported for Austria (AUT), Belgium (BEL), Finland (FIN), France (FRA), Germany (DEU), Greece (GRC), Ireland (IRL), Italy (ITA), Netherlands (NLD), Portugal (PRT), Spain (ESP), Slovakia (SVK), and Slovenia (SVN). Note that CDSs for Cyprus, Luxembourg, and Malta are not available.

Table 10.2 Sovereign ratings vs. CDS-IRs, 1 January 2009

| | 10-Year CDS (bps) | Fitch actual rating | CDS–Fitch IR | Moody's actual rating | CDS–Moody's IR | S&P actual rating | CDS–S&P IR |
|---|---|---|---|---|---|---|---|
| DEU | 50.2 | AAA | AAA | Aaa | Aaa | AAA | AAA |
| FRA | 59.0 | AAA | AAA | Aaa | Aaa | AAA | AAA |
| FIN | 65.5 | AAA | AAA | Aaa | Aaa | AAA | AAA |
| BEL | 83.9 | AA+ | AAA | Aa1 | Aaa | AA+ | AA+ |
| NLD | 93.5 | AAA | AA | Aaa | Aa2 | AAA | AA |
| PRT | 100.4 | AA | AA | Aa2 | Aa2 | AA– | AA |
| ESP | 104.6 | AAA | AA | Aaa | Aa2 | AA | AA |
| SVN | 117.2 | AA | AA | Aa2 | Aa2 | AA | AA |
| AUT | 135.0 | AAA | AA | Aaa | Aa2 | AAA | AA– |
| ITA | 161.1 | AA– | AA– | Aa2 | Aa2 | A+ | AA– |
| SVK | 165.0 | A+ | AA– | A1 | A1 | A+ | AA– |
| IRL | 185.0 | AAA | A+ | Aaa | A1 | AAA | A |
| GRC | 239.5 | A | A– | A1 | A1 | A | A– |

Sources: Author's computations, http://www.fitchratings.com, http://www.moodys.com, http://www.standardandpoors.com, and http://www.datastream.com

participants overweighted the risk of a banking crisis in these two countries: the CDS-IRs for Ireland are four or five notches lower than the actual ratings, and there is a three-notch gap between the Austria's CDS-IR and the actual S&P rating. On 1 December 2009 (several days prior to the wave of rating cuts that hit Greece), significant gaps are observed for three countries: Spain, Ireland, and Greece (see Table 10.3). Ireland's CDS-IRs are much lower (by three and five notches) than the actual ratings assigned by Fitch, Moody's, and S&P. Examination of Greece's CDS-IRs and agency ratings reveals a divergence between the views of Moody's and the investors. These remarks apply also to Fitch regarding the credit position of Spain. A comparison between the CDS-IRs and actual ratings as of 1 January 2010 (several days after the wave of downgrades of Greece's ratings) amplifies the conclusions made for 1 December 2009 (Table 10.4). Market makers have much more pessimistic views of Spain, Ireland, and Greece than do the CRAs. It is worth remarking that all three of Greece's CDS-IRs are already in the speculative-grade category. Starting on 1 March 2010, it is evident that the views of the market and the CRAs diverge with respect to Spain, Ireland, and Greece as well as a fourth country, Portugal, whose CDS rose 50% in 2 months (see Table 10.5). Clearly, there is disagreement between Moody's and market participants about the credit position of Greece. On 30 April 2010 (i.e., within 3 days of S&P downgrading Spain, Portugal, and Greece by one, two, and three notches, respectively; see Table 10.1), market anxiety spreads to a fifth country: Italy (Table 10.6).

The data reveal that investors "classify" eurozone members into two categories. On the one hand, Finland, Netherlands, Germany, France, Slovenia, Austria, Belgium, and Slovakia exhibit CDS-IRs in the AAA/AA categories. On the other hand, Italy, Spain, Ireland, Portugal, and Greece have CDS-IRs in the BBB or speculative-grade categories. The discrimination made by Fitch, Moody's, and S&P is not especially sharp. It is interesting that among the three agencies the Moody's sovereign risk perception diverges the most from that of the market. This finding stems in part from the low number of rating downgrades announced by Moody's during the period 1 December 2009 to 30 April 2010 (Table 10.1). The CDS-IRs evolved very little between 30 April and 17 May 2010 (i.e., a week after the European Union/IMF support package for Greece was launched). However, observe that the CDS-IRs of Italy and Spain are one notch higher (Table 10.7).

This section sheds new light on the Greek debt crisis. Most of the eurozone members' CDSs widened between 1 December 2009 and 17 May 2010 (+69% on average). In the meantime, Moody's, Fitch, and S&P announced two, three, and four downgrades, respectively. These diverging perceptions of sovereign risk explain why, on 17 May 2010, the CDS-IRs of the riskiest countries (Greece, Ireland, Portugal, and Spain) were much lower than the Fitch, Moody's, and S&P ratings. More astonishingly, the ratings assigned to Greece, Ireland, and Spain by Fitch, Moody's, and S&P on 17 May 2010 were actually higher than the CDS-IRs of Greece, Ireland, and Spain on 1 January 2010. These findings demonstrate that the downgrades announced during 1 January 2010 to 17 May 2010 were not even sufficient to yield credit ratings that reflected, at the end of the Greek debt crisis, the risk associated with the CDS-IRs at the beginning of this crisis. In short, the agencies' ratings were "sticky" rather than procyclical during the Greek debt crisis.

**Table 10.3** Sovereign ratings vs. CDS-IRs, 1 December 2009

| | 10-Year CDS (bps) | Fitch actual rating | CDS–Fitch IR | Moody's actual rating | CDS–Moody's IR | S&P actual rating | CDS–S&P IR |
|---|---|---|---|---|---|---|---|
| DEU | 29.23 | AAA | AAA | Aaa | Aaa | AAA | AAA |
| FIN | 32.11 | AAA | AAA | Aaa | Aaa | AAA | AAA |
| FRA | 32.96 | AAA | AAA | Aaa | Aaa | AAA | AAA |
| NLD | 38.58 | AAA | AAA | Aaa | Aaa | AAA | AAA |
| BEL | 56.16 | AA+ | AA+ | Aa1 | Aa1 | AA+ | AA+ |
| SVN | 72.31 | AA | AA | Aa2 | Aa1 | AA | AA+ |
| AUT | 80.71 | AAA | AA | Aaa | Aa1 | AAA | AA |
| PRT | 82.97 | AA | AA | Aa2 | Aa1 | A+ | AA |
| SVK | 83.59 | A+ | AA | A1 | Aa2 | A+ | AA |
| ESP | 95.22 | AAA | AA– | Aaa | Aa2 | AA+ | AA |
| ITA | 98.27 | AA– | AA– | Aa2 | Aa2 | A+ | AA |
| IRL | 165.71 | AA– | A– | Aa1 | A3 | AA | BBB+ |
| GRC | 184.02 | A– | BBB+ | A1 | Baa1 | A– | BBB |

*Sources*: Author's computations, http://www.fitchratings.com, http://www.moodys.com, http://www.standardandpoors.com, and http://www.datastream.com

**Table 10.4** Sovereign ratings vs. CDS-IRs, 1 January 2010

| | 10-Year CDS (bps) | Fitch actual rating | CDS–Fitch IR | Moody's actual rating | CDS–Moody's IR | S&P actual rating | CDS–S&P IR |
|---|---|---|---|---|---|---|---|
| DEU | 31.1 | AAA | AAA | Aaa | Aaa | AAA | AAA |
| FIN | 34.5 | AAA | AAA | Aaa | Aaa | AAA | AAA |
| NLD | 38.9 | AAA | AAA | Aaa | Aaa | AAA | AAA |
| FRA | 39.9 | AAA | AAA | Aaa | Aaa | AAA | AAA |
| BEL | 60.8 | AA+ | AA+ | Aa1 | Aa1 | AA+ | AA+ |
| SVN | 80.8 | AA | AA | Aa2 | Aa1 | AA | AA |
| AUT | 88.6 | AAA | AA | Aaa | Aa1 | AAA | AA |
| SVK | 89.0 | A+ | AA | A1 | Aa1 | A+ | AA |
| PRT | 98.5 | AA | AA | Aa2 | Aa1 | A+ | AA |
| ITA | 115.8 | AA− | A | Aa2 | A1 | A+ | A |
| ESP | 119.6 | AAA | A | Aaa | A1 | AA+ | A |
| IRL | 160.4 | AA− | BBB+ | Aa1 | A3 | AA | BBB+ |
| GRC | 279.4 | BBB+ | SG | A2 | SG | BBB+ | SG |

*Sources*: Author's computations, http://www.fitchratings.com, http://www.moodys.com, http://www.standardandpoors.com, and http://www.datastream.com

**Table 10.5** Sovereign ratings vs. CDS-IRs, 1 March 2010

| | 10-Year CDS (bps) | Fitch actual rating | CDS–Fitch IR | Moody's actual rating | CDS–Moody's IR | S&P actual rating | CDS–S&P IR |
|---|---|---|---|---|---|---|---|
| FIN | 32.01 | AAA | AAA | Aaa | Aaa | AAA | AAA |
| NLD | 40.95 | AAA | AAA | Aaa | Aaa | AAA | AAA |
| DEU | 42.23 | AAA | AAA | Aaa | Aaa | AAA | AAA |
| FRA | 54.91 | AAA | AA+ | Aaa | Aaa | AAA | AAA |
| AUT | 65.80 | AA+ | AA+ | Aaa | Aaa | AAA | AA+ |
| BEL | 66.75 | AA+ | AA+ | Aa1 | Aaa | AA+ | AA+ |
| SVN | 83.72 | AA | AA | Aa2 | Aa1 | AA | AA |
| SVK | 88.44 | A+ | AA | A1 | Aa1 | A+ | AA |
| ESP | 123.12 | AAA | A | Aaa | A1 | AA+ | A |
| ITA | 123.33 | AA– | A | Aa2 | A1 | A+ | A |
| IRL | 140.61 | AA– | BBB+ | Aa1 | A2 | AA | BBB+ |
| PRT | 148.13 | AA | BBB+ | Aa2 | A3 | A+ | BBB+ |
| GRC | 307.99 | BBB+ | SG | A2 | SG | BBB+ | SG |

*Sources*: Author's computations, http://www.fitchratings.com, http://www.moodys.com, http://www.standardandpoors.com, and http://www.datastream.com

10.2 Perception of Sovereign Risk During the Greek Debt Crisis: Ratings vs. CDS-IRs 181

**Table 10.6** Sovereign ratings vs. CDS-IRs, 30 April 2010

| | 10-Year CDS (bps) | Fitch actual rating | CDS–Fitch IR | Moody's actual rating | CDS–Moody's IR | S&P actual rating | CDS–S&P IR |
|---|---|---|---|---|---|---|---|
| FIN | 30.48 | AAA | AAA | Aaa | Aaa | AAA | AAA |
| NLD | 44.91 | AAA | AAA | Aaa | Aaa | AAA | AAA |
| DEU | 44.95 | AAA | AAA | Aaa | Aaa | AAA | AAA |
| FRA | 64.37 | AAA | AA+ | Aaa | Aaa | AAA | AA+ |
| SVN | 68.18 | AA | AA+ | Aa2 | Aaa | AA | AA+ |
| AUT | 72.60 | AAA | AA | Aaa | Aaa | AAA | AA+ |
| BEL | 81.29 | AA+ | AA | Aa1 | Aa2 | AA+ | AA+ |
| SVK | 81.39 | A+ | AA | A1 | Aa3 | A+ | AA |
| ITA | 137.41 | AA– | BBB+ | Aa2 | A2 | A+ | A– |
| ESP | 160.36 | AAA | BBB– | Aaa | Baa1 | AA | BBB |
| IRL | 185.01 | AA– | BBB– | Aa1 | Baa2 | AA | BBB |
| PRT | 259.23 | AA– | SG | Aa2 | SG | A– | SG |
| GRC | 531.65 | BBB– | SG | A3 | SG | BB+ | SG |

*Sources*: Author's computations, http://www.fitchratings.com, http://www.moodys.com, http://www.standardandpoors.com, and http://www.datastream.com

**Table 10.7** Sovereign ratings vs. CDS-IRs, 17 May 2010

| | 10-Year CDS (bps) | Fitch actual rating | CDS–Fitch IR | Moody's actual rating | CDS–Moody's IR | S&P actual rating | CDS–S&P IR |
|---|---|---|---|---|---|---|---|
| FIN | 35.12 | AAA | AAA | Aaa | Aaa | AAA | AAA |
| NLD | 51.22 | AAA | AAA | Aaa | Aaa | AAA | AAA |
| DEU | 52.96 | AAA | AAA | Aaa | Aaa | AAA | AAA |
| AUT | 70.64 | AAA | AA+ | Aaa | Aaa | AAA | AA+ |
| FRA | 79.34 | AAA | AA+ | Aaa | Aaa | AAA | AA+ |
| SVN | 82.04 | AA | AA+ | Aa2 | Aa1 | AA | AA+ |
| SVK | 93.17 | A+ | AA | A1 | Aa2 | A+ | AA+ |
| BEL | 104.63 | AA+ | AA | Aa1 | Aa2 | AA+ | AA– |
| ITA | 136.28 | AA– | A– | Aa2 | A1 | A+ | A– |
| ESP | 180.74 | AAA | BBB | Aaa | A3 | AA | BBB+ |
| IRL | 195.05 | AA– | BBB– | Aa1 | Baa2 | AA | BBB |
| PRT | 246.10 | AA– | SG | Aa2 | SG | A– | SG |
| GRC | 544.89 | BBB– | SG | A3 | SG | BB+ | SG |

*Sources*: Author's computations, http://www.fitchratings.com, http://www.moodys.com, http://www.standardandpoors.com, and http://www.datastream.com

These comments are particularly relevant to Moody's. On 17 May 2010, Greece was still rated A3 by Moody's vs. BBB− and BB+ by Fitch and S&P, respectively. In light of the preceding discussion, the four-notch rating downgrade of Greece that Moody's announced on 14 June 2010 is puzzling. It may support the view that Moody's was initially unaware of the seriousness of the crisis and eventually downgraded Greece to be in line with Fitch and S&P. Alternatively, it could mean that Moody's – although it realized Greece was likely to default – was reluctant to downgrade massively in a time of high risk aversion. Section 10.3 addresses this question by providing evidence to show why Moody's (and, more generally, all three rating agencies) failed to anticipate the Greek debt crisis and delayed negative rating actions.

## 10.3 How CRAs Were Cornered

This section argues that the rating policy of Moody's before and during the Greek debt crisis reveals the two fundamental limits of sovereign ratings. First, the CRAs lost themselves in their own rating methodologies, believing until 2010 that an advanced economy like Greece was unlikely to default. Second, Greece's credit ratings were not significantly modified until the end of April 2010 because the CRAs have become captive to the lawmakers and regulators that use their opinions for financial regulatory purposes.

### 10.3.1 The Daedalean Labyrinth

On 1 January 2001, Greece joined the third stage of the EMU (Economic and Monetary Union). To reach this objective, then Prime Minister Kostas Simitis had to adopt several major economic, financial, and monetary measures: the Greek drachma was devalued by 14% in 1998; inflation was reduced to an annual rate of 3.2% in 2000, down from 8.2% in 1996; the Greek government sold majority stakes in large public enterprises; and the ratios of fiscal deficit to GDP and of public debt to GDP fell (respectively) from 7.4 and 111.3% in 1996 to 2 and 106.2% in 2000.

Believing that the Greek fiscal consolidation was successful and that macroeconomic discipline within the EMU would assist the country in catching up with other European Union states, Moody's and S&P announced several upgrades of Greece's rating (see Table 10.8).

However, a major problem arose in 2004 when the newly elected Prime Minister Kostas Karamanlis revised the fiscal deficit for 2003 from 1.7 to 4.6% of GDP and the public debt for 2003 from 102.4 to 109.9% of GDP [for exhaustive details on the revision of Greek fiscal data, see Eurostat 2004; Sibert 2010]. S&P and Fitch reacted by lowering Greece's rating one notch on 17 November and 16 December 2004, respectively. The negative rating actions by Fitch (2004) and S&P (2004) were

**Table 10.8** Upgrades affecting Greece, 1 January 1996 to 31 December 2003

| Date | Moody's rating action | Date | S&P rating action |
|---|---|---|---|
| 23 December 1996 | Baa3 → Baa1 | 30 November 1998 | BBB- → BBB |
| 14 July 1999 | Baa1 → A2 | 24 November 1999 | BBB → A- |
| 4 November 2002 | A2 → A1 | 13 March 2001 | A- → A |
| | | 10 June 2003 | A → A+ |

Sources: http://www.moodys.com and http://www.standardandpoors.com

consequences of the deepening deterioration of public finances and lack of progress in lowering public debt. From then until 2009, Fitch, Moody's, and S&P left Greece's rating unchanged. Surprisingly, Moody's (2007a) and Fitch (2007a) revised their rating outlook for Greece from stable to positive in (respectively) January and March 2007 on the grounds that the country's economic growth forecast was strong and its public debt ratios had declined. For these agencies, the strengths of the Greek economy were its convergence with higher-rated sovereigns, the country's membership in the eurozone, and commitment to further structural reforms (Fitch 2007a; Moody's 2007a; S&P 2007). The rating agencies evidently tended to overweight the alleged "advanced economy" status of Greece and neglected the possible unreliability of reported debt ratios. It is also possible that the AAA/Aaa rating assigned to all EMU members' country ceilings[2] confused the rating agencies by suggesting that the eurozone was free of sovereign default risk.

The second fiscal data revision – made by the newly elected Prime Minister, George Papandreou, in October 2009 – triggered the Greek debt crisis. At that time, the sovereign ratings assigned to Greece were high, but why were they so sticky when the crisis was intensifying?

### 10.3.2 The Icarus Syndrome

Flandreau et al. (2010) show how CRAs became the gatekeepers of bond markets in 1931 when the US Office of the Comptroller of the Currency incorporated credit ratings into regulatory rules in order to prevent the collapse of financial markets. The rationale for this decision was that ratings were considered to be independent and reliable opinions with likely countercyclical effects. Since then, CRAs have been installed at the center of financial systems (Bank for International Settlements 2009). However, CRAs derive their influence not only from the incorporation of their credit ratings into regulatory rules, but also from the use of those credit ratings by market participants. For any investor, holding a high-rated security is tantamount to riskless investment because default rates for investment-grade rating categories are extremely low (Type I errors – i.e., rating too highly an issuer that subsequently

---

[2] Recall that S&P refers to the "Country T&C assessments" (see Chap. 3).

defaults – are uncommon). In contrast, investors holding lower-rated bonds are required to maintain higher levels of capital reserves than when holding higher-rated bonds. This means that Type II errors (i.e., underrating an issuer that does not subsequently default) are harmful to investors when they must consequently hold more collateral than is actually needed.

The result is that regulators, investors, and debt issuers need high ratings: regulators because they want to avoid financial contagion, investors because they want to save capital, and debt issuers because they want low interest rates. Thus, CRAs have three types of incentives to inflate their ratings. The phenomenon of rating inflation may well have been magnified in the sovereign rating area. Because there were so few sovereign issuers that had defaulted on their bond debt since the 1990s, the main challenge for Fitch, Moody's, and S&P was to avoid Type II errors. That objective may have led them to overrate investment-grade issuers, thus imposing even smaller "haircuts" for issuers whose securities were already eligible as collateral by most central banks. This view is supported by the very low default rates for investment-grade issuers, the accuracy ratios higher for sovereign issuers than for corporate issuers, and the downward rigidity of investment-grade ratings (discussed in Chap. 8).

The Moody's rating policy in effect during the Greek debt crisis exemplifies the tendency to avoid Type II errors. On 29 April 2010 (2 days after Greece was downgraded to speculative-grade status by S&P), Moody's announced that it expected to complete its review of Greece's A3 sovereign bond rating shortly after details of the EMU/IMF program were unveiled. Moody's opinion was that "Greece's short-term liquidity and restructuring risks [were] negligible given the depth of international commitment to maintaining regional financial stability." These remarks indicated that Moody's was unlikely to downgrade Greece's rating in the very short term. Four days later, on 3 May 2010, the European Central Bank (ECB) decided to drop the minimum credit threshold (BBB–/Baa3) of its collateral framework policy and to accept Greek government bonds as collateral even if they had a speculative-grade rating. It is clear that the rating decision by Moody's was countercyclical because it prevented massive sales of Greek government bonds. It also enabled the ECB, the European Union, and the IMF to come to the rescue of Greece in "better market conditions." In return, the ECB's laxer collateral rules relieved the pressure on CRAs by rendering any further downgrades of Greece's rating (relatively) painless.

## 10.4 Concluding Remarks

The Greek debt crisis smoldered long before it burst. Multi-notch downgrades should have followed the 2004 revision of fiscal data, but the rating firms were reluctant to make them. Eventually, in 2010, they paid for those past mistakes. Looking at Greece now, it must be acknowledged that the country is most likely to restructure its debt, since the episodes of large debt reversals have been uncommon so far (Reinhart & Rogoff 2009). More importantly, one should wonder to what extent the Greek economy's collapse heralds the demise of some unsustainable welfare states, particularly in Southern European countries. This possibility, in line with the views expressed by Buiter and Rahbari (2010), means that Fitch, Moody's, and S&P will have to discriminate more sharply among advanced economies in the coming years.

The 2010 financial turmoil also sheds new light on the behavior of CRAs during times of high risk aversion. Credit ratings were more stable than market-based indicators (e.g., CDS-IRs). Moody's really "missed" the Greek debt crisis, but its ratings had countercyclical effects and served as a shield to avoid contagion. In contrast, S&P and Fitch ratings were slightly more correlated with the CDSs. These findings support the view that paradoxically the use of credit ratings for regulatory purposes is more suitable than one would expect.

## References

Bank for International Settlements (2009), "Stocktaking on the use of credit ratings", *Basel Committee on Banking Supervision – The Joint Forum*, June.

Breger L., Goldberg L. and Cheyette O. (2003), "Market Implied Ratings", *Barra Credit Series, Research Insights*.

Buiter W. and Rahbari E. (2010), "Is Sovereign Default 'Unnecessary, Undesirable and Unlikely' For All Advanced Economies?", *Global Economic View, Citigroup Global Markets*, 16 September.

Cantor R. and Packer F. (1994), "The Credit Rating Industry", *Federal Reserve Bank of New York Quarterly Review*, Summer-Fall.

Cottarelli C., Forni L., Gottschalk J. and Paolo M. (2010), "Default in Today's Advanced Economies: Unnecessary, Undesirable, and Unlikely", *IMF Staff Position Note*, 1st September.

Eichengreen B. and Hausmann R. (1999), "Exchange Rates and Financial Fragility", paper presented at the symposium *New Challenges for Monetary Policy*, 26–28 August, Jackson Hole, WY.

Eichengreen B., Hausmann R. and Panizza U. (2005a), "The Pain of Original Sin", in Eichengreen B. and Hausmann R. (eds.), *Other People's Money*, Chicago University Press, Chicago.

Eichengreen B., Hausmann R. and Panizza U. (2005b), "The Mystery of Original Sin", in Eichengreen B. and Hausmann R. (eds.), *Other People's Money*, Chicago University Press, Chicago.

Eurostat (2004), *Report by Eurostat on the Revision of the Greek Government Deficit and Debt Figures*, 22 November.

Financial Stability Board (2010), *Principles for Reducing Reliance on CRA Ratings*, 27 October.

Fitch Ratings (2004), "Fitch Downgrades Greece to 'A' from 'A+'", 16 December.

Fitch Ratings (2007a), "Fitch Changes Greece's Outlook to Positive", 5 March.

Fitch Ratings (2007b), "Fitch CDS Implied Ratings (CDS-IR) Model", 13 June.

Flandreau M., Flores J. H., Gaillard N. and Nieto-Parra S. (2010), "The End of Gatekeeping: Underwriters and the Quality of Sovereign Bond Markets, 1815-2007", in Reichlin L. and West K. (eds), *NBER International Seminar on Macroeconomics 2009*, NBER and University of Chicago Press, Chicago.

Hausmann R. and Panizza U. (2010), "Redemption or Abstinence? Original Sin, Currency Mismatches and Counter Cyclical Policies in the New Millenium", *CID Working Paper No.194*, Harvard University.

# References

Kou J. and Varotto S. (2008), "Timeliness of Spread Implied Ratings", *European Financial Management*, Vol.18, Issue 3.

Moody's Investors Service (2003), "Measuring the Performance of Corporate Bond Ratings", April.

Moody's Investors Service (2007a), "Moody's Changes Outlook on Greece's A1 Bond Ratings to Positive", 11 January.

Moody's Investors Service (2007b), "Moody's Market Implied Ratings – Description, Methodology, and Analytical Applications", December.

Partnoy F. (2002), "The Paradox of Credit Ratings" in Ratings, Rating Agencies and the Global Financial System, edited by Levich R., Majnoni G. and Reinhart C., Kluwer, Boston.

Partnoy F. (2009), "Historical Perspectives on the Financial Crisis: Ivar Kreuger, the Credit-Rating Agencies, and Two Theories About the Function, and Dysfunction, of Markets", *Yale Journal on Regulation*, Vol.26.

Qian R., Reinhart C. and Rogoff K. (2011), "On Graduation from Default, Inflation and Banking Crises: Elusive or Illusion?", in Acemoglu D. and Woodford M. (eds), *NBER Macroconomics Annual 2010*, NBER and University of Chicago Press, Chicago.

Reinhart C. and Rogoff K. (2009), *This Time is Different*, Princeton University Press, Princeton.

Reinhart C., Rogoff K. and Savastano M. (2003) "Debt Intolerance", *Brookings Papers on Economic Activity*, Vol.34 (1).

Sibert A. (2010), "The EFSM and the EFSF: Now and What Follows", *Directorate General for Internal Policies*, 8 September.

Standard & Poor's (2004), "Greece Outlook Revised to Negative as Public Finances Crisis Deepens; Ratings Affirmed", 13 September.

Standard & Poor's (2007), "Hellenic Republic", 6 March.

# Chapter 11
# Conclusion

Sovereign rating experienced two periods of high activity: the interwar years and the period since the mid-1980s. During the 1920s and 1930s, the four main credit rating agencies (Fitch, Moody's, Poor's, and Standard Statistics) failed to anticipate the sovereign debt crisis that broke out in 1931, and they overreacted by making massive downgrades well into 1933. Even so, the very low default rates for sovereign bonds rated in the first two rating classes indicate that the four agencies successfully discriminated among foreign government bonds. Because there were so few rated sovereigns that defaulted during the period 1986–2010, it is not possible to make reliable comparisons between the modern era's sovereign ratings and those issued during the interwar years. Despite this reserve, an examination of default rates and accuracy ratios indicates (not surprisingly) that the ratings issued by Fitch, Moody's, and S&P during the past 25 years have been more accurate than those from the interwar period.

With regard to the idiosyncratic rating policy of Fitch, Moody's, and S&P in the modern era, the following observations are noteworthy.

Ratings are assigned by Moody's "through the cycle"; its rating changes are less frequent but are of greater magnitude than those announced by Fitch and S&P. The Moody's ratings perform best in the medium term, as shown by 3- and 5-year cumulative default rates and accuracy ratios. The S&P ratings are more in line with market participants' views; they are more volatile and perform best in the short term. Fitch ratings are highly correlated with those issued by S&P but perform slightly less well. Two reasons may explain this finding.

First, Fitch has seldom employed innovative rating policies, especially when compared with its competitors. For example, rating outlooks and rating reviews for sovereign issuers were introduced by S&P in 1989 and 1991, respectively. Moody's pioneered in terms of measuring the accuracy of sovereign credit ratings by providing default rates and accuracy ratios in the early 2000s. Moreover, Moody's spurred revision of the country ceiling policy in 2001 and implemented the first-ever empirical model to assess sovereign risk in 2003–2004. In contrast, Fitch did not launch sovereign recovery ratings until 2005.

Second, Fitch tends to lag behind Moody's and S&P. During the past years, the most stunning rating actions came from Moody's or S&P, not Fitch. Which agency first boosted Singapore and Hong Kong to the AAA top rating in 1995 and 2010 (respectively) and threatened the United Kingdom's AAA rating by revising the country's rating outlook to negative from stable in May 2009? S&P. Which agency first downgraded Greece in November 2004 and first lowered the country's rating to the speculative-grade category in April 2010? S&P. Which agency first upgraded Brazil to the investment-grade category in April 2008? S&P. Which agency is the most prompt to downgrade the countries that subsequently default? S&P. Which agency announced the most massive multi-notch upgrades (in November 2002)? Moody's. Which agency first upgraded Russia to the investment-grade category in October 2003? Moody's. In short, Fitch needs to overcome its "challenger" status and differentiate its rating policy in order to improve the accuracy of its credit ratings.

Beyond these specific conclusions, one of the most striking findings in this book is the "timelessness" of sovereign rating methodologies. During the interwar years and also during the past two decades, the determinants of sovereign ratings have remained the same: GDP per capita, the ratio of foreign currency debt to exports or revenues, inflation, the indicator for default history, and institutional stability. This methodological framework has led CRAs to assign investment-grade ratings to most advanced economies and to assign speculative-grade ratings to most emerging countries. Yet this rating policy seems to have reached its limits, and CRAs face a major challenge. It is time they realize that several so-called advanced countries are burdened with social and economic structures that have become unable to generate long-term growth prospects. The very likely default of Greece, which will reduce the accuracy ratios of the three CRAs (particularly those of Moody's), should drive Fitch, Moody's and S&P to update their methodologies.

Finally, this research sheds new light on the debate concerning the possible overreliance on CRA ratings in standards, laws, and regulatory rules. Credit ratings are certainly no substitute for institutional investors' due diligence. However, when considering sovereign ratings, the use of credit ratings for regulatory purposes is supported by their lesser procyclicality than market-based indicators during the past decade. These findings are crucial because they demonstrate how credit ratings may actually be able to alleviate market volatility.

# Appendix 1
# Sovereign Bonds in USD or in GBP Listed on the NYSE That Defaulted in 1931–1938

| Sovereign bonds | Date of default |
| --- | --- |
| Austria International Loan 7s of 1930 | 31 May 1938 |
| Bolivia National Government 6s of 1917 | 1 April 1931 |
| Bolivia National Government 7s of 1927 | 1 January 1931 |
| Bolivia National Government 7s of 1928 | 1 March 1931 |
| Bolivia National Government 8s of 1922 | 1 May 1931 |
| Brazil Federal Government 8s of 1921 | 1 December 1931 |
| Brazil Federal Government 7s of 1922 | 1 December 1931 |
| Brazil Federal Government 6.5s of 1926 | 1 April 1932 |
| Brazil Federal Government 6.5s of 1927 | 15 April 1932 |
| Brazil Federal Government 5s of 1931 | 1 January 1938 |
| Bulgaria National Government 7.5s of 1928 | 15 November 1932 |
| Bulgaria National Government 7s of 1926 | 1 July 1933 |
| Chile National Government 6s of 1926 | 1 October 1931 |
| Chile National Government 6s of 1928–January 1961 | 1 January 1932 |
| Chile National Government 6s of 1927 | 1 August 1931 |
| Chile National Government 6s of 1928–September 1961 | 1 September 1931 |
| Chile National Government 6s of 1929 | 1 September 1931 |
| Chile National Government 6s of 1930 | 1 November 1931 |
| Chile National Government 7s of 1922 | 1 November 1931 |
| Colombia National Government 6s of 1927 | 1 July 1933 |
| Colombia National Government 6s of 1928 | 1 October 1933 |
| Costa Rica National Government 7s of 1926 | 1 November 1936 |
| Costa Rica National Government 7.5s of 1927 | 1 September 1937 |
| Costa Rica National Government 5s of 1932 | 1 November 1936 |
| Costa Rica National Government Pacific Railway 5s of 1933 | 1 September 1936 |
| Cuba National Government Public Works 5.5s of 1930 | 31 December 1933 |
| Cuba National Government 5.5s of 1927 | 1 July 1937 |
| Dominican Republic National Government 5.5s of 1922 | October 1931 |
| Dominican Republic National Government 5.5s of 1926 | October 1931 |
| Germany National Government 7s of 1924 | 15 October 1934 |
| Germany National Government 5.5s of 1930 | 1 December 1934 |

(continued)

(continued)

| Sovereign bonds | Date of default |
| --- | --- |
| Greece National Government 7s of 1924 | 1 May 1932 |
| Greece National Government 6s of 1928 | 1 August 1932 |
| Greece National Government 8s of 1925 | 1 October 1932 |
| Guatemala National Government 8s of 1927 | 1 November 1933 |
| Hungary National Government 7.5s of 1924 | 1 February 1934 |
| Panama National Government 7s of 1927 | 31 July 1932 |
| Panama National Government 5s of 1928 | 15 May 1933 |
| Peru National Government 7s of 1927 | 1 September 1931 |
| Peru National Government 6s of 1927 | 1 June 1931 |
| Peru National Government 6s of 1928 | 1 April 1931 |
| Poland National Government 6s of 1920 | 1 October 1936 |
| Poland National Government 8s of 1925 | 1 January 1937 |
| Poland National Government 7s of 1927 | 15 April 1937 |
| Romania National Government 4s of 1922 | 1 October 1933 |
| Salvador National Government 7s of 1924 | 1 July 1932 |
| Salvador National Government 8s of 1923 | 1 January 1933 |
| Uruguay National Government 8s of 1921 | 1 August 1933 |
| Uruguay National Government 6s of 1926 | 1 November 1933 |
| Uruguay National Government 6s of 1930 | 1 November 1933 |
| Uruguay National Government 5s of 1915 | 1 January 1934 |
| Yugoslavia National Government 8s of 1922 | 1 November 1932 |
| Yugoslavia National Government 7s of 1922 | 1 November 1932 |

*Sources*: Author's classification based on *Moody's Manuals* (1931 through 1939)

# Appendix 2
# Sources Used in Chap. 5

*Ratings*

1925 ratings: *Moody's Manual* (1925)

1929 ratings: *Moody's Manual* (1929)

2006 ratings: Moody's (2006), "Sovereign Ratings Summary," December

Other ratings: *Moody's Manuals* (1918–1987); Moody's (2007), "Sovereign Default and Recovery Rates, 1983–2006," June; http://www.moodys.com

*Per capita income*

1925 and 1929: wealth per capita figures from *Moody's Manuals* (1925 and 1929), except for Dominican Republic, Ecuador, Haiti, Panama and Salvador: GDP per capita figures, author's calculations from Maddison (2003)

2006: 2004 GDP per capita (PPP) figures for all countries from "Moody's Statistical Handbook – Country Credit," May 2006

*Growth*

1925 and 1929: GDP growth estimations for all countries. For Bolivia, China, Cuba, Dominican Republic, Ecuador, Haiti, Panama, and Russia: author's calculations from Maddison (2003). For Colombia, Nicaragua, Salvador, and Uruguay: Oxford Latin American Economic History Database (http://oxlad.qeh.ox.ac.uk). For Poland and Romania, I used the wealth growth of Yugoslavia. For other countries: Maddison (2003)

2006: GDP growth on a year-to-year basis from "Moody's Statistical Handbook – Country Credit," May 2006

*Inflation*

1925 and 1929: for Austria, Canada, China, Czechoslovakia, Denmark, Finland, France, Germany, Italy, Japan, Netherlands, Norway, Peru, Poland, Romania, Russia, Sweden, Switzerland, and United Kingdom: price movements from League of Nations (1925 and 1932). Bolivia, Ecuador, Hungary, Nicaragua, Salvador, Uruguay: money circulation growth, League of Nations (1925 and 1932). Belgium and Greece: consumer price indices from Mitchell (1992). Argentina, Brazil, and Chile: consumer price indices from Mitchell (1993). Colombia, Cuba, and Mexico: consumer price indices from Oxford Latin American Economic History Database

2006: CPI, % change, December/December from "Moody's Statistical Handbook – Country Credit," May 2006

*Fiscal balance*

1925 and 1929: *Moody's Manuals* (1925 and 1929)

2006: "Moody's Statistical Handbook – Country Credit," May 2006

(continued)

(continued)

*External balance*

1925 and 1929: author's calculations from *Moody's Manuals* (1925 and 1929)

2006: "Moody's Statistical Handbook – Country Credit," May 2006

*Debt*

1925 and 1929: foreign currency debt from *Moody's Manuals* (1925 and 1929)

2006: general government debt from "Moody's Statistical Handbook – Country Credit," May 2006

*Exports*

1925 and 1929: *Moody's Manuals* (1925 and 1929)

2006: not applicable

*General government revenue*

1925 and 1929: not applicable

2006: "Moody's Statistical Handbook – Country Credit," May 2006

*Indicator for economic development*

1925 and 1929: *Moody's Manuals* (1925 and 1929)

The indicator for economic development used by Cantor and Packer (1996) was the IMF classification as an industrialized country. I managed to find an equivalent indicator for the interwar period. *Moody's Manuals* used to classify countries into four groups, according to the predominant feature of their economic activity: "manufacturing countries," "commercial countries," "agricultural countries," and "miscellaneous countries." This subdivision was based on Mulhall's *Industry and Wealth of Nations* (1896) who had grouped countries into nine sectors ("manufacturing," "agriculture," "minerals, forestry and fisheries," "commerce," "transport," "house-rent," "domestic servants," "public service" and "professional services"). The countries I considered as industrialized were called "manufacturing countries" by Moody's: Belgium, France, Germany, Switzerland, United Kingdom, and United States

2006: Moody's classification from "Moody's Statistical Handbook – Country Credit," May 2006

*Indicator for default history*

The indicator for default history is the most comparable variable from the 1920–1930s through the 1990s–2000s. For each reference year, the indicator assesses the occurrence of a default on foreign currency debt during the previous 25 years

1925: *Moody's Manuals* (1918 through 1925) and *Annual Report* of the Corporation of Foreign Bondholders (various issues between 1900 and 1924)

1929: *Moody's Manuals* (1918 through 1929) and *Annual Report* of the Corporation of Foreign Bondholders (various issues between 1904 and 1928)

2006: Standard & Poor's (2004), "Sovereign Defaults Set to Fall Again in 2005," September 28; Moody's (2007), "Sovereign Default and Recovery Rates, 1983–2006," June

*Institutional indicator*

1925 and 1929: scoring based on *Moody's Manuals* (various issues) and "Moody's Investment Letters" (various issues); see Table 5.14

2006: not applicable

*Governance index*

1925 and 1929: not applicable

2006: average of six indicators ("voice and accountability," "political stability," "government effectiveness," "regulatory quality," "rule of law," "control of corruption") implemented by Kaufmann, Kraay and Mastruzzi, *Governance Matters IV: Governance Indicators for 1996–2004, World Bank* (2005); see Table 5.17

# Appendix 3
# List of the 135 Bonds Included in the Sample Used in Chap. 7

| Sovereign bonds | Maturity | Sovereign bonds | Maturity |
|---|---|---|---|
| Argentina 5% Int Gold 1909 | 1945 | Brazil Ext gold 8s 1921 | 1941 |
| Argentina gold 7s 1922 | 1927 | Brazil Central Ry 7s 1922 | 1952 |
| Argentina 6s of 1923 | 1957 | Brazil Coffee 7.5s 1922 | 1952 |
| Argentina 6s of 1924 | 1958 | Brazil Ext 6.5s 1926 | 1957 |
| Argentina 6s of 1925 | June 1959 | Brazil Ext 6.5s 1927 | 1957 |
| Argentina 6s of 1925 | October 1959 | Brazil Fund 5s 1931 | 1951 and 1971 |
| Argentina 6s of 1926 | 1960 | Bulgaria 7s 1927 | 1967 |
| Argentina 6s 1926 (Pub W) | 1960 | Bulgaria 7.5s 1928 | 1968 |
| Argentina 6s 1927 (Pub W) | 1961 | Canada 5s 1915 | 1935 |
| Argentina 6s 1927 (State Ry) | 1960 | Canada P S 5s 1916 | 1921/1926/1931 |
| Argentina 6s 1927 (Sani W) | 1961 | Canada 5.5s 1919 | 1921/1929 |
| Argentina 5.5s 1928 | 1962 | Canada 5s 1922 | 1952 |
| Argentina 4.5s 1936 | 1971 | Canada 4.5s 1926 | 1936 |
| Argentina 4s 1937 | 1972 | Canada 4s Gold 1930 | 1960 |
| Australia 5s 1925 | 1955 | Canada 2.5s 1935 | 1945 |
| Australia 5s 1927 | 1957 | Canada 3.25s 1936 | 1961 |
| Australia 4.5s 1928 | 1956 | Canada 2.5s 1937 | 1944 |
| Austria Guar G 7s 1923 | 1943 | Canada 3s 1937 | 1967 |
| Austria 7s Inter 1930 | 1957 | Chile 8s 1921 | 1941 |
| Belgium 7.5s 1920 | 1945 | Chile 5s 1921 | 1926 |
| Belgium 8s 1921 | 1941 | Chile 8s 1921 | 1946 |
| Belgium 6.5s 1924 | 1949 | Chile Ext 7s 1922 | 1942 |
| Belgium Ext 6s 1924 | 1955 | Chile Ext 6s 1926 | 1960 |
| Belgium Ext 7s 1925 | 1955 | Chile Ext 6s 1927 | 1961 |
| Belgium Stab 7s 1926 | 1956 | Chile Ext 6s 1928 | 1961 |
| Bolivia Dollar 6s 1917 | 1940 | Chile Ry 6s 1928 | 1961 |
| Bolivia Dollar 6s 1920 | 1921–1934 | Chile Ext 6s 1929 | 1962 |
| Bolivia Ext 8s 1922–1924 | 1947 | Chile Ext 6s 1930 | 1963 |
| Bolivia Ext 7s 1927 | 1958 | China Ry 5s 1911 | 1951 |
| Bolivia Ext 7s 1928 | 1969 | Colombia Ext 6s 1927 | 1961 |

(continued)

(continued)

| Sovereign bonds | Maturity | Sovereign bonds | Maturity |
|---|---|---|---|
| Colombia Ext 6s 1928 | 1961 | Italy 7s 1925 | 1951 |
| Costa Rica Ext 7s 1926 | 1951 | Japan Stlg 4s 1905 | 1931 |
| Costa Rica Pac Ry 7.5s 1927–1929 | 1949 | Japan Gold 6.5s 1924 | 1954 |
| | | Japan Gold 5.5s 1930 | 1965 |
| Cuba Ext Gold 5s 1904 | 1944 | Mexico 5s 1899 | 1945 |
| Cuba Gold 4.5s 1909 | 1949 | Mexico 4s 1904 | 1954 |
| Cuba Ext Gold 5s 1914 | 1949 | Netherlands 6s 1922 | 1972 |
| Cuba Ext 5.5s 1923 | 1953 | Netherlands 6s 1924 | 1954 |
| Cuba 5.5s 1927 | 1929–1937 | Norway 6s 1922 | 1952 |
| Cuba Pub W 5.5s 1928 | 1931–1932 | Norway 6s 1923 | 1943 |
| Cuba Pub W 5.5s 1930 | 1945 | Norway 6s 1924 | 1944 |
| Czechoslovakia Ext 8s 1922 | 1951 | Norway 5.5s 1925 | 1965 |
| Czechoslovakia Ext 8s 1924 | 1952 | Norway 5s 1928 | 1963 |
| Denmark Ext 6s 1922 | 1942 | Norway 4.5s 1936 | 1956 |
| Denmark Ext 5.5s 1925 | 1955 | Norway 4.25s 1936 | 1965 |
| Denmark Ext 4.5s 1928 | 1962 | Norway 4s 1937 | 1963 |
| Dominican Rep 5% Cust Ad 1908 | 1958 | Panama 5s 1928 | 1963 |
| | | Peru 6s 1927 | 1960 |
| Dominican Rep 5.5s 1922 | 1942 | Peru 7s 1927 | 1959 |
| Dominican Rep Cust 5.5s 1926 | 1940 | Peru 6s 1928 | 1961 |
| | | Poland 6s 1920 | 1940 |
| Estonia Bk Currency 7s 1927 | 1967 | Poland 8s 1925 | 1950 |
| Finland Ext 6s 1923 | 1945 | Poland 7s 1927 | 1947 |
| Finland Ext 7s 1925 | 1950 | Russia 5.5% 1916 | 1921 |
| Finland 6.5s 1926 | 1956 | Russia 6.5% 1916 | 1919 |
| Finland 6.5s 1928 | 1958 | Salvador 8s 1923 | 1948 |
| Finland 4.5s 1934 | 1936–1940 | Salvador 7s 1924 | 1957 |
| France Ext 8s 1920 | 1945 | Sweden 6s 1919 | 1939 |
| France 7.5s 1921 | 1941 | Sweden 5.5s 1924 | 1954 |
| France 7s 1924–1925 | 1949 | Switzerland 5.5s 1919 | 1929 |
| Germany 7s 1924 | 1949 | Switzerland 8s 1920 | 1940 |
| Germany 5.5s Inter Loan 1930 | 1965 | Switzerland 5.5s 1924 | 1946 |
| | | United Kingdom 5.5s 1917 | 1937 |
| Greece Refugee 7s 1924 | 1964 | United Kingdom 5.5s 1919 | 1929 |
| Greece 6s 1928 | 1968 | United Kingdom Funding 4s 1919 | 1990 |
| Guatemala 8s 1927 | 1948 | | |
| Haiti Gold 6s 1922 | 1952 | Uruguay 8s 1921 | 1946 |
| Haiti Gold 6s 1923 | 1953 | Uruguay 6s 1926 | 1960 |
| Hungary 7s 1924 | 1944 | Uruguay SF 6s 1930 | 1964 |
| Irish Free State 5s 1927 | 1929–1960 | Yugoslavia 8s 1922 | 1962 |

Printed by Publishers' Graphics LLC
MRO20120913-2130-19